World Risk Society

ULRICH BECK

Polity

First published in 1999 by Polity Press in association with
Blackwell Publishers Ltd.

Reprinted 2000, 2001

Editorial office:
Polity Press
65 Bridge Street
Cambridge CB2 1UR, UK

Marketing and production:
Blackwell Publishers Ltd
108 Cowley Road
Oxford OX4 1JF, UK

Published in the USA by
Blackwell Publishers Inc.
350 Main Street
Malden, MA 02148, USA

ISBN 0-7456-2220-8
ISBN 0-7456-2221-6 (pbk)

A catalogue record for this book is available from the British Library and has been
applied for from the Library of Congress.

Typeset in 10.5 on 12pt Sabon
by Graphicraft Limited, Hong Kong
Printed in Great Britain by
TJ International Ltd, Padstow, Cornwall

This book is printed on acid-free paper.

Contents

Acknowledgements   vii

1 Introduction: The Cosmopolitan Manifesto   1

2 World Risk Society as Cosmopolitan Society?
   Ecological Questions in a Framework of Manufactured
   Uncertainties   19

3 From Industrial Society to Risk Society:
   Questions of Survival, Social Structure and
   Ecological Enlightenment   48

4 Risk Society and the Welfare State   72

5 Subpolitics: Ecology and the Disintegration of
   Institutional Power   91

6 Knowledge or Unawareness? Two Perspectives on
   'Reflexive Modernization'   109

Contents

7 Risk Society Revisited: Theory, Politics, Critiques and
   Research Programmes   133

Notes   153

References   161

Index   168

Acknowledgements

The author and publishers wish to thank the following for use of copyright material:

'Introduction: The Cosmopolitan Manifesto', enlarged and revised version, first published in English in *The New Statesman*, 20 March 1998, copyright © *The New Statesman*, reprinted by permission of *The New Statesman*.

'World Risk Society as Cosmopolitan Society? Ecological Questions in a Framework of Manufactured Uncertainties', revised version, first published in German, © Ulrich Beck, in *Kölner Zeitschrift für Soziologie und Sozialpsychologie*, special issue 36, *Umweltsoziologie*; English translation by Ulrich Beck first published in *Theory, Culture & Society*, vol. 13 (4) (1996), © Sage 1996, reprinted by permission of the Editor, *Kölner Zeitschrift für Soziologie und Sozialpsychologie*, and Sage Publications Ltd.

'From Industrial Society to Risk Society: Questions of Survival, Social Structure and Ecological Enlightenment', revised version, first published in German by Bundeszentrale fur Politische Bildung, 1990, © Ulrich Beck 1990; English translation by Mark Ritter first published in *Theory, Culture & Society*, vol. 9 (1992), © Sage 1992, reprinted by permission of Sage Publications Ltd.

'Risk Society and the Welfare State', original version published in German as 'Risikogesellschaft und Vorsorgestaat – Zwischenbilanz einer Diskussion' in François Ewald *Der Vorsorgestaat*, © Suhrkamp Verlag, Frankfurt am Main, 1993; English translation by Martin

Chalmers in S. Lash, B. Szerszynski and B. Wynne (eds), *Risk, Environment and Modernity: Towards a New Ecology* (Sage, 1996), reprinted by permission of Suhrkamp Verlag and Sage Publications Ltd.

'Subpolitics: Ecology and the Disintegration of Institutional Power', revised version, first published in English in *Organization and Environment*, vol. 10 (1) (1997), © 1997 by Sage Publications, reprinted by permission of Sage Publications, Inc.

'Knowledge or Unawareness? Two Perspectives on "Reflexive Modernization"', revised and enlarged version, first published in German as 'Wissen oder Nicht-Wissen' by Suhrkamp in *Reflexive Modernisierung* by Ulrich Beck, Anthony Giddens and Scott Lash, © Suhrkamp, 1996; English translation by Mark Ritter, first published as 'Misunderstanding Reflexivity: The Controversy on Reflexive Modernization' as chapter 7 of *Democracy without Enemies*, © Polity Press, 1997.

'Risk Society Revisited: Theory, Politics, Critiques and Research Programmes', first published in English in Barbara Adam, Ulrich Beck and Joost van Loon (eds), *Repositioning Risk*, © Sage 1999, reprinted by permission of Sage Publications Ltd.

1

Introduction:
The Cosmopolitan Manifesto

All around the world, contemporary society is undergoing radical change that poses a challenge to Enlightenment-based modernity and opens a field where people *choose* new and unexpected forms of the social and the political. Sociological debates of the nineties have sought to grasp and conceptualize this reconfiguration. Some authors lay great stress on the openness of the human project amid new contingencies, complexities and uncertainties, whether their main operative term is 'postmodernity' (Bauman, Lyotard, Harvey, Haraway), 'late modernity' (Giddens), the 'global age' (Albrow) or 'reflexive modernization' (Beck, Giddens, Lash). Others have prioritized research into new forms of experimental identity (Melucci) and sociality (Maffesoli), the relationship between individualization and political culture (Touraine), the 'post-national constellation' (Habermas) or the preconditions of 'cosmopolitan democracy' (Held). Others still have contributed a wave of books on the 'politics of nature' (Vandana Shiva, Gernot Böhme, Maarten Hajer, John S. Dryzek, Tim Hayward, Andrew Dobson, Barbara Adam, Robin Grove-White and Brian Wynne). All agree that in the decades ahead we will confront profound contradictions and perplexing paradoxes; and experience hope embedded in despair.

In an attempt to summarize and systematize these transformations, I have for some time been working with a distinction between first modernity and second modernity. The former term I use to describe the modernity based on nation-state societies, where social relations, networks and communities are essentially understood in a territorial sense. The collective patterns of life, progress and controllability, full employment and exploitation of nature that were typical of this first modernity have now been undermined by five interlinked processes: globalization, individualization, gender revolution, underemployment and global risks (as ecological crisis and the crash of global financial markets). The real theoretical and political challenge of the second modernity is the fact that society must respond to all these challenges *simultaneously*.

If the five processes are considered more closely, it becomes clear what they have in common: namely, they are all unforeseen consequences of the victory of the first, simple, linear, industrial modernization based on the national state (the focus of classical sociology from Durkheim, Weber and Marx to Parsons and Luhmann). This is what I mean by talking of 'reflexive modernization'. Radicalized modernization undermines the foundations of the first modernity and changes its frame of reference, often in a way that is neither desired nor anticipated. Or, in the terms of system theory: the unforeseen consequences of functional differentiation can no longer be controlled by further functional differentiation. In fact, the very idea of controllability, certainty or security – which is so fundamental in the first modernity – collapses. A new kind of capitalism, a new kind of economy, a new kind of global order, a new kind of society and a new kind of personal life are coming into being, all of which differ from earlier phases of social development. Thus, sociologically and politically, we need a paradigm-shift, a new frame of reference. This is not 'postmodernity' but a second modernity, and the task that faces us is to reform sociology so that it can provide a new framework for the reinvention of society and politics. Research work on reflexive modernization does not deal only with the *decline* of the Western model. The key question is how that model relates to the *different modernities* in other parts of the world. Which new and unexpected forms of the social are emerging? Which new social and political forces, and which lines of conflict, are appearing on the horizon?

In world risk society, non-Western societies share with the West not only the same space and time but also – more importantly – the same basic challenges of the second modernity (in different places and with different cultural perceptions). To stress this aspect of sameness – and not otherness – is already an important step in revising the evolutionary bias that afflicts much of Western social science to this day, a bias whereby contemporary non-Western societies are relegated to the category of 'traditional' or 'pre-modern' and thus defined not in their own terms, but as the opposite or the absence of modernity. (Many even believe that the study of pre-modern Western societies can help us understand the characteristics of non-Western societies today!) To situate the non-Western world firmly within the ambit of a second modernity, rather than of tradition, allows a *pluralization of modernity*, for it opens up space for the conceptualization of divergent trajectories of modernities in different parts of the world. This idea of multiple modernities recalls Nehru's image of a 'garb of modernity' that can be worn in a number of ingeniously different ways.[1]

The increasing speed, intensity and significance of processes of transnational interdependence, and the growth in discourses of economic, cultural, political and societal 'globalization', suggest not only that non-Western societies should be included in any analysis of the challenges of the second modernity, but also that the specific refractions and reflections of the global need to be examined in these different sites of the emerging global society.

Reversing Marx's judgement, we could say with Shalini Randeria that many parts of the 'Third World' today show Europe the image of its own future. On the positive side, we could list such features as the development of multi-religious, multi-ethnic and multi-cultural societies, the cross-cultural models and the tolerance of cultural difference, the legal pluralism observable at a number of levels, and the multiplication of sovereignties. On the negative side, we could point to the spread of the informal sector and the flexibilization of labour, the legal deregulation of large areas of the economy and work relations, the loss of legitimacy by the state, the growth of unemployment and underemployment, the more forceful intervention by multinational corporations, and the high rates of everyday violence and crime. All these aspects, together with related questions and arguments, imply that we need a new frame of reference for the world risk society (including non-Western countries) in which we live if we are to understand the dynamics and contradictions of the second modernity (see *Korean Journal of Sociology*, 1998).

As the bipolar world fades away, we are moving from a world of enemies to one of dangers and risks. But what does 'risk' mean? Risk is the modern approach to foresee and control the future consequences of human action, the various unintended consequences of radicalized modernization. It is an (institutionalized) attempt, a cognitive map, to colonize the future. Every society has, of course, experienced dangers. But the risk regime is a function of a new order: it is not national, but global. It is rather intimately connected with an administrative and technical decision-making process. Risks presuppose decision. These decisions were previously undertaken with fixed norms of calculability, connecting means and ends or causes and effects. These norms are precisely what 'world risk society' has rendered invalid. All of this becomes very evident with private insurance, perhaps the greatest symbol of calculation and alternative security – which does not cover nuclear disaster, nor climate change and its consequences, nor the breakdown of Asian economies, nor the low-probability high-consequences risk of various forms of future technology. In fact, most controversial technologies, like genetic engineering, are not privately insured.

What has given rise to this new prominence of risk? The concept of risk and risk society combines what once was mutually exclusive – society and nature, social sciences and material sciences, the discursive construction of risk and the materiality of threats. Margaret Thatcher, the former British Prime Minister, once said: there is no such thing as society. Most sociologists believe in what can be called a 'reverse Thatcherism', namely there is *nothing but society*. This 'nothing but society' sociology is blind to the ecological and technological challenges of second modernity. Risk society theory breaks with this self-sufficiency and self-centredness. It argues that there is at the same time the immateriality of mediated and contested definitions of risk *and* the materiality of risk as manufactured by experts and industries world-wide. This has many implications. For example, risk analysis needs an interdisciplinary approach. Risk science without the sociological imagination of constructed and contested risk is *blind*. Risk science that is not informed about the technologically manufactured 'second nature' of threats is *naïve*. The ontology of risk as such does not grant privilege to any specific form of knowledge. It forces everyone to combine different and often divergent rationality-claims, to act and react in the face of 'contradictory certainties' (Schwarz and Thompson, 1990).

In world risk society the politics and subpolitics of risk definition become extremely important. Risks have become a major force of political mobilization, often replacing references to, for example, inequalities associated with class, race and gender. This highlights the new *power game* of risk and its meta-norms: who is to define the riskiness of a product, a technology, and on what grounds in an age of manufactured uncertainties? When, in 1998, the Greens entered Gerhard Schröder's government in Germany, they began to act upon and change some of those power relations of risk definition by, for example, a strategy of pluralization of experts, calling counter-experts into governmental commissions for security who had previously been excluded; or by raising the level of acceptable insurance; or by enforcing legal norms which so far have not really been taken seriously; and so on. This, within the common framework, looks of minor, negligible importance. But this is exactly the point: in risk society seemingly unimportant areas of political intervention and action are becoming extremely important and seemingly 'minor' changes do induce basic long-term transformations in the power game of risk politics.

Thus the framework of risk society again connects what have been strictly discrete areas: the question of nature, the democratization of democracy and the future role of the state. Much political debate over the last twenty years has centred on the decline in the power and legitimacy of government and the need to renew the culture of democracy. Risk society demands an opening up of the decision-making process, not only of the state but of private corporations and the sciences as well. It calls for institutional reform of those 'relations of definition', the hidden power-structure of risk conflicts. This could encourage environmental innovations and help to construct a better developed public sphere in which the crucial questions of value that underpin risk conflicts can be debated and judged (see Jacobs, 1997).

But at the same time new prominence of risk connects, on the one hand, individual autonomy and insecurity in the labour market and in gender relations, and, on the other hand, the sweeping influence of scientific and technological change. World risk society opens public discourse and social science to the challenges of ecological crisis, which, as we now know, are global, local and personal at one and the same time. Nor is this all. In the 'global age', the theme of risk unites many otherwise disparate areas of new transnational politics with the question of cosmopolitan democracy: with the new political economy of uncertainty, financial markets, transcultural conflicts over food and other products (BSE), emerging 'risk communities', and, last but not least, the anarchy of international relations. Personal biographies as well as world politics are getting 'risky' in the global world of manufactured uncertainties.

But the globality of risk does not, of course, mean a global equality of risk. The opposite is true: the first law of environmental risks is: *pollution follows the poor*. In the last decade poverty has intensified everywhere. The UN says more than 2,400 million people now live without sanitation, a considerable increase on a decade ago; 1,200 million have no safe drinking water; similar numbers have inadequate housing, health and education services; more than 1,500 million are now undernourished, not because there is no food, or there is too much drought, but because of the increasing marginalization and exclusion of the poor.

Not only has the gap between rich and poor grown, but more people are falling into the poverty trap. Free-market economic policies, imposed on indebted countries by the West, worsen the situation by forcing countries to develop expert industry to supply the rich, rather than to protect, educate or care for the weakest. The poorest countries now spend more servicing their debt to the richest countries than they do on health and education in their own countries.

The past decade has shown that the dogmatic free-market economics imposed throughout the 1980s – and to which every world and nation forum has since signed up – has exacerbated environmental risks and problems just as much as central planning from Moscow ever did. Indeed free-market ideology has increased the sum of human misery. On the back of crucial free-trade pacts like the WTO and NAFTA, for example, consumption is now virtually out of control in the richest countries. It has multiplied six times in less than twenty-five years, according to the UN. The richest 20 per cent of the people are consuming roughly six times more food, energy, water, transportation, oil and minerals than their parents were.

Risk and *responsibility* are intrinsically connected, as are risk and *trust*, risk and *security* (insurance and safety). To whom can responsibility (and therefore costs) be attributed? Or do we live in a context of 'organized irresponsibility'? This is one of the major issues in most of the political conflicts of our time. Some believe that risk induces control, so that the greater the risk the greater the need for controllability. The concept of 'world risk society', however, draws attention to the *limited* controllability of the dangers we have created for ourselves. The main question is how to take decisions under conditions of manufactured uncertainty, where not only is the knowledge-base incomplete, but more and better knowledge often means more uncertainty.

We now have to recognize and act upon the *new global market risk* which is highlighted by the Asian crisis and which demonstrates the social and political dynamics of the *economic* world risk society. The global market (risk) is a new form of 'organized irresponsibility' because it is an institutional form so impersonal as to have no responsibilities, even to itself. Enabled by the information revolution, the global market risk allows the near-instant flow of funds to determine who, if anyone, will prosper, and who will suffer. Like the competitive terms of economic theory, no one component is large enough to shift the overall flow; nobody controls the global market risk. The components follow their own self-interest, and the results resemble those predicted by theory. Because there is no global government, the global market risk cannot be regulated like national markets. Nor can any national market resist it with impunity. But at the same time the constructed fatalism is an illusion too. Most recently, the spotlight has been on the IMF as it has tried to push the Asian countries into the Procrustean mould of classical economics.

One trouble with this new liberal global economic policy is that too few policy-makers in international economics have noticed that the world is increasingly democratic. Voters have a tendency to vote against policies that hurt them; they are frequently too shortsighted to wait for the economist-assured improvement that will come in the Keynesian long run, when they all are dead. Right now the so-called 'Asian crisis' has set the Asian middle class adrift. Waves of bankruptcies and unemployment are battering the region. Western investors and commentators often view the Asian financial crisis in terms of how big a threat it is to the financial markets. But, like the global ecological risks, the global financial risks cannot be 'kept on one side' but flood and transform themselves into social and political risks, that is, risks for the middle class, the poor or the political elites. To illustrate this very briefly: in Asia, the crisis is wrecking so many lives that the focus has shifted from a purely economic frame of reference to what some might call a 'class plunge'. This again has destabilized governments and states, the social and political situation of minority groups, and so on.

Political analysts say it is still very difficult to predict exactly how the new social and political risks will spill over in individual countries. But many now argue that the risk of backlash against the West, internal crisis or even conflict between nations has increased across the region. And what was unthinkable a year or so ago is becoming real now: the global free market is falling apart and the global free-market ideology is collapsing. All over the world, politicians, including European leaders, are taking tentative steps towards a new policy: protectionism is being reinvented; some are asking for new transnational institutions to control global financial flow, while others plead for a transnational insurance system or a new politics of the existing transnational institutions and regimes. The consequence is that the era of free-market ideology is a fading memory and is being superseded by its opposite: a *politicization* of global market economy.

Today you can illustrate the constitutive components of the global market risks by the experience of the Asian crisis as you could in

1986 the basic aspects of the global technological and ecological risk society with the anthropological shock of Chernobyl. So in the global financial as well as in the global ecological risk society:

- two conflicts, two logics of distribution are interconnected: the distribution of *goods* and the distribution of *bads*;
- the foundations of 'risk calculation' are undermined: damages like millions of unemployed and poor cannot, for example, be compensated financially – it makes no sense to insure oneself against a global recession;
- the '*social explosiveness*' of global financial risks is becoming real: it sets off a dynamic of cultural and political change that undermines bureaucracies, challenges the dominance of classical economics and neoliberalism and redraws the boundaries and battlefields of contemporary politics;
- the institutions of the nation-state collapse;
- risk always involves the question of responsibility, so the need for 'responsible globalization' becomes a world-wide public and political issue;
- new options are emerging: national and regional protectionism, transnational institutions and democratization.

Here is the reason why I call myself neither an optimist nor a pessimist, but a pessimistic optimist: the world risk society is the opposite of a 'postmodern constellation'; it is a self-critical, highly political society in a new sense: the transnational dialogue of politics and democracy – perhaps even sociology – has to be reinvented.

The focus of this book, however, is much more limited. It includes neither the global political economy of uncertainty and risk, nor risk biographies, nor the dangers of international anarchy in the aftermath of the Cold War. Instead, it mainly concentrates on ecological and technological questions of risk, and their sociological and political implications. Along the way, it discusses and answers some of the basic criticisms that my earlier book *Risk Society* has provoked.[2] The thesis is that we now have an 'earth politics' which we did not have some years ago, and that it can be understood and organized in terms of the dynamics and contradictions of a world risk society. What is the environment? What is nature? What is wilderness? What is 'human' in human beings? These and similar questions have to be remembered, reposed, reconsidered and rediscussed in a transnational setting, even if nobody has the answers.

*

We live in an age of risk that is global, individualistic and more moral than we suppose. The ethic of individual self-fulfilment and achievement is the most powerful current in modern Western society. Choosing, deciding, shaping individuals who aspire to be the authors of their lives, the creators of their identities, are the central characters of our time.

This 'me-first' generation has been much criticized, but I believe its individualism is moral and political in a new sense. In many ways this is a more moral time than the 1950s and 1960s. Freedom's children feel more passionately and morally than people used to do about a wide range of issues – from our treatment of the environment and animals, to gender, race and human rights around the world.

It could be that this provides the basis for a new cosmopolitanism, by placing globality at the heart of political imagination, action and organization. But any attempt to create a new sense of social cohesion has to start from the recognition that individualization, diversity and scepticism are written into our culture.

Let us be clear what 'individualization' means. It does *not* mean individualism. It does *not* mean individuation – how to become a unique person. It is *not* Thatcherism, not market individualism, not atomization. On the contrary, individualization is a *structural* concept, related to the welfare state; it means '*institutionalized* individualism'. Most of the rights and entitlements of the welfare state, for example, are designed for individuals rather than for families. In many cases they presuppose employment. Employment in turn implies education, and both of these presuppose mobility. By all these requirements people are invited to constitute themselves as individuals: to plan, understand, design themselves as individuals and, should they fail, to blame themselves. Individualization thus implies, paradoxically, a collective lifestyle.

When this is coupled with the language of ethical globalization, I am convinced that a cosmopolitan democracy is a realistic, if utopian, project – though in an age of side-effects, we must also reflect on the dark side, on the ways it can be used politically as a front for old-style imperial adventures.

Are we a 'me-first' society? One might think so from the catch-phrases that dominate public debate: the dissolving of solidarity, the decline of values, the culture of narcissism, entitlement-oriented hedonism, and so on. On this view, modern society lives off moral resources it is unable to renew; the transcendental 'value ecology', in which community, solidarity, justice and ultimately democracy are 'rooted', is decaying; modernity is undermining its own indispensable moral prerequisites.

But this conception of modern society is false. Morality, including Christian morality, and political freedom are not mutually exclusive but mutually inclusive, even if this means that an insoluble contradiction is lodged within Christian traditions.

The question is: what is modernity? And the answer is: not only capitalism (Marx), rationalization (Weber), functional differentiation (Parsons, Luhmann), but also the dynamics of political freedom, citizenship and civil society. The point of this answer is that morality and justice are not extra-territorial variables for modern society. Quite the reverse is true. Modernity has an independent (simultaneously ancient and very modern) well-spring of meaning in its midst, which is political freedom. This spring is not exhausted by daily use – indeed, it bubbles up all the more vigorously as a result. Modernity, from this point of view, means that a world of traditional certainty is perishing and being replaced – if we are fortunate – by a legally sanctioned individualism for all.

In what we have called the first modernity, the issue of who has and who has not a right to freedom was answered through recourse to such matters as the 'nature' of gender and ethnicity; contradictions between universal claims and particular realities were settled by an ontology of difference. Thus until the early 1970s, even in Western countries, women were denied civil rights such as the control of property and of their own bodies.

In the second modernity, the structure of community, group and identity loses this ontological cement. After *political* democratization (the democratic state) and *social* democratization (the welfare state) a *cultural* democratization is changing the foundations of the family, gender relations, love, sexuality and intimacy. Our words about freedom start to become deeds and to challenge the basis of everyday life, as well as of global politics. Being freedom's children, we live under conditions of radicalized democracy for which many of the concepts and formulas of the first modernity have become inadequate.

No one knows how the ever-growing demand for family intimacy can be tied in with the new demands for freedom and self-realization for men, women and children. No one knows whether the exigencies of mass organization (political parties, trade unions) are compatible with the claims for participation and self-organization.

People are better adapted to the future than are social institutions and their representatives. The decline of values which cultural pessimists are so fond of decrying is in fact opening up the possibility of an escape from the 'bigger, more, better' creed, in a period that is living beyond its means both ecologically and economically. Whereas, in the old system of values, the self always had to be subordinated to patterns of the collective, the new orientations towards the 'we' are creating something like a cooperative or altruist individualism. Thinking of oneself and living for others – once considered by definition contradictory – are revealed as internally and substantively connected with each other (see Wuthnow, 1991). Living alone means living socially.

As well as ignoring these aspects of institutionalized individualism most moral preachers also fail to mention that an ever larger number of men and women are compelled to treat the future as a threat, rather than as a shelter or a promised land. All we can do here is offer a few notes about how such a *political economy* of uncertainty, the political economy of world risk society, might be developed.[3]

First, the new power-play between territorially fixed political actors (government, parliament, unions) and non-territorial economic actors (representatives of capital, finance, trade) is the central element expressed in the political economics of uncertainty and risk. To provide a simple formula: capital is global, work is local. All around the world, at the same time, *fragile* work increases rapidly, that is, part-time, self-employed work, limited-term jobs and other forms for which we have barely found proper descriptions. If this dynamic continues, in ten to fifteen years about half the employable population of the West will work under conditions of uncertainty. What used to be the exception is becoming the rule.

Second, this leads to a well-founded impression that states no longer have any leeway except to choose between (a) social protection of the growing numbers of the poor, at the price of high unemployment (as in most European countries), and (b) acceptance of glaring poverty to achieve slightly lower unemployment (as in the United States).

Third, this is bound up with the end of the work society as more and more human beings are replaced by intelligent technologies. Rising unemployment can no longer be attributed to cyclical economic crisis, but rather to the *success* of technologically advanced capitalism. Since the early 1970s the relationship between GDP growth and employment has become tenuous in all OECD countries. Considerable increases in per capita GDP have been accompanied by little or no employment growth. The old instruments of economic policy therefore fail to achieve results, and work today is, so to speak, a daily rehearsal of redundancy.

Fourth, the political economy of uncertainty describes and analyses a *domino effect*. Things which used to supplement and reinforce one another in good times – full employment, pension savings, high tax revenue, leeway for government action – now tend *mutatis mutandis* to endanger one another. As employment grows more precarious, the bases of the welfare state decay and 'normal' biographies come apart;

the ever-growing pressure on welfare cannot be financed from a public purse full of holes.

Fifth, orthodox defensive strategies are therefore put under pressure. 'Flexibility' is demanded everywhere – or, in other words, an 'employer' should be able to fire 'employees' more easily. 'Flexibility' also means a redistribution of risks from state and economy to individuals. The jobs available become more and more short-term and 'renewable' – which is to say, 'terminable'. People are just asked to smile and accept it: 'Your skills and abilities are obsolete, and no one can tell you what to learn so that you will be needed in the future.' Consequently, the more work relations are 'deregulated' and 'flexibilized', the faster work society turns into a risk society that is not open to calculation by individuals or by politics. At the same time, it becomes increasingly important to resolve the contradictions that the political economy of risk[4] implies for economics, politics and society (Beck, 1999a). One thing is clear. Endemic uncertainty is what will mark the lifeworld and the basic existence of most people – including the apparently affluent middle classes – in the years that lie ahead. So, the expression 'precarious freedoms' denotes a basic ambivalence between the cultural script of individual self-fulfilment and the new political economy of uncertainty and risk. All too swiftly, the 'elective', 'reflexive' or 'do-it-yourself' biography can become the breakdown biography.

Let us link these points up with our previous theme. How can a secular society exposed to the rigours of a global market, based on institutionalized individualization amidst a global communications explosion, also foster a sense of belonging, trust and cohesion? It can do this only through a source which, instead of being exhausted by daily use, pours forth all the stronger – only through cultural democratization and political freedom. Yet there is a basic contradiction between political freedom and the political economy of risk and uncertainty. On the road to the uncontested rule of the political economy of risk, republican institutions and the liveliness of democratic culture are the first to go by the board. As Zygmunt Bauman (1999) has put it:

> The purpose of the republic is not an imposition of a preconceived model of the 'good' life, but the enabling of its citizens to discuss freely the models of life they prefer and to practise them. . . . The decoupling of income entitlements from paid work and from the labour market may serve the republic in only one, but a crucial, way: *by taking out the awesome fly of insecurity from the ointment of freedom.* But this limitation of risks and damages is precisely the most crucial of the basic-income objectives.[5]

When, or if, this objective is reached, men and women no longer afraid to use their freedom may find the time, will and courage to tackle the challenges of the second modernity. Let there be no misunderstanding. I am not arguing for a basic assured income to raise the poor from their poverty – that is an important issue, but one relating to a special (interest) group. My argument is, I believe, stronger: namely, that we need a basic assured income as a *sine qua non* of a political republic of individuals who will create a sense of cohesion and fellow-feeling through public conflict and commitment (see Beck, 1998a).

With political freedom placed at its centre, modernity is not an age of decline of values but an age *of* values, in which the hierarchical certainty of ontological difference is displaced by the creative uncertainty of freedom. Freedom's children are the first to live in a post-national cosmopolitan world order. But what does this mean politically? Living in an age of side-effects, we have to ask very early what are the unforeseen and unwanted consequences of the new rhetoric of 'global community', 'global governance' and 'cosmopolitan democracy'. What are the risks if the cosmopolitan mission succeeds?

The collapse of the Soviet bloc has not only made it easier to effect a collective name-change from 'the West' to 'global neighbourhood'. Its importance is greater than that. For whereas the West's promotion of universal values such as human rights or democracy used always to be open to challenge and was often discredited in practice – in the case of the Vietnam War, for example – today, for the first time, the West has *carte blanche* to define and promote universal values. With the removal of any challenge to the dominance of the world's major economic powers, these moral arguments too can be posited on uncontested grounds. The themes of global civil society and an ethical foreign policy have provided a new ideological cement for the project of Western power.

Globalization implies the weakening of state structures, of the autonomy and power of the state. This has a paradoxical result. On the one hand, it is precisely collapses of the state which have produced most of the really grave human conflicts of the 1990s, whether in Somalia, East Africa, Yugoslavia, Albania or the former Soviet Union; on the other hand, the idea of 'global responsibility' implies at least the possibility of a new Western *military humanism* – to enforce human rights around the globe. Consequently, the greater the success of neoliberal politics on a global level – that is, the greater the erosion of state structures – the more likely it is that a 'cosmopolitan façade' will emerge to legitimize Western military intervention. The striking feature here is that imperial power-play can coexist harmoniously with a cosmopolitan mission. For the subordination of weak states to institutions of 'global governance' actually creates the space for power strategies disguised as humane intervention.

Of course, there are also double standards of morality involved here. Take the example of cosmopolitan democracy itself. What would happen if the European Union wanted to become a member of the European Union? Naturally it would have to be refused. Why? Because of its glaring lack of democracy! But it must also be asked whether EU member-states such as France, Germany, Britain or Italy can really be considered democracies, when roughly half the laws passed in their parliaments merely transplant directives issued by Brussels, the World Trade Organization, and so on.

In the age of globalization, there is no easy escape from this democratic dilemma. It cannot be solved simply by moving towards 'cosmopolitan democracy'. The central problem is that without a politically strong cosmopolitan consciousness, and without corresponding institutions of global civil society and public opinion, cosmopolitan democracy remains, for all the institutional fantasy, no more than a necessary utopia. The decisive question is whether and how a consciousness of cosmopolitan solidarity can develop. The *Communist Manifesto* was published a hundred and fifty years ago. Today, at the beginning of a new millennium, it is time for a Cosmopolitan Manifesto. The *Communist Manifesto* was about class conflict. The Cosmopolitan Manifesto is about transnational–national conflict and dialogue which has to be opened up and organized. What is to be the object of this global dialogue? The goals, values and structures of a cosmopolitan society. The possibility of democracy in a global age.

Who will raise this question? The 'me-first' generation, freedom's children. We have been witnessing a global erosion of the authority of national states and a general loss of confidence in hierarchical institutions. But at the same time, active intervention by citizens has been growing more common and breaking the bounds of past convention – especially among younger and more educated sections of the population. The spaces in which people think and act in a morally responsible manner are becoming smaller and more likely to involve intense personal relationships. They are also, however, becoming more global and difficult to manage. Young people are moved by issues that national politics largely rules out. How can global environmental destruction be avoided? How can one live and love with the threat of AIDS? What do tolerance and social justice mean in the global age?

These questions slip through the political agendas of national states. The consequence is that freedom's children practise a highly political disavowal of politics.

The key idea for a Cosmopolitan Manifesto is that there is a new dialectic of global and local questions which do not fit into national politics. These 'glocal' questions, as we might call them, are already part of the political agenda – in the localities and regions, in governments and public spheres both national and international. But only in a transnational framework can they be properly posed, debated and resolved. For this there has to be a reinvention of politics, a founding and grounding of the new political subject: that is, of *cosmopolitan parties*. These represent transnational interests transnationally, but also work within the arenas of national politics. They thus become possible, both programmatically and organizationally, only as national–global movements *and* cosmopolitan parties.

The underlying basis here is an understanding that the central human worries are 'world' problems, and not only because in their origins and consequences they have outgrown the national schema of politics. They are also 'world' problems in their very concreteness, in their very location here and now in this town, or this political organization.

Let us take the case of all the various regulation-intensive industries that have been liberalized in recent years: telecommunications is the main example; others include energy, financial services and food. Increased competition in these areas has brought the domestic regimes that regulate them into conflict, but meanwhile the problems have become global. And this is just the start. Looming ahead are new issues – environmental and labour legislation – in which regulation is even more sensitive, even more crucial. This is the challenge of the years to come. A first wave of national deregulation enforces a second wave of transnational regulation. Without a decisive step towards cosmopolitan democratization, we are heading for a post-political technocratic world society.[6]

The first expressions of a cosmopolitan politics are already taking shape within the framework of national states – expressions that require specific points to crystallize as political movements within and between national states. This creates the opportunities for cosmopolitan movements and parties which, even if they initially win over and mobilize only minorities for cosmopolitan interests, have the basis of their power in the act of opening out the transnational domain.

This is a difficult task. The resolution of problems in all these areas is already providing conflict enough between the US and the EU – for example, over food safety questions. Difficulties will be even greater between countries that are more divergent in their cultural assumptions, political forms and income levels. So cosmopolitan parties will have to organize global debates on these highly controversial issues, both from within and from outside individual countries. Just like corporate agrarian societies and nationally based industrial or service societies, so too world society develops its own forms of social inequality and notions of justice, its own political values and ideas, its own hysterias and dilemmas, and its own questions of organization and representation.

As I learned from Martin Albrow and his group, non-territorial communities that are organized, for example, around a transnational division of labour should be understood as 'socio-scapes' (Albrow, 1996; Eade, 1997). But again the question arises: how are post-national communities possible as bases for political action and collectively binding decision-making? There are many risks in life, and only some are suitable as the basis of community. But *risk-sharing* or a *'socialization of risk'* (Elkins, 1995) can, in my view, become a powerful basis of community, one which has both territorial and non-territorial aspects. So far, risk has seemed a purely negative phenomenon, to be avoided or minimized. But it may be seen at the same time as a positive phenomenon too, when it involves the sharing of risks without borders. Post-national communities could thus be constructed and reconstructed as communities of risk. Cultural definitions of appropriate types or degrees of risk define the community, in effect, as those who share the relevant assumptions. 'Risk-sharing' further involves the taking of responsibility, which again implies conventions and boundaries around a 'risk community' that shares the burden. And in our high-tech world, many risk communities are potentially political communities in a new sense – because they have to live with the risks that others take. There is a basic power structure within world risk society, dividing those who produce and profit from risks and the many who are afflicted with the same risks.

This idea of non-territorial communities of shared risk cannot be developed here in all its aspects. But the key questions it poses are the following. Should risks and their attendant costs be shared among certain categories of citizens or among residents of a certain place? How can global risks ever be shared? What does it mean when the socialization of risk occurs across generations? Models of post-national risk communities may be found, for example, in regional ecological treaties (for example, among states bordering the North Sea or the Mediterranean), in transnational communities, non-governmental organizations or global movements, such as ecological or feminist networks.

These movements form a 'world party' in a threefold sense. First, their values and goals have not a national but a cosmopolitan foundation: their appeal (*liberty, diversity, toleration!*) is to human values and traditions in every culture and religion; they feel an obligation towards the planet as a whole. National parties, on the other hand, appeal to national values, traditions and solidarities.

Second, they are world parties because they place globality at the heart of political imagination, action and organization. Both programmatically and institutionally, they propose a politics of concrete alternatives to the firmly established and firmly guided priorities of the national sphere. Thus, for cosmopolitan parties what is at issue is never just a certain content, but always also a new concept, new structures, new institutions of politics, which for the first time offer a platform for the negotiation and enforcement of transnational issues from below.

Third, they are world parties in the sense that they are possible only as *multinational* parties. Thus, there have to be cosmopolitan movements and parties of French, North American, Polish, German, Japanese, Chinese, South African and other provenances which, by interacting with one another in the various areas of world society, struggle to bring about cosmopolitan values, mutualities and institutions. This involves strengthening the existing independent transnational institutions against national egoisms, but above all else it involves the democratization of transnational regimes and regulators.

Which groups come into consideration as bearers of such a cosmopolitan movement to expand democracy? Where are the voters who feel they are addressed and represented by cosmopolitan parties and could be mobilized and organized by them? Where globality becomes an everyday problem or the object of cooperation – in the big cities, the transnational organizations and movements, schools and universities – the milieu and mentality of a self-conscious world citizenship take shape with a post-national understanding of politics, responsibility, the state, justice, art, science and public interchange. However, the extent to which this is already so, or likely in the future, is still open, both empirically and politically.

This expanding 'world citizenship' (Kant) with national cultural hues should not be confused with the rise of a global managerial class. A distinction must be drawn between 'global capitalists' and 'global citizens'. Yet a plural world citizenship is soaring with the wind of global capital at its back. For the bourgeois must already learn to operate in his or her own interests in a transnational framework, while the citizen must still think and act within the categories of the national state.

Nevertheless, in the milieu of transnational structures, experts and counter-experts, transnational movements and networks, we can see experimental forms of organization and the expression of a cosmopolitan common sense. It comprises a mixture of scepticism about national egoisms masquerading as universal necessities, and scepticism about the mistakes and defects of national bureaucracies. Voluntary organizations play a crucial role in building a global civil society. They help to generate the public-mindedness and civic trust to open up the national agendas for transnational, cosmopolitan concerns. And they constitute a human flourishing in their own right.

How can cosmopolitan movements become possible and powerful? In the end, this question can be answered only where people ask and listen to it – in the space of political experimentation. Citizens of the world, unite!

2

World Risk Society as Cosmopolitan Society?

Ecological Questions in a Framework of Manufactured Uncertainties

Risk society, fully thought through, means world risk society. For its axial principle, its challenges, are dangers produced by civilization which cannot be socially delimited in either space or time. In this way the basic conditions and principles of the first, industrial modernity – class antagonism, national statehood, as well as the images of linear, technical-economic rationality and control – are circumvented and annulled (the concept '*world* risk society' was first introduced in Beck, 1992, see also Beck, 1995 and chapter 3 below).

It is clear, then, which concepts will *not* be employed here. The focus will not be on 'nature' or the 'destruction of nature', nor on 'ecological' or 'environmental problems'. Does this have to do with a systematic setting of goals? Yes, it does – as we shall see. In fact, we shall propose – for the sociological analysis of ecological questions – a conceptual framework which allows us to grasp them as problems not of the *environment* or surrounding world, but of the *inner* world of society. In place of the seemingly self-evident key concepts of 'nature', 'ecology' and 'environment', which have their ground in an opposition to the social, this framework starts beyond the dualism of society and nature. Its central themes and perspectives have to do with *fabricated uncertainty* within our civilization: risk, danger, side-effects, insurability, individualization and globalization.

It has often been objected that such talk of a world risk society encourages a kind of neo-Spenglerism and blocks any political action. We shall see, however, that the opposite is also the case. In the self-understanding of world risk society, society becomes *reflexive* in three senses (on reflexive modernization see the various positions of Beck, Giddens and Lash in Beck et al., 1994). First, it becomes an issue and problem for itself: global dangers set up global mutualities, and indeed the contours of a (potential) world public sphere begin to take shape. Second, the perceived globality of the self-endangerment of civilization triggers a politically mouldable impulse towards the development of cooperative international institutions. Third, the boundaries of the political come to be removed: constellations appear of a subpolitics at once global and direct, which relativizes or circumvents the coordinates and coalitions of nation-state politics and may lead to world-wide 'alliances of mutually exclusive beliefs'. In other words, 'cosmopolitan society' (Kant) can take shape in the perceived necessity of world risk society.

Elements of a Theory of World Risk Society

The Indeterminacy of the Concepts of 'Nature' and 'Ecology'

The concept of 'ecology' has had quite a success story. Today, responsibility for the condition of nature is laid at the door of ministers and managers. Evidence that the 'side-effects' of products or industrial processes are endangering the basic conditions of life can cause markets to collapse, destroying political confidence as well as economic capital and belief in the superior rationality of experts. This success, in many respects thoroughly subversive, disguises the fact that 'ecology' is a quite vague concept; everyone gives a different answer to the question of what should be preserved.[1]

'Again I came up against all the claptrap about nature', writes the German poet Gottfried Benn (1986: 71ff).

> Snow, even when it does not melt, hardly provides any linguistic or emotional themes: you can fully grasp its indisputable monotony without going out of doors. Nature is empty and desolate; only petty-bourgeois minds see something in it – poor devils who have to keep taking the air. For example, forests lack any thematic material and everything below 1500 metres is old hat, ever since you have been able to see and experience Mount Palü in the cinema for one mark.... Steer clear of nature! It messes up your thoughts and has a notoriously

bad effect on your style! *Natura* – a feminine noun, of course! Always concerned to draw off the male's semen, to copulate with him and tire him out. But is nature at all natural? It starts something and then lets it lie: beginnings and just as many interruptions, changes of direction, failures, desertions, contradictions, things flaring up, meaningless deaths, experiments, games, appearances of reality – the classroom example of the unnatural! And it is also uncommonly laborious, marching up the hill and down again: ascents that are ever cancelling each other out, clear views all around that continually become blurred, hitherto unknown and then forgotten lookout points – stupid tricks, in other words.

If someone uses the word 'nature', the question immediately arises: what *cultural model* of 'nature' is being taken for granted? Nature 'in hand', driven to exhaustion by industry? Or the country life of the 1950s (as it appears today in retrospect or as it appeared then to people living in the country)? Mountain solitude before there was a book called *Wandering in the Solitary Mountains*? The nature of the natural sciences? Or as it is sold in the tourist supermarket brochures of world solitude? The 'hard-headed' view of businessmen that industrial operations on nature can always be fully compensated? Or the view of 'sensitive' people stirred by nature, who consider that even small-scale operations may cause irreparable damage?

So, nature itself is not nature: it is a concept, a norm, a recollection, a utopia, an alternative plan. Today more than ever. Nature is being rediscovered, pampered, at a time when it is no longer there. The ecological movement is reacting to the global state of a contradictory fusion of nature and society, which has superseded both concepts in a relationship of mutual linkages and injuries of which we do not yet have any idea, let alone any concept. In the ecological debate, attempts to use nature as a standard against its own destruction rest upon a *naturalistic misunderstanding*. For the nature invoked is no longer there (Oechsele, 1988; Beck, 1992: 81; 1995: 58–72). What is there, and what creates such a political stir, are different forms of socialization and different symbolic mediations of nature (and the destruction of nature). It is these *cultural concepts* of nature, these opposing views of nature and their (national) cultural traditions, which, behind the disputes among experts and the technical formulae and dangers, have a determining influence on ecological conflicts in Europe, as well as between Europe and 'Third World' countries and within those countries themselves.[2]

But if nature 'in itself' cannot be the analytic reference for the ecological crisis and for a critique of the industrial system, what can play this role? A number of answers are possible. The most common is: the *science* of nature. Technical formulae – toxicity of air, water and food, climatological models, or feedback loops of the ecosystem conceived along cybernetic lines – are supposed to be decisive for whether damage and destruction are tolerable. This approach, however, has at least three drawbacks. First, it leads straight towards 'ecocracy', which differs from technocracy through its greater extent of power (global management), crowned with a distinctively good conscience.

Second, it ignores the significance of cultural perceptions and of intercultural conflict and dialogue. For the same dangers appear to one person as dragons, and to another as earthworms. The best example of this is the assessment of the hazards of atomic energy. For our French neighbours, nuclear power stations symbolize the pinnacle of modernity; adults take their children to them on bank-holiday pilgrimages of awe. Meanwhile, on the other side of the border, the German government is now changing its politics in order to exit the atomic age.

Third, natural-science approaches to ecological questions again imply hidden cultural models of nature (for example, the model characteristic of scientific systems, which clearly differs from the earlier one of natural conservation).

Of course, everyone has to think in the concepts of natural science simply to perceive the world as ecologically threatened. Everyday ecological consciousness is thus the exact opposite of some 'natural' consciousness: it is a totally scientific view of the world, in which chemical formulae determine everyday behaviour.[3]

And yet, all manner of experts can never answer the question: how do we want to live? What people are and are not prepared to go on accepting does not follow from any technical or ecological diagnosis of dangers. This must rather become the object of a global dialogue between cultures. And it is precisely that which appears as the aim in a second perspective, associated with the science of *culture*. Here, the scale and urgency of the ecological crisis vary according to intracultural and intercultural perceptions and evaluations.

What kind of truth is it – we might ask with Montaigne – which ends on the border with France and is then regarded as pure illusion? Dangers, it would seem, do not exist 'in themselves', independently of our perceptions. They become a political issue only when people are generally aware of them; they are social constructs which are strategically defined, covered up or dramatized in the public sphere with the help of scientific material supplied for the purpose. Not by chance, two Anglo-Saxon social anthropologists – Mary Douglas and

Aaron Wildavsky – have been developing this analysis since their book *Risk and Culture* was published in 1982. Douglas and her co-author argue there (as an affront to the rising ecological consciousness) that there is no substantive difference between the dangers posed in early history and in developed civilization – except in the mode of cultural perception and the way in which it is organized in world society.

True and important though this view may be, it is still not satisfactory. First, it highlights the (mistakes of the) 'nothing but society' sociology which ignores the 'and' characteristic of risk's immateriality (social definition) *and* materiality (product of action). Second, we know that people in the Stone Age did not have the capacity for nuclear and ecological annihilation, and that the dangers posed by lurking demons did not have the same political dynamic as the man-made hazards of ecological self-destruction.[4]

The Realism–Constructivism Debate

This is where the theory of world risk society begins. If it is asked what is the justification for this concept, two answers are possible: one *realist* and one *constructivist* (for an interpretation and critique see Szerszynski et al., 1996; Wynne, 1996a). In the realist view, the consequences and dangers of developed industrial production 'are' now global. This 'are' supports itself upon scientific findings and debates about ongoing destruction (of the ozone layer, for example); the development of productive forces is intertwined with the development of destructive forces, and together these are generating – in the shadow of latent side-effects – the novel dynamic of conflict of a world risk society. This dynamic is expressed in such things as the Chernobyl disaster, when an 'atomic cloud' terrified the whole of Europe and forced people to make major changes even in their day-to-day private lives.[5] But it is also expressed in the knowledge of every mature newspaper-reader or TV viewer in Western societies that the poisoning of air, water, soil, plants and foodstuffs 'knows no boundaries'.

In this 'realist' perspective, then, talk of a world risk society reflects the forced global socialization due to dangers produced by civilization. The new state of the world is the basis for the growing importance of transnational institutions. To the global dangers correspond, 'realistically', global models of perception, world fora of public life and action, and finally – if the supposed objectivity gives sufficient impetus for action – transnational actors and institutions.

The strength of realism can also be seen in its clear historical 'story-line', in which the development of industry or industrial society has gone through two distinct phases. In a first phase it was class or social questions that were paramount; in a second phase it is ecological questions. Yet it would be much too simple to assume that ecology has supplanted the class question; it is quite apparent, and needs to be stressed, that the ecological, labour-market and economic crises are overlapping and may well aggravate one another. A phase model stands to gain in persuasive force, however, if it counterposes the global reach of ecological questions to the issues of poverty and class that dominated the national phase of industrial capitalism. For in this way, the patterns of conflict of industrial society are rendered null and void. To assume the objectivity of global dangers is to further the construction of (centralized) transnational institutions. This point of view, often suspected of being naïve, thus involves – or even produces – a considerable impetus to power, in order to carry through a policy of 'sustainable development', as it is called in a new magic phrase.

A superficial look at such realist ways of grounding the world risk society is enough to show how feeble they really are. In the first place, the unreflexive realist viewpoint forgets or suppresses the fact that its 'realism' is sedimented, fragmented, mass-media collective consciousness. Of course, as Bryan Wynne argues, public knowledge about risk is often not expert but lay knowledge, from which social recognition has been withheld.[6] But ecological images and symbols do not at all have intrinsic certainty: they are culturally perceived, constructed and mediatized; they are part of the social fabric of knowledge, with all its contradictions and conflicts (social movements, television, daily press, environmental organizations, research institutes, and so on). The definitional power of realism rests upon exclusion of questions that speak more for the interpretative superiority of constructivist approaches. How, for example, is the borrowed self-evidence of 'realistic' dangers actually produced? Which actors, institutions, strategies and resources are decisive in its *fabrication*? These questions can be meaningfully asked and understood only within an anti-realist, constructivist perspective.

In a social-constructivist view, then, talk of a 'world risk society' rests not on a (scientifically diagnosed) globality of problems but on *transnational 'discourse coalitions'* (Hajer, 1996), which assert within public space the issues of a global environmental agenda. These coalitions were forged and became powerful only in the 1970s and 1980s, and in the present decade – especially since the Rio Earth

Summit – they have begun to reshape the thematic landscape around problems of the planet. This obviously requires institutionalization of the environmental movement and the building of networks and transnational actors (IUN, WWF, Greenpeace, but also environment ministries, national and international legislation and agreements, and industries and big science rising to the task of global management of world problems). Nor is that all. Such actors must also be *successful* in what they do, and continually assert themselves against powerful counter-coalitions.

So far, the global approach to problems – the very talk of a world risk society – has encountered three types of counter-argument. First, it is argued that the relevant (lay and expert) knowledge is far from clear about the global hazards; many also refer to discrepancies between the actual state of expert knowledge and the public drama of danger and crisis. Second, the global definition of environmental problems is criticized as a kind of ecological neo-imperialism, especially by actors and governments in the so-called 'Third World'. The idea here is not only that Western states thereby assure themselves of a lead in knowledge and development over poorer countries, but above all that they cover up their own primary responsibility for world-wide threats to civilization. Third, the objection is raised that the global definition of ecological questions leads to a perversion of 'nature conservation' into its opposite, a kind of world-management. This then sets up new monopolies of knowledge – the hi-tech 'global circulation models' of the International Panel for Climate Change (IPCC), with their inbuilt forms of politics and their demands for disciplinary interpretation and control (especially of the natural and computer sciences).

Furthermore, it is becoming noticeable that talk of a world risk society does not go together with the overcoming of ethnic-nationalist conflicts of perception and evaluation. On the contrary, it seems to accompany the emergence of new ones (for example, in disputes over 'degrees' of danger, or who is 'responsible', or the need for counter-measures), which serve to define the future winners and losers among nations.

However contradictory the essentialist-realist and constructivist approaches may be in their methods and basic assumptions, they agree with each other in their diagnoses. For, in different ways, they both justify talk of a world risk society. This should by no means lead us to minimize the differences. It is particularly remarkable that realism lays the stress on *world risk* society, and constructivism on world risk *society*. In the constructivist optic, transnational actors must already have *pushed through* their discursive politics, so that the globality of environmental issues is decisive for social perceptions and demands for action. On the 'realist' side, by contrast, this globality is based *only* upon the floating ostensible self-authority of objective dangers. We might say that realism conceives the ecological problematic as 'closed', whereas constructivism maintains its *openness* in principle. For the one, it is the *dangers* (the doomsday scenarios) of the world risk society that are the central focus; for the other, it is the *opportunities*, the contexts in which actors operate. For the one, global dangers must first of all give rise to international institutions and treaties. For the other, talk of global environmental dangers already assumes supranational discourse coalitions engaging in successful action.

But another question poses itself here. Is it really true that realism and constructivism, in their approaches to world risk society and their ways of explaining it, are in every respect mutually exclusive? This is the case only as long as both sides are assumed to play *naïvely*. For just as there is a belief that nature and reality simply exist as such, there is also a belief in pure constructivism that is nothing but constructivist. As long as we remain at this level, we will fail to recognize the interpretative content of *reflexive realism*, and hence its potential role in *strategies of power*. Such a reflexive realism does delve into the sources which make of 'reality constructs' a 'reality' for the first time; it investigates how self-evidence is produced, how questions are curtailed, how alternative interpretations are shut up in black boxes, and so on.

If one distrusts simple counter-positions, it is thus possible to counterpose or juxtapose 'reflexive' realism and 'naïve' constructivism. Naïve constructivism is unable to see the game of constructivist realism, and so remains stuck in what one might call a realist misunderstanding of its mere constructivism. It fails to recognize, as it were, that constructions of reality which are meant to last (and to guide action) must cancel their very constructedness – otherwise they will be constructed as *constructions* of reality and not as *reality*. Similarly, naïve constructivism does not grasp the characteristic materiality or compulsiveness of global dangers, which is in every way as powerful as economic constraints. Constructivist analyses, if they are blind to the difference between destruction as an *event* and *talk* about that event, may cognitively play down dangers. For it is possible that, in leaving 'cognitive elements' out of account, they will overlook the fact that dangers have destructive, painful and disintegrative effects and therefore a chaotic-diabolic significance.

How is the Nature–Society Distinction Socially Constructed and Sociologically Reconstructed?

A number of sociological research programmes, starting from different points, are working on this question of how the old dualism between nature and society can be superseded, at the same time that it is redefined and reconceptualized in the sense of symbolically mediated social relations with nature.

From a context of scientific and technological research, Bruno Latour (1993) and Donna Haraway (1991) have suggested dropping the nature–society dualism in favour of a *sociology of artefacts* or – as they put it – of *hybrids*. As to what is to replace the basic distinction between society and nature (society and technique), Latour and Haraway reply: the new unity of their indistinguishability. They can spell this out quite convincingly in *negative terms*, but not when it comes to its positive meaning. The reader is left feeling as the angel does in Walter Benjamin's parable. To decipher the meaning of the text, all you can do is stand with your back to the headwind of the arguments. If you want to know and understand more, you have to consult, for example, Latour's empirical-historical studies relating to actor-network theory.[7]

In the field of gender research, a number of thoroughly competitive attempts at a *feminist eco-sociology* have recently been produced. What they have in common is the assumption of a special relationship between woman and nature – where 'special' implies a concept of the 'normal' or 'other'. This is found in the patriarchally determined relationship between man and nature. Technical-industrial domination of nature thus has its parallel (its basis?) in the domination of men over women, and the former can only be eradicated along with the latter. The special relationship between woman and nature is conceived in either essentialist or constructivist terms, or as a combination of the two. In any case it is women who – not least because of their experience of motherhood – appear to be closer to nature. This is sometimes understood symbolically or spiritualistically – for instance, in the sense that 'women have always thought like mountains' (Doubiago, 1989: 41).

In the view of Charlene Spretnak (1989: 128f), experiences of women living together point to

the truths of naturalism and the holistic proclivities of women. . . . I do not mean 'merely' our power to form people from our very flesh and blood and then to nourish them from our breasts. . . . I mean that there are many moments in a woman's life wherein she gains experiential knowledge, in a powerful body/mind union, of the holistic truths of spirituality.

Ynestra King (1989: 22f) turns this essentialist view into a political one. Assuming that the supposed proximity of women to nature is a social construct, there are three options for feminists. First, women can be integrated into the world of men, so that the woman–nature bond is severed. Second, women can strengthen this bond. And third:

> although the nature–culture dualism is a product of culture, we can nonetheless *consciously choose* not to sever the woman–nature connection by joining male culture. Rather, we can use it as a vantage point for creating a different kind of culture and politics that would integrate intuitive, spiritual and rational forms of knowledge, embracing both science and magic insofar as they enable us to transform the nature–culture distinction and to envision and create a free, ecological society.

In an approach that combines the sociology of technology with feminist ecology, Donna Haraway (1991: 150) has demonstrated to great intellectual and political effect how the traditional boundaries between the sexes (as well as between nature and culture, man and animal, man and machine) are generally fading under the influence of computer and bio-technologies. She argues that this should not be mourned as a loss, but rather seized as a chance for 'pleasure in the confusion of boundaries and responsibility in their construction'.

As Barbara Adam's work (1995, 1996, 1998) so finely shows, an explicit focus on *social time* both deepens eco-feminist analysis and emphasizes the acculturation of nature.

> As rhythmicity and synchronization, growth and decay, 'natural time' is implicated in human being-becoming, experience and knowledge. As memory and anticipation, it constitutes our temporal horizon. As physical measure and source for synchronization, it is integral to social organization and the regulation of cultural activity. As externalized machine, time is linked to industrial production, to the role of abstract exchange-value, and to the social control of time. To recognize ourselves as having evolved and thus *being* and *creating* the times of nature allows for the humanly constructed and symbolized aspects of time to become one expression among others.
>
> (*Adam, 1996: 92*)

The meanings and dimension of 'natural' and 'social' time connect the realist and constructivist views in a most thoughtful manner.

Following on from the theory of late capitalism, some authors working on theoretical and empirical research in the field of *social ecology* have identified what they call a *social crisis in the relationship to nature*. While coming out against the dead-ends of naturalism and socio-centrism, they nevertheless try to combine the achievements of both. Neither the material problems describable by the natural sciences, nor the cultural-symbolic (over-)patterning of natural destruction on which constructivism lays such stress, can alone constitute the kernel of the ecological crisis. What is central, they argue, is that these apparently exclusive approaches and certainties should be considered together and combined in concrete research, with all the historically inevitable conflicts between scientific disciplines.

The social-ecological approach thus seeks to resolve the dilemma of naturalism or socio-centrism through the interaction between different forms of *science* and *knowledge*.

> The distinguishing features of this approach are, first, that a number of different natural relationships are each grasped as specific fields to be fought over; second, that their scientific handling is bound up with the demand for a new *interdisciplinarity*, a new relationship between the natural and social sciences; and third, that plurality is embedded in a general explanatory model of society, a model of 'transformational kernel and cultural shell'.
>
> (*Scharping and Görg, 1994: 190; see also Becker, 1990*)

To be properly understood and assessed, however, these three themes of a 'crisis of social relationships to nature' would have to be formulated and translated within the context of (social-)scientific research.

The essentialist meaning in talk of nature and the destruction of nature is here replaced by corresponding *expert and anti-expert knowledge*: such is the view of Bryan Wynne and Maarten Hajer. The latter, in criticizing mainly Anglo-American discourse and cultural theory, has developed an approach to this dimension of knowledge that is both politically and analytically more radical. Paradoxical though it may seem, the naturalist-essentialist content in talk of 'the destruction of nature' thereby changes into *action-related theory of actors and institutions*. At the centre of things now are '*discourse coalitions*' that stretch across the boundaries of classes, nation-states and systems. They are, as it were, discursive landscape architects: they create, design and alter 'cognitive maps', 'story-lines' or 'taboos'. Reality becomes, strictly speaking, project and product of action, so that a long-unclarified ambiguity in talk of the 'production' or 'fabrication' (*Herstellen*) of reality assumes considerable importance. For the main stress in such talk may be *cognitive* (in which case it refers *only* to the construction of knowledge), or it may fall more narrowly on *action* (decision, work, material production [*Produktion*]) and thus on the changing or shaping of realities. It may often be very difficult in concrete cases to demarcate these two aspects of production (*Herstellen*), but they refer to different modes of the 'creation of reality', of the 'shaping of the world'. Hajer's achievement is, among other things, to have corrected the cognitive bias of discourse and culture theory within an action–institution perspective. The point is no longer simply how realities are constructed in the world risk society (for example, in the public sphere, through media reporting of dangers); there is also the question of how reality-in-itself is (re-)produced by discourse politics and coalitions within institutional contexts of decision, action and work.

'Constructions of reality' may, so to speak, be distinguished according to whether they have more or less 'reality'. The closer they are to and in institutions (understood as the institutionalization of social practices), the more powerful and closer to decision and action they are – and therefore the more 'real' they become or appear. Essentialism, when illuminated by the sociology of knowledge, turns into a kind of strategic institutionalism geared to power and action. In a world civilization that dissolves everything into decisions, reality-in-itself derives from powerful structures of action, deep-rooted decision and work routines, in which cognitive maps are 'realized' or just redrawn. The straightforward way in which people now talk in daily life of 'nature' and the 'destruction of nature' may indicate a paradoxical strategy of the construction of deconstruction. The impression of having been constructed is thereby (to a greater or lesser extent) reflexively and powerfully destroyed, and the appearance of reality-in-itself is produced.

Maarten Hajer only touches upon these questions concerning the possibility of 'really real' (and thus deconstructed) constructions of social reality. But in a number of international comparative studies, he brings out and illustrates a whole range of discursive (political) strategies: the symbolic politics of passing fads; selective definition of certain themes and issues as 'unique'; attempts to inspire confidence by pictorial representation of threats; discursive building up of macro-actors; social constructions of ignorance; the use of 'black boxing' (especially important as a measure of power) to produce self-evident truths, which then really are self-evident; the drawing of functional analogies to cover up contradictions and so create the appearance of integratability, and so on. 'In my terms the ecological crisis is then a "discourse of self-confrontation" that calls for a reconsideration of the institutional practices that brought it about.'[8]

Beyond Insurability

With these points in mind, the theory of world risk society can be made somewhat more concrete. It shares in the farewell to the society–nature dualism that Bruno Latour, Donna Haraway and Barbara Adam conduct with such intellectual flair. The only question is: how do we handle nature *after* it ends? This question, which both eco-feminism and the crisis theory of social–natural relations attempt to illuminate in various ways, is further developed in the theory of world risk society (picking up Hajer's political-institutional twist to discourse theory) in the direction of *institutional constructivism*. 'Nature' and the 'destruction of nature' are institutionally produced and defined (in 'lay–expert conflicts') within industrially internalized nature. Their essential content correlates with institutional power to act and to mould. Production and definition are thus two aspects of the material *and* symbolic 'production' of 'nature and the destruction of nature'; they refer, one might say, to discourse coalitions within and between quite different, ultimately world-wide, action networks. It will be the task of future research to examine in detail *how* – and with what discursive and industrial resources and strategies – these differences in the 'naturalness' of nature, in its 'destruction' and 're-naturalization', are produced, suppressed, normalized and integrated within institutions and in the conflict between cognitive actors.

The theory of world risk society translates the question of the destruction of nature into another question. How does modern society deal with self-generated manufactured uncertainties? The point of this formulation is to distinguish between decision-dependent *risks* that can in principle be brought under control, and *dangers* that have escaped or neutralized the control requirements of industrial society. This latter process may take at least two forms.

First, there may be a failure of the norms and institutions developed within industrial society: risk calculation, insurance principle, the concept of an accident, disaster prevention, prophylactic after-care (Ewald, 1991; Bonß, 1995). Is there a ready indicator of this? Yes, there is. Controversial industries and technologies are often those which not only do not have private insurance but are completely cut off from it. This is true of atomic energy, genetic engineering (including research), and even high-risk sectors of chemical production. What goes without saying for motorists – not to use their car without insurance cover – seems to have been quietly dropped for whole industrial branches and sunrise technologies, where the dangers simply present too many problems. In other words, there are highly reliable 'technological pessimists' who do not agree with the judgement of technicians and relevant authorities about the harmlessness of their product or technology. These pessimists are the insurance actuaries and insurance companies, whose economic realism prevents them from having anything to do with a supposed 'nil risk'. World risk society, then, balances its way along *beyond the limits of insurability*. Or, conversely, the criteria that industrial modernity uses in making provision for its self-generated dangers can be turned around into yardsticks of criticism.[9]

Second, the pattern of decisions in industrial society, and the globality of their aggregate consequences, vary between two distinct epochs. To the extent that the decisions bound up with the scientific, technical-economic dynamic are still organized at the level of the nation-state and the individual enterprise, the resulting threats make us all members of a world risk society. To assure the health and safety of citizens, no task can be performed at national level in the developed system of danger-industrialism. This is one of the essential lessons of the ecological crisis. With the appearance of ecological discourse, there is talk every day about the end of 'foreign politics', the end of 'internal affairs of another country', the end of the national state. Here we can see immediately a central strategy in the production of difference and lack of difference. The established rules of allocation and responsibility – causality and guilt – break down. This means that their undaunted application in administration, management and legal terminology now produces the opposite result: dangers grow *through* being made anonymous. The old routines of decision, control and production (in law, science, administration, industry and politics) effect the material destruction of nature *and* its symbolic normalization. The two complement and accentuate each other. Concretely, it is not rule-breaking but the rules themselves which 'normalize' the death of species, rivers or lakes.

This circular movement between symbolic normalization and permanent material threats and destruction is indicated by the concept of 'organized irresponsibility'. The state administration, politics, industrial management and research negotiate the criteria of what is 'rational and safe' – with the result that the ozone hole grows bigger, allergies spread on a mass scale, and so on.

Alongside (and independently of) physical explosiveness, discourse-strategic action tends to make *politically* explosive the dangers normalized in the legitimation circle of administration, politics, law and management, which spread uncontrollably to assume global dimensions. We might say, both with and against Max Weber, that purposive-rational bureaucracy transforms all-round guilt into acquittal – and thereby, as an unintended consequence, threatens the very basis of its claim to rational control.

The theory of world risk society thus replaces talk of the 'destruction of nature' with the following key idea. The conversion of the unseen side-effects of industrial production into global ecological flashpoints is not strictly a problem of the world surrounding us – not a so-called 'environmental problem' – but rather *a deep institutional crisis of the first (national) phase of industrial modernity* ('reflexive modernization'). So long as these new developments are grasped within the conceptual horizon of industrial society, they continue to be seen as negative side-effects of seemingly accountable and calculable action ('residual risks'), rather than as trends which are eroding the system and delegitimating the bases of rationality. Their central political and cultural signific-ance becomes clear only in the concept and vantage-point of world risk society, where they draw attention to the need for reflexive self-definition (and redefinition) of the Western model of modernity.

In the phase of discourse about world risk society, it may become accepted that the threats generated through technological-industrial development – as measured by the existing institutional yardsticks – are neither calculable nor controllable. This forces people to reflect on the bases of the democratic, national, economic model of the first modernity, and to examine prevailing institutions (the externalization of effects in economics, law, science, and so on) and their historical devaluation of the bases of rationality. Here arises a truly global challenge, out of which new world flashpoints and even wars – but also supranational institutions of cooperation, conflict regulation and consensus-building – can be 'forged' (see the next section).

The situation of the economy also undergoes radical change. Once upon a time – in the early-capitalist entrepreneurial paradise – indus-try could launch projects *without* submitting to special checks and provisions. Then came the period of state regulation, when economic activity was possible only in the framework of labour legislation, safety ordinances, tariff agreements, and so on. In the world risk society – and this is a decisive change – all these agencies and regula-tions can play their role, and all the valid agreements can be hon-oured, without this resulting in any security. Even though it respects the norms, a management team may suddenly find itself put into the dock by world public opinion and treated as 'environmental pigs'.

Markets for goods and services become in principle unstable – that is, out of the control of firms using household remedies. Manufactured insecurity thus appears in the core areas of action and management based upon economic rationality. The normal reactions to this are the blocking of demands for serious thought, and the condemnation as 'irrational' or 'hysterical' of the storm of protest that breaks out *in spite of* official agreements. The way is now open to a series of errors. Filled with pride at representing Reason itself in a sea of irrationalism, people stumble into the trap of risk conflicts that are hard to bring under control (on the logic of risk conflict see Lau, 1989; Nelkin, 1992; Hildebrandt et al., 1994).

In world risk society, industrial projects become a *political* venture, in the sense that large investments presuppose long-term consensus. Such consensus, however, is no longer guaranteed – but rather jeopardized – with the old routines of simple modernization. What could previously be negotiated and implemented behind closed doors, through the force of practical constraints (for example, waste disposal problems, and even production methods or product design), is now potentially exposed to the crossfire of public criticism.[10]

For there is probably no longer any incentive for the old 'progress coalition' of state, economy and science. This is certainly and most significantly the case when the Greens get into government, as happened in Germany in 1998. Then the mostly informally constructed and sustained state–science–economy structure of first modernity threatens to collapse. The main consequence is a politicization of taken-for-granted assumptions and institutions alike. For example, who has to 'prove' what under conditions of manufactured uncertainties? What is to count as sufficient proof? Who is to decide on compensation? Industry certainly raises productivity, but at the same time it is at risk of losing legitimacy. The legal order no longer guarantees social peace, because it generalizes and legitimizes the threats to life – and to politics as well.

A Typology of Global Threats

Three types of global threats may be distinguished in the application of this theory.

First, there are conflicts over what we might call 'bads' (as opposed to 'goods'): that is, *wealth-driven* ecological destruction and technological-industrial dangers, such as the hole in the ozone layer, the greenhouse effect or regional water shortages, as well as the unpredictable risks involved in the genetic engineering of plants and humans.

A second category, however, comprises risks that are directly related to poverty. The Brundtland Commission was the first to point out that not only is environmental destruction the danger shadowing growth-based modernity, but the exact opposite is also the case: a close association exists between poverty and environmental destruction. 'This inequality is the planet's main "environmental" problem; it is also its main "development" problem' (World Commission on Environment and Development, 1987: 6). Accordingly, an integrated analysis of habitation and food, loss of species and genetic resources, energy, industry and human population shows that all these things are connected with one another and cannot be treated separately.

Michael Zürn (1995: 51), from whom the ideas and data for this typology have been drawn, writes:

> Between environmental destruction as a result of well-being and environmental destruction as a result of poverty there is, however, an essential difference. Whereas many wealth-driven ecological threats stem from the *externalization of production costs*, in the case of poverty-driven ecological destruction it is *the poor who destroy themselves* with side-effects for the rich. In other words, wealth-driven environmental destruction is distributed evenly around the globe, whereas poverty-driven environmental destruction strikes at particular spots and becomes international only in the form of side-effects appearing over the medium term.

The best-known example of this is the felling of the tropical rainforests, where some 17 million hectares are currently being lost every year. Other examples are toxic waste (sometimes imported from other countries) and obsolete technologies (for example, in the chemical, nuclear and – in the future – genetic industry, as well as in genetic engineering research). These hazards are a feature of modernization processes that have been started up or broken off. Industries thus grow which are technologically capable of endangering the environment and human life, while the countries in question do not have the institutional and political means to prevent possible destruction.

Wealth-driven or poverty-driven dangers are, as it were, 'normal': they usually arise in conformity with the rules, through the application of safety norms that have been introduced precisely because they offer no protection at all or are full of loopholes. The *third* threat, however, from NBC (nuclear, biological, chemical) *weapons of mass destruction*, is actually deployed (rather than used for the purposes of terror) in the exceptional situation of war. Even after the end of the

East–West confrontation, the danger of regional or global self-destruction through NBC weapons has by no means been exorcized – on the contrary, it has broken out of the control structure of the 'atomic pact' between the superpowers. To the threat of military conflict between states is now added the (looming) threat of fundamentalist or private terrorism. It can less and less be ruled out that the private possession of weapons of mass destruction, and the potential they provide for political terror, will become a new source of dangers in the world risk society.

These various global threats may very well complement and accentuate one another: that is, it will be necessary to consider the interaction between ecological destruction, wars and the consequences of uncompleted modernization. Thus, ecological destruction may promote war, either in the form of armed conflict over vitally necessary resources such as water, or because eco-fundamentalists in the West call for the use of military force to stop destruction already under way (such as the clearing of tropical forests). It is easy to imagine that a country which lives in growing poverty will exploit the environment to the hilt. In desperation (or as political cover for desperation), a military attempt might be made to grab resources vital to another country's existence. Or, ecological destruction (for example, the flooding of Bangladesh) might trigger mass emigration which in turn leads to war. Or, again, states threatened with defeat in war might turn to the 'ultimate weapon' of blowing up their own or other countries' nuclear or chemical plants, in order to threaten nearby regions or cities with annihilation. There are no limits in our imagination to the horror scenarios that could bring the various threats into relationship with one another. Zürn speaks of a 'spiral of destruction', which could build up into one great crisis in which all other crisis phenomena converge.[11]

All this confirms the diagnosis of a world risk society. For the so-called 'global threats' have together led to a world where the basis of established risk-logic has been whittled away, and where hard-to-manage dangers prevail instead of quantifiable risks. The new dangers are removing the conventional pillars of safety calculation. Damage loses its spatio-temporal limits and becomes global and lasting. It is hardly possible any more to blame definite individuals for such damage: the principle of a guilty party has been losing its cutting edge. Often, too, financial compensation cannot be awarded for the damage done; it has no meaning to insure oneself against the worst-case effects of spiralling global threats. Hence there are no plans for aftercare if the worst should happen.

Looked at in this way, it is clear that there are no global threats as such; rather, they are charged and mixed in with the ethnic, national and resource conflicts that have beset the world especially since the end of the East–West confrontation – to the point that they become unrecognizable. This is one of the points made by Eva Senghaas-Knobloch. In the post-Soviet republics, ruthless diagnosis of environmental destruction goes hand in hand with political criticism of the imperial exploitation of natural resources. Talk of 'native soil' becomes, in this sense, a claim on both natural resources *and* national sovereignty.

> It is no accident if militant, separatist movements for autonomy in the former republics of the Soviet Union – as in Brittany, Occitania or Corsica – generally cluster around two issues: language and conservation of the natural environment. Both are themes of protection of the homeland, directed first of all against the consequences of an industrial growth model which are experienced as economically unjust but are also associated with questions of cultural identity. . . . The new lines of conflict . . . are not mainly established along the 'risk-winner'/ 'risk-loser' axis. Insofar as this axis has any meaning at all, it is rather a question of mass flows of refugees – which may subsequently contribute to new social, political and cultural conflicts. Awareness of environmental damage and threats to the natural conditions of life is regionally and locally bound up with strivings for autonomy and demands for justice. Especially in regions where a self-standing 'civil society' has not yet been able to develop (above all, in the 'state societies' of the former Eastern bloc), this connection may lead to the supercharging of global threats with ethnic-nationalist, partly militant, separation conflicts.
>
> (*Senghaas-Knobloch, 1992: 66*)

The Emergence of a World Public and a Global Subpolitics

The Concept of 'Subpolitics'

When we speak of a world risk *society*, it is also necessary to say that global threats cause, or will cause, people to act. Two distinct perspectives – arenas or actors – are possible here: in the first, globalization *from above* (for example, through international treaties and institutions), in the second, globalization *from below* (for example, through new transnational actors operating beyond the system of parliamentary politics and challenging established political organizations and interest groups). There is weighty evidence for both kinds of globalization. Thus, it can be shown that the majority of international accords on the environment have been reached over an extremely short period – the last twenty years in fact (on the question of basic conditions under which international regulations can be established, see Zürn, 1995: 49–56).

Richard Falk identifies a number of political arenas in which globalization from above is negotiated and pushed through:

> The response to threats against strategic oil reserves in the Middle East, the efforts to expand the GATT framework, the coercive implementation of the nuclear nonproliferation regime, the containment of South–North migration and refugee flows.... The legal implications of globalization-from-above would tend to supplant interstate law with a species of global law, but one at odds in most respects with 'the law of humanity'.
>
> (*Falk, 1994: 137*)

There is hardly need of further proof that, in the field of global environmental politics, it has long been a question (at best) of proverbial drops in the ocean. At the same time, however, a number of spectacular boycott movements operating world-wide across cultures have made it clear that the impotence of official politics in dealing with the industrial bloc is impotence with regard to the classical stage-setting. For powerful actors of a globalization *from below* have also appeared on the scene, especially non-governmental organizations (NGOs) such as Robin Wood, Greenpeace, Amnesty International or Terre des Hommes. The UN estimates that there are now some 50,000 such groups in the world, but that does not mean much because each one, or almost each, is different. *Die Zeit* speaks of the 'New International',[12] which, by definition, falls between two stools, market and state, but which, as a third force, is gaining more and more influence and displaying its political muscle-power in relation to governments, international corporations and authorities. Here we can see the first outlines of a 'global citizenship' (Richard Falk and Bart van Steenbergen) – or, as we would put it, the new constellation of a global subpolitics. We must now examine how this has become possible and how it is now actually emerging.

With the victory march of industrial modernity, a purposive-rational system of politics is everywhere asserting itself. The common sense of this epoch is drawn from an everything-under-control mentality, which applies even to the uncontrollability that it itself produces. However, the accomplishment of this form of order and control brings about its opposite – the return of uncertainty and insecurity.

'Second-order dangers' (Bonß, 1995) then appear as the other side of any attempt to 'get on top' of this. Unintentionally, in the shadow of the 'side-effects' of global dangers, society thus opens out into the (sub)political. In every sphere – the economy as well as science, private life and the family as well as politics – the bases of action reach a decisive turning-point: they have to be rejustified, renegotiated, rebalanced. How is this to be conceptualized?

'Crisis' is not the right concept, any more than 'dysfunction' or 'disintegration', for it is precisely the *victories* of unbridled industrial modernization that call it into question. This is just what is meant by the term '*reflexive* modernization': theoretically, application to itself; empirically, self-transformation (through individualization and globalization processes, for example); politically, loss of legitimacy and a vacuum of power. What this means may be clarified by Thomas Hobbes, the theorist of the state. As is well known, he argued for a strong, authoritarian state, but he also mentioned *one* individual right of civil resistance. If a state brings about conditions threatening to life, or if it commands a citizen 'to abstain from the use of food, ayre, medicine, or any other thing, without which he cannot live', then, according to Hobbes (1968: 269), 'hath that man the Liberty to disobey'.

In terms of social politics, then, the ecological crisis involves a *systematic violation of basic rights*, a crisis of basic rights whose long-term effect in weakening society can scarcely be underestimated. For dangers are being produced by industry, externalized by economics, individualized by the legal system, legitimized by the natural sciences and made to appear harmless by politics. That this is breaking down the power and credibility of institutions only becomes clear when the system is put on the spot, as Greenpeace, for example, has tried to do. The result is the subpoliticization of world society.

The concept of 'subpolitics' refers to politics outside and beyond the representative institutions of the political system of nation-states. It focuses attention on signs of an (ultimately global) self-organization of politics, which tends to set all areas of society in motion. Subpolitics means '*direct*' politics – that is, *ad hoc* individual participation in political decisions, bypassing the institutions of representative opinion-formation (political parties, parliaments) and often even lacking the protection of the law. In other words, subpolitics means the shaping of society from below. Economy, science, career, everyday existence, private life, all become caught up in the storms of political debate. But these do not fit into the traditional spectrum of party-political differences. What is characteristic of the subpolitics of world society are precisely *ad hoc* '*coalitions of opposites*' (of parties, nations, regions, religions, governments, rebels, classes). Crucially, however, subpolitics sets politics free by changing the rules and boundaries of the political so that it becomes more open and susceptible to new linkages – as well as capable of being negotiated and reshaped.

The Symbolic Mass Boycott: A Case Study of Global Subpolitics

In the summer of 1995 Greenpeace, the latter-day crusader for good causes, first succeeded in getting Shell to dispose of one of its obsolete oil rigs on land rather than in the sea. Then this campaigning multinational tried to halt a resumption of French nuclear tests by publicly pillorying President Jacques Chirac for deliberate breach of international regulations. Many asked whether it was not the end of certain basic rules of (foreign) politics, if an unauthorized actor such as Greenpeace could conduct its own domestic world politics without regard for national sovereignty or diplomatic norms. Perhaps it would be the Moonies' turn tomorrow, and then of a third private organization hoping in its way to make the rest of the world happy.

What such jibes overlooked was that the oil multinational was brought to its knees not by Greenpeace but by a mass public boycott, put together through world-wide televised indictments. Greenpeace is not itself shaking the political system, but it is making visible a vacuum of power and legitimacy that has many parallels with what happened in the GDR.

Everywhere there are signs of this coalition model of global subpolitics or 'direct politics'. Alliances of forces 'totally' incapable of allying with one another are coming into being. Thus the then German Chancellor, Helmut Kohl, protesting as a citizen who was also head of government, supported the Greenpeace action against the then British Prime Minister, John Major. Suddenly political elements were discovered and deployed in everyday activity – in the filling of petrol tanks, for example. Car drivers banded together against the oil industry (you only need to try it once to 'get a taste for it'). And in the end the state joined in with the illegitimate action and its organizers, thereby using its power to legitimize a deliberate, extra-parliamentary violation of the rules, while for their part the protagonists of direct politics sought to escape – through a kind of 'self-administered ecological justice' – the narrow framework of indirect, legally sanctioned agencies and rules. The anti-Shell alliance eventually led to a scene-switch between the politics of the first and the second modernity. National governments sat on the benches and watched, while unauthorized actors of the second modernity directed the course of the action.

In the case of the world-wide movement against President Chirac's decision to resume nuclear testing, a spontaneous global alliance actually developed between governments, Greenpeace activists and the most diverse protest groups. The French miscalculation was reflected in two aspects of the situation: (a) the Mururoa decision coincided with commemorations of the fiftieth anniversary of Hiroshima and Nagasaki; and (b) it was roundly condemned by a meeting of the ASEAN Forum, including both the USA and Russia. All this pointed to a temporary, direct-politics alliance stretching across national, economic, religious and political-ideological differences. Thus a global coalition of contradictory symbolic and economic forces emerged. A special feature of this politics of the second modernity is that in practice its 'globality' does not exclude anyone or anything – not only socially, but also morally or ideologically. It is, in the end, a politics *without opponents or opposing force*, a kind of 'enemyless politics'.

The political novelty was not that David had beaten Goliath, but that David *plus Goliath*, acting at a global level, successfully joined together, first against a world corporation, then against a national government and one of its policies. What was new was the alliance all around the globe between extra-parliamentary and parliamentary forces, citizens and governments, for a cause that is in the higher sense legitimate: the saving of the world environment (*(Um)Welt*).

Something else has become apparent. The post-traditional world only appears to be breaking up into individualization. Paradoxically, the challenge of global dangers provides it with a fountain of youth – for a new transnational morality and activism, for new forms (and forums) of protest, but also for new hysterias. Status or class-consciousness, belief in progress or decline, the enemy image of communism – all these could be replaced by the humanity-wide project of saving the world environment. Global threats generate global risk communities – at least *ad hoc* ones for the historical moment.

Of course, the anti-Shell alliance was morally suspect. In fact, it was based on downright hypocrisy. Kohl, for instance, could use this symbolic action (which cost him nothing) to divert attention from his no-speed-limit policy on German autobahns, which was polluting the air over Europe (and continues to do so under his successor, Gerhard Schröder, and his Green Minister of the Environment, Jürgen Trittin).

German-Green nationalism and know-all attitudes also made themselves felt here beneath the surface. Many Germans want a kind of green Greater Switzerland. They dream of a Germany that will be the world's ecological conscience. Perhaps a second, ecologically motivated round of 'reparations' has here appeared from behind the scenes, mixed up with a fresh dose of 'superiority' over environmental questions that are anything but environmental – namely, a kind of new religion of secularized, individualized society. Still, the lessons of politics are different from those of morality. Precisely in the alliance between mutually exclusive beliefs – from Chancellor Kohl to Greenpeace activists, from Porsche fetishists to throwers of incendiary devices – the new quality of the political is beginning to show. How far this extends has been evident since 1998 in Germany, where the Greens, now in a new position of influence within Gerhard Schröder's government, are beginning to enforce an 'environment tax' which is to be used to reduce the costs of waged labour. In addition, they have proposed the scrapping of nuclear power nationally.

For the economy, too, there has been a radical change in the situation. Shell, for example, did everything from its point of view to control the problem. An agreement had been reached with government, experts and managers to go for dumping at sea, and that was the optimal solution for Shell itself. But when it tried to implement it, the exact opposite happened: the markets threatened to collapse. So the lesson is: there are no expert solutions in risk discourse, because experts can only supply factual information and are never able to assess which solutions are culturally acceptable.

This too is new. Politics and morality are gaining priority over expert reasoning. Whether such politicization can go beyond single issues to constitute an authoritative environmental politics is quite another matter. Here, probably, are the limits of global subpolitics, which should not be confused with the policy of national governments. (This changes, of course, when, as in Germany, Green subpolitics is becoming state politics.) On the other hand, the process of subpoliticization should not at all be considered as irrational, because it has all the marks of republican modernity in contrast to the representative, national-parliamentary democracy of parties. The activity of world corporations and national governments is becoming subject to the pressure of a world public sphere. In this process, individual-collective participation in global action networks is striking and decisive; citizens are discovering that the act of purchase can be a direct ballot which they can always use in a political way. Through the boycott, an active consumer society thus combines and allies with direct democracy – at a world level.

This is coming close, in an exemplary manner, to what Kant outlined around two hundred years ago in his 'Perpetual Peace' essay as the utopia of a cosmopolitan society, as opposed to what he called the 'despotism' of representative democracy. It would be a global nexus of responsibility, in which individuals – and not only their organizational representatives – could directly participate in political decisions. This allows us to grasp at once what is currently discussed in the USA as 'technological citizenship': namely, the recovery of basic democratic rights against the 'no-man's-rule' of technological developments.

In his book *Autonomous Technology*, Langdon Winner (1992) draws the conclusion that most social science analysis of technological development fails to recognize the difference between 'technology *requires* legislation' and 'technology *is* legislation'. Lewis Mumford, more than thirty years ago, wrote that large-scale technological systems are the most influential forms and sources of tyranny in the modern world. And in the view of Andrew Zimmerman (1995: 88), social autonomy is being hollowed out by technological autonomy; whereas in the first modernity, the well-being and 'freedom' of the citizen were a function of the well-being and freedom of technical systems. The contrasting approach of Philip Frankenfeld seeks to justify the demand for technological participation:

> The status of technological citizenship may be enjoyed at the national, state, local, or global level or at levels in between. Hence one can be a technological citizen of . . . the Chernobyl ecosphere, of the plastic explosives production and use 'noosphere' – which is global in scale – of a particular nuclear-free zone in the noncontiguous network of them, of the realm covered by the non-proliferation treaty. . . . However, one *would* be a technological citizen *of* any of these spheres of impact *if* their inhabitants deigned to create a set of agencies, a cocoon of protections or benefits, or a cocoon of rights and responsibilities granting subjects status in relation to impacts of technologies with a specific overarching purpose.
>
> (*Frankenfeld, 1992: 463f, quoted in Zimmerman, 1995: 89;*
> *see also van Steenbergen, 1994; Archibuggi and Held, 1995*)

As normatively overarching goals of citizenship, Frankenfeld names: '(1) autonomy, (2) dignity, (3) assimilation – versus alienation – of members of the polity'. It therefore includes: '1. rights to knowledge or information; 2. rights to participation; 3. rights to guarantees of informed consent; and 4. rights to limitation on the total amount of endangerment of collectivities and individuals' (Frankenfeld, 1992: 462, 465).

The directness of global technological participation is established, for example, in the *unity of the acts of purchase and casting a ballot*. Here there are no organizational intermediaries, no representative agencies of the popular will, no bureaucracy, no electoral registration, no shopping police, no water cannons, no application forms to hold a demonstration! It is a direct, anarchistic form of politics and protest, here, now and everywhere, which often costs nothing and can, so to speak, be incorporated into the menu. Politics can thus become an integral part of everyday activity, and at the same time involve active integration into the (post-traditional) cosmopolitan (non-)order.

But what are the sites, the instruments and the media of this direct politics of 'global technological citizenship'? The political site of the world risk society is not the street but *television*. Its political subject is not the working class and its organization, not the trade union. Instead *cultural symbols are staged in the mass media*, where the accumulated bad conscience of the actors and consumers of industrial society can be offloaded. There are three ways of illustrating this appreciation.

First, in the abstract omnipresence of dangers, destruction and protest are symbolically mediated. Second, in acting against ecological destruction, everyone is also their own enemy. Third, the ecological crisis is breeding a cultural Red Cross consciousness. Those, like Greenpeace, who inscribe this on their banner are raised to the ecological nobility and given a blank cheque for an almost unlimited store of trust – which has the advantage that, in cases where there is doubt, one's own information and not that of industrial agencies is believed.

Here lies a crucial limitation of direct politics. We are children lost in a 'forest of symbols' (Baudelaire). In other words, we have to rely on the symbolic politics of the media. This is true especially in the abstractness and omnipresence of destruction that keep the world risk society going. Tangible, simplifying symbols, in which cultural nerve fibres are touched and alarmed, here acquire a key political significance. These symbols must be produced or concocted, in the open fire of conflict provocation, before the strained-terrified television eyes of the public. The decisive question is: who discovers (or invents), and how, symbols that disclose or demonstrate the structural character of the problems as well as creating the capacity for action? This capacity should be all the greater, the simpler and neater is the staged symbol, the fewer are the individual costs of public protest actions, and the more easily each person can thereby clear his or her conscience.

Simplicity means a lot. First, *transmissibility*. We are all environmental sinners; just as Shell wanted to dump its oil rig in the sea, so
do 'all' our fingers itch to toss cans of coke out of the car window.
This is the everyman situation which makes the Shell case (according
to the social construction) so 'transparent'. Yet there is an essential
difference, in that the likelihood of official acquittal becomes more
tempting with the size of the sin. Second, *moral outrage*. 'Those at
the top' get the approval of government and experts to dump in the
Atlantic an oil rig filled with toxic waste, yet 'we down below' – as
German-Green ideology could be characterized ironically – have to
save the world by dividing every teabag into three – paper, string and
leaves – and disposing of them separately. Third, *political expediency*. Will Chancellor Schröder support Greenpeace in its actions
against French national nuclear policy? Hardly. For that is a question
of national power-poker and not just of Shell's market interests.
Fourth, *simple alternative actions*. To hit at Shell, one would have
had to fill up with 'morally clean' petrol from one of its competitors.
If governments throughout the world had led the boycott of French
goods, then of course everything would have taken on a new dimension. Fifth, *selling of ecological indulgences*. The boycott gained importance from the bad conscience of industrial society, because it
allowed a kind of personally directed *ego te absolvo* to be granted at
no cost to oneself.

Global ecological dangers, far from intensifying a general lack of
meaning in the modern world, create a meaning-filled horizon of
avoidance, protection and assistance, a moral climate that grows
sharper with the scale of the perceived danger, and in which a new
political significance attaches to the roles of hero and villain. If the
world is perceived within the coordinates of ecological-industrial self-
endangerment, then a universal drama can be made out of morality,
religion, fundamentalism, desperation, tragedy and tragi-comedy
– always intertwined with their opposites: salvation, assistance, liberation. In this world tragi-comedy, the economy is free either to
take the role of poison-stirrer or to slip into the part of hero and
helper. This is the background against which Greenpeace, using the
ruse of impotence, manages to occupy the stage. What it practises is
a kind of *judo politics*, designed to mobilize the superior strength of
environmental sinners against themselves.

The Greenpeace people are multinational media professionals;
they know how cases of contradictory promulgation and violation of
the norms of safety and inspection need to be presented so that the
great and powerful (corporations, governments) walk right into them

and wriggle telegenically for the enjoyment of the world's public. Thoreau and Gandhi would have beamed with delight to see Greenpeace using the methods of the media age to stage world-wide civil resistance. Greenpeace is also a smithy turning out political symbols. The artificial means of the Black–White conflict are used to forge cultural sins and sin-symbols which, in binding protests together, may become lightning conductors of the collective guilty conscience. Such are the ways in which new certainties and new outlets for rage are constructed in the enemyless democracy that has succeeded the enemy-images of the East–West conflict. This process is and remains part of the world fairground of symbolic politics. Is it not all an absurd distraction from the central challenges of the world risk society?

Yet if we focus not on single issues but on the new political constellation, then the incentive for a sense of success is clear enough. In the playful confluence of opposites in transcultural civil resistance, cosmopolitan society feels its direct power. It is well known that nothing is as infectious as success. Those who would like to get on the right trail soon discover that mass sport and politics here directly fuse with each other on a world scale. It is a kind of political boxing match with active audience participation, all around the world. No normal TV entertainment could compete with that; it would lack not only the extra kick of reality, but also the modern ecological aura of world salvation which in the end has nothing opposing it. At any event, it is clear from *this* case study that the widespread talk of the end of politics and democracy, or the collapse of all values – in short, the whole canon of cultural criticism – is foolish because it is so historically blind. People have only to get a taste of direct participation with 'tangible' success and they're up and away.

As awareness of the dangers spreads, the world risk society becomes self-critical. Its bases, coordinates and pre-stamped coalitions are thrown into a state of turbulence. Politics breaks out in a new and different way, beyond the reach of formal responsibilities and hierarchies. So, we are sometimes looking for politics in the wrong place, with the wrong concepts, on the wrong floors, on the wrong pages of the daily newspapers. The very areas of decision-making that the model of industrial capitalism places in the slipstream of politics – advertising, economics, administration, consumption, science, private life – are swept by reflexive risk-modernity into the storms of political argument. If you want to understand why, you must look at the cultural-political meaning of manufactured dangers.

Internal danger too is alienated, concentrated subjectivity and history. It is a kind of obsessional collective memory of the fact that our decisions and mistakes lie hidden in what we now find ourselves facing. Global threats are the embodiment of the errors of a whole epoch of industrialism; they are a kind of collective return of the repressed. In their conscious investigation lies perhaps a chance of breaking the spell of industrial fatalism. If someone wanted to build a machine to counteract the mechanization of society, they would have to use the plan of ecological self-endangerment. It is the reification that cries out to be overcome. This is the admittedly tiny chance for global (sub)politics in the world risk society (Beck, 1994).

If the need for a world environmental politics from above is also included, then it is clearly still possible to conceive within an active perspective the vacuum that Europe and the world became after the end of the East–West conflict. Our fate is that we have to invent the political anew.

3

From Industrial Society to Risk Society:
Questions of Survival, Social Structure and Ecological Enlightenment

Are Risks Timeless?

Aren't risks at least as old as industrial society, possibly even as old as the human race itself? Isn't all life subject to the risk of death? Aren't and weren't all societies in all epochs 'risk societies'?

On the contrary, should we not (or must we not) be discussing the fact that since the beginning of industrialization, threats – famines, epidemics or natural catastrophes – have been continually reduced? To list only a few key advances: the reduction of infant mortality, the 'bonus years' (Imhof), the achievements of the welfare state, the enormous progress in technological perfection over the past hundred years. Isn't the Federal Republic of Germany, in particular, an Eldorado of bureaucratically organized care and caution?

At a conference on risk at Cardiff University in February 1996, the British sociologist Hilary Rose suggested that 'risk society' has a German taste, a flavour of wealth and security. Perhaps only a few countries, and certainly not Britain, can *afford* to be risk societies? A few weeks later, the 'BSE crisis', a textbook example of risk society, began. Even today, in 1999, this crisis is far from played out. No one knows how many other countries may be affected by the disease, or what its long-term consequences may be. Thus BSE highlights the growing importance of 'aware unawareness' in risk production and risk definition because the precise mode of its transmission across species is a mystery and it may have a long gestation period (Adam, 1998: 163–92). Meanwhile, its purely economic impact has been considerable. The latest estimate from the BSE inquiry in 1998 puts its costs, in the UK alone, at £3 billion, measured in terms of compensation paid to farmers and the costs of destroying infected cattle and disposing of their remains. The BSE crisis also provides ample evidence of how risks and their contested social definitions cut across borders – of states and of scientific disciplines. If, for example, you had gone into the mountains of southern Bavaria in the summer of 1996 and visited a lonely *Wirtshaus* (small local restaurant), your menu would probably have borne a photograph showing the local farmer, arm in arm with his smiling family and surrounded by family cattle, as a means of building personal trust to counter the omnipresence of the BSE risk. The implicit message: 'Please trust me. You can enjoy this family steak safely here. Forget about that risky British BSE beef!' However, the BSE crisis cannot be 'kept on one side' politically either and has flooded into key areas of politics – health politics, agricultural politics, foreign politics, trade politics, European politics – illustrating again the specific 'and'-characteristic of risk conflicts.

Still, it may be objected, certainly there are 'new risks', such as nuclear power, chemical and biotechnical production, but, considered mathematically or physically, aren't these dangers not of great scope, but also of exceedingly small, actually negligible, probability? Looking at them coolly and rationally, does that not imply that they should be given a lesser status than long-accepted risks, such as the incredible carnage on the highways or the risks to smokers?

Certainly, ultimate security is denied to us human beings. But is it not also true that the unavoidable 'residual risks' are the downside of the opportunities – for prosperity, relatively high social security and general comfort – that developed industrial society offers to the majority of its members in a historically unparalleled manner? Isn't risk primarily an 'energizing principle' (Giddens) for the active exploration of new worlds and markets? Is the mostly negative dramatization of such risks not in the end a typical media spectacle, ignoring established expert opinion, a 'new German anxiety', or a millennium fever, as untenable and just as short-lived as the débâcle regarding the 'railroad sickness' from the end of the previous century?

And finally, aren't risks a central concern of the engineering and physical sciences? What business has the sociologist here? Isn't that once again typical?

The Calculus of Risk: Predictable Security in the Face of an Open Future

Human dramas – plagues, famines and natural disasters, the looming power of gods and demons – may or may not quantifiably equal the destructive potential of modern mega-technologies in hazardousness. They differ essentially from 'risks' in my sense since they are not based on decisions, or, more specifically, decisions that focus on techno-economic advantages and opportunities and accept hazards as simply the dark side of progress. This is my first point: risks presume industrial, that is, techno-economic, decisions and considerations of utility. They differ from 'war damage' by their 'normal birth', or, more precisely, their 'peaceful origin' in the centres of rationality and prosperity with the blessings of the guarantors of law and order. They differ from pre-industrial natural disasters by their origin in decision-making, which is of course conducted never by individuals but by entire organizations and political groups.[1]

The consequence is fundamental: pre-industrial hazards, no matter how large and devastating, were 'strokes of fate' raining down on humankind from 'outside' and attributable to an 'other' – gods, demons or Nature. Here too there were countless accusations, but they were directed against the gods or God, 'religiously motivated', to put it simply, and not – like industrial risks – politically charged. For with the origin of industrial risks in decision-making the problem of social accountability and responsibility irrevocably arises, even in those areas where the prevailing rules of science and law permit accountability only in exceptional cases. People, firms, state agencies and politicians are responsible for industrial risks. As we sociologists say, the social roots of risks block the 'externalizability' of the problem of accountability.[2]

Therefore, it is not the number of dead and wounded, but rather a social feature, their industrial self-generation, which makes the hazards of mega-technology a political issue. The question remains, however: must one not view and assess the past two hundred years as a period of continual growth in calculability and precautions in dealing with industrially produced insecurities and destruction? In fact, a very promising approach, and one barely explored to date, is to trace the (political) institutional history of evolving industrial society as the conflict-laden emergence of a system of rules for dealing with industrially produced risks and insecurities (see Ewald, 1986, 1991; Böhret, 1987; Evers and Nowotny, 1987; Lau, 1989; Schwarz and Thompson, 1990; Hildebrandt et al., 1994; Yearley, 1994; Bonß, 1995; Lash et al., 1996; Wynne, 1996a, 1996b).

The idea of reacting to the uncertainties that lie in opening and conquering new markets or in developing and implementing new technologies with collective agreements – insurance contracts, for instance, which burden the individual with general fees just as much as they relieve him or her from dramatic damage cases – is hardly a new social invention. Its origins go back to the beginnings of inter-continental navigation, but with the growth of industrial capitalism, insurance was continually perfected and expanded into nearly all problem areas of social action. Consequences that at first affect only the individual become 'risks', systematically caused, statistically de-scribable and in that sense 'predictable' types of events, which can therefore also be subjected to supra-individual and political rules of recognition, compensation and avoidance.

The calculus of risks connects the physical, the engineering and the social sciences. It can be applied to completely disparate phenomena not only in health management – from the risks of smoking to those of nuclear power – but also to economic risks, risks of old age, of unemploy-ment and underemployment, of traffic accidents, of certain phases of life, and so forth. In addition, it permits a type of 'technological moral-ization' which no longer need employ moral and ethical imperatives directly. To give an example, the place of the 'categorical imperative' is taken by the mortality rates under certain conditions of air pollution. In this sense, one could say that the calculus of risk exemplifies a type of ethics without morality, the mathematical ethics of the technolo-gical age. The triumph of the calculus of risks would probably not have been possible if fundamental advantages were not tied to it.

The first of these lies in the fact that risks open the opportunity to document statistically consequences that were at first always person-alized and shifted onto individuals. In this way risk de-individualizes. Risks are revealed as systematic events, which are accordingly in need of a general political regulation. Through the statistical descrip-tion of risks (say in the form of accident probabilities) the blinkers of individualization drop off – and this is not yet sufficiently the case with environmental diseases such as pseudo-croup, asthma or even cancer. A field for corresponding political action is opened up: acci-dents on the job, for instance, are not blamed on those whose health they have already ruined anyway, but are stripped of their individual origin and related instead to the plant organization, the lack of pre-cautions, and so on.

A second advantage is closely connected to the first: insurance payments are agreed on and guaranteed on a no-fault basis (setting aside the extreme cases of gross negligence or intentional damage). In that way, legal battles over causation become unnecessary and moral outrage is moderated. Instead, an incentive for prevention is created for businesses, in proportion to the magnitude of the insurance costs – or perhaps not.

The decisive thing, however, is ultimately that in this manner the industrial system is made capable of dealing with its own unforeseeable future. The calculus of risks, protection by insurance liability laws, and the like, promise the impossible: future events that have not yet occurred become the object of current action – prevention, compensation or precautionary after-care. As the French sociologist François Ewald (1986) shows in detailed studies, the 'invention' of the calculus of risks lies in making the incalculable calculable, with the help of accident statistics, through generalizable settlement formulae as well as through the generalized exchange principle of 'money for damages'. In this way, a norm system of rules for social accountability, compensation and precautions, always very controversial in its details, creates present security in the face of an open uncertain future. Modernity, which brings uncertainty to every niche of existence, finds its counter-principle in a *social compact against industrially produced hazards and damages*, stitched together out of public and private insurance agreements; and, thus, activating and renewing *trust* in corporations and government.

Politically and programmatically, this pact for the containment and 'just' distribution of the consequences of the standard industrial revolution is an early *Third Way* because it is situated somewhere between socialism and liberalism. On the one side it is based on the systematic creation of consequences and hazards, but at the same time it involves public and private insurance (welfare state) *and* active individuals in preventing and compensating for them. The consensus that can be achieved with it always remains unstable, conflict-laden and in need of revision. For that very reason, however, it represents the core, the inner 'social logic' of the consensus on progress, which – in principle – legitimated techno-economic development in the first industrial modernity. Where this 'security pact' is violated wholesale, flagrantly and systematically, the consensus on progress itself is consequently at stake.

Risk and Threat: On the Overlapping of Normal and Exceptional Conditions

My decisive idea, and the one that leads us further, is that this is precisely what has happened in a series of technological challenges with which we are concerned today – nuclear power, many types of chemical and bio-technological production as well as the continuing and threatening ecological destruction. The foundations of the established risk logic are being subverted or suspended.[3]

Put another way, since the middle of the twentieth century the social institutions of industrial society have been confronted with the historically unprecedented possibility of the destruction through decision-making of all life on this planet. This distinguishes our epoch not only from the early phase of the industrial revolution, but also from all other cultures and social forms, no matter how diverse and contradictory these may have been in detail. If a fire breaks out, the fire brigade comes; if a traffic accident occurs, the insurance pays. This interplay between beforehand and afterwards, between the future and security in the here and now, because precautions have been taken even for the worst imaginable case, has been revoked in the age of nuclear, chemical and genetic technology. In all the brilliance of their perfection, nuclear power plants have suspended the principle of insurance not only in the economic, but also in the medical, psychological, cultural and religious sense. *The residual risk society has become an uninsured society*, with protection paradoxically diminishing as the danger grows. Turned around politically, this implies, as demonstrated by the 'nuclear exit-politics' of Germany's current Red–Green government, that raising the insurance level of nuclear power plants is a 'safe' ticket out of the atomic age.

Ultimately, there is no institution, neither concrete nor probably even conceivable, that would be prepared for the 'WIA', the 'worst imaginable accident', and there is no social order that could guarantee its social and political constitution in this worst possible case.[4] There are many, however, which are specialized in the only remaining possibility: denying the dangers. For after-care, which guarantees security even against hazards, is replaced by the dogma of technological infallibility, which will be refuted by the next accident. The queen of error, science, becomes the guardian of this taboo. Only 'communist' reactors, but not those in West Germany, are empirical creations of the human hand which can toss all their theories onto the scrap-heap. Even the simple question 'What if it does happen after all?' ends up in the void of unpreparedness for after-care. Correspondingly, political stability in risk societies is the stability of not thinking about things.

Put more precisely, nuclear, chemical, genetic and ecological megahazards abolish the four pillars of the calculus of risks. First, one is concerned here with global, often irreparable, damage that can no longer be limited; the concept of monetary compensation therefore fails. Second, precautionary after-care is excluded for the worst imaginable accident in the case of fatal hazards; the security concept of anticipatory monitoring of results fails. Third, the 'accident' loses its delimitations in time and space, and therefore its meaning. It becomes an event with a beginning and no end; an 'open-ended festival' of creeping, galloping and overlapping waves of destruction. But that implies: standards of normality, measuring procedures and therefore the basis for calculating the hazards are abolished; incomparable entities are compared and calculation turns into obfuscation.

The problem of the incalculability of consequences and damage becomes clear with particular vividness in the lack of accountability for them. The scientific and legal recognition and attribution of hazards takes place in our society according to the principle of causality, the polluter-pays principle. But what strikes engineers and lawyers as self-evident, even virtually demanded by ethics, has extremely dubious, paradoxical consequences in the realm of mega-hazards. One example: the legal proceedings against the lead crystal factory in the community of Altenstadt in the Upper Palatinate.[5]

Flecks of lead and arsenic the size of a penny had fallen on the town, and fluoride vapours had turned leaves brown, etched windows and caused bricks to crumble away. Residents were suffering from skin rashes, nausea and headaches. There was no question where all of that originated. The white dust was pouring visibly from the smokestacks of the factory. A clear case. A clear case? On the tenth day of the trial the presiding judge offered to drop charges in return for a fine of DM 10,000, a result which is typical of environmental crimes in the Federal Republic (1996: 21,000 investigations, forty-nine convictions with prison terms, thirty-one of those suspended, the rest dropped).

How is that possible? It is not only the lack of laws and not merely the legendary shortcomings in applying them which protect the criminals. The reasons lie deeper and cannot be eliminated by the staunch appeals to the police and the law-makers that issue ever more loudly from the ranks of the environmentalists. A conviction is blocked by the very thing that was supposed to achieve it: the strict application of the (individually interpreted) polluter-pays principle.

In the case of the lead crystal factory, the commission of the crime could not be and was not denied by anyone. A mitigating factor came into play for the culprits: there were three other glass factories in the vicinity which emitted the same pollutants. Notice: the more pollution is committed, the less is committed.

More precisely: the more liberally the acceptable levels are set, the greater the number of smokestacks and discharge pipes through which pollutants and toxins are emitted, the lower the 'residual probability' that a culprit can be made responsible for the general sniffling and coughing, that is to say, the less pollution is produced. Whereas at the same time – one does not exclude the other – the general level of contamination and pollution is increasing. Welcome to the real-life travesty of the hazard technocracy![6]

This example illustrates three points: first, the importance of meta-norms of risk definitions, here the legal norms of how to attribute causes and consequences to actors under conditions of high complexity and contingency. If it is necessary to name one and only one actor, in the overwhelming majority of cases *no* actor can be named.

This is even more true because, second, a significant number of technologically induced hazards, such as those associated with chemical pollution, atomic radiation and genetically modified organisms, are characterized by an inaccessibility to the human senses. They operate outside the capacity of (unaided) human perception. Everyday life is 'blind' in relation to hazards which threaten life and thus depends in its inner decisions on experts and counter-experts. Not only the potential harm but this *'expropriation of the senses'* by global risks makes life insecure.

Third, there is a significant interrelationship between *ignoring* a risk which cannot be attributed according to the meta-norms of risk definition in law and science and *enforcing* risk production as a consequence of industrial action and production.

This organized irresponsibility is based fundamentally on a confusion of centuries. The hazards to which we are exposed date from a different century than the promises of security which attempt to subdue them. Herein lies the foundation for both phenomena: the periodic outbreak of the contradictions of highly organized security bureaucracies and the possibility of normalizing these 'hazard shocks' over and over again. At the threshold of the twenty-first century, the challenges of the age of atomic, genetic and chemical technology are being handled with concepts and recipes that are derived from early industrial society of the nineteenth and the early twentieth centuries.[7]

Is there an operational criterion for distinguishing between risks and threats? The economy itself reveals the boundary line of what is tolerable with economic precision, through the refusal of private insurance. Where the logic of private insurance disengages, where the economic risks of insurance appear too large or too unpredictable to insurance concerns, the boundary that separates 'predictable' risks from uncontrollable threats has obviously been breached again and again in large and small ways.

Two types of consequences are connected in principle to this overstepping of the bounds. First, the *social* pillars of the calculus of risks fail; security degenerates into mere technical safety. The secret of the calculus of risks, however, is that technical *and* social components work together: limitation, accountability, compensation, precautionary after-care. These are now running in neutral, and social and political security can be created solely by means of a contradictory maximizing of technical superlatives.

Second, a central part of this political dynamic is the social contradiction between highly developed safety bureaucracies, on the one hand, and the open legalization of previously unseen, gigantic threats, on the other, without any possibility of after-care. A society which is oriented from top to toe towards security and health is confronted with the shock of their diametrical opposites, destruction and threats which scorn any precautions against them.

Two contrary lines of historical development are converging in late twentieth-century Europe: a level of security founded on the perfection of techno-bureaucratic norms and controls, and the spread and challenge of historically new hazards which slip through all the meshes of law, technology and politics. This contradiction, which is not of a technical, but of a social and political character, remains hidden in the 'confusion of centuries' (Günther Anders). And this will continue so long as the old industrial patterns of rationality and control last. It will break up to the extent that improbable events become probable. 'Normal accidents' is the name Charles Perrow (1984) gives in his book to this predictability with which what was considered impossible occurs – and the more emphatically it is denied, the sooner, more destructively and shockingly it occurs. In the chain of publicly revealed catastrophes, near-catastrophes, whitewashed security faults and scandals the technically centred claim to the control of governmental and industrial authority shatters – quite independently of the established measure of hazards: the number of dead, the danger of the contaminations, and so on.

The central social-historical and political potential of ecological, nuclear, chemical and genetic hazards lies in the collapse of administration, in the collapse of techno-scientific and legal rationality and of institutional political security guarantees which those hazards conjure up for everyone. That potential lies in the unmasking of the concretely existing anarchy which has grown out of the denial of the social production and administration of mega-hazards.[8]

Hazards of the nuclear and chemical age, therefore, have a social as well as a physical explosiveness. As the hazards appear, the institutions which are responsible for them, and then again not responsible, are pressed into competition with the security claims they are compelled to issue, a competition from which they can only emerge as losers. On the one hand, they come under permanent pressure to make even the safest things safer; on the other hand, this overtaxes expectations and sharpens attention, so that in the end not only accidents, but even the suspicion of them, can cause the façades of security claims to collapse. The other side of the recognition of hazards is the failure of the institutions that derive their justification from the non-existence of hazard. That is why the 'social birth' of a hazard is an event which is equally improbable and dramatic, traumatic and unsettling to the entire society.

Precisely because of their explosiveness in social and political space, hazards remain distorted objects, ambiguous, interpretable, resembling modern mythological creatures, which now appear to be an earthworm, now again a dragon, depending on perspective and the state of interests. The ambiguity of risks also has its basis in the revolutions which their official unambiguity had to provoke. The institutions of developed industrial society – politics, law, engineering sciences, industrial concerns – accordingly command a broad arsenal for 'normalizing' non-calculable hazards. They can be underestimated, compared out of existence or made anonymous causally and legally. These instruments of a symbolic politics of detoxification enjoy correspondingly great significance and popularity (this is shown by Fischer, 1989).

Ministers of the environment, no matter what their party affiliation, are not to be envied. Hampered by the scope of their ministry and its financial endowment, they must keep the causes largely constant and counter the cycle of destruction in a primarily symbolic fashion. A 'good' minister of the environment ultimately is the one who stages activities in a publicity-grabbing way, piling up laws, creating bureaucratic jurisdictions, centralizing information. He or she may even dive into the Rhine with a daredevil smile or try a spoonful of contaminated whey powder, provided the media eyes of a frightened public are trained upon him/her. Dogged adherence to a line must be sold with the same TV smile and 'good arguments' as a 180-degree shift in direction.

But gradually, one accident at a time, the logic of the institutionalized non-management of problems can turn into its opposite: what does probability-based safety – and thus the entire scientific diagnosis – mean for the evaluation of the worst imaginable accident, whose occurrence would leave the experts' theories intact but destroy their lives?

Sooner or later the question will arise as to the value of a legal system that regulates and pursues every detail of the technically manageable minor risks, but legalizes the mega-hazards by virtue of its authority, to the extent they cannot be minimized technically, and burdens everyone with them, including those who resist.

How can a democratic political authority be maintained which must counter the escalating consciousness of hazards with energetic safety claims, but in that very process puts itself constantly on the defensive and risks its entire credibility with every accident or sign of an accident?

The Role of Technology and the Natural Sciences in Risk Society

There is a public dispute over a new ethics of research in order to avoid incalculable and inhuman results. To limit oneself to that debate is to misunderstand the degree and type of involvement of the engineering sciences in the production of hazards. An ethical renewal of the sciences, even if it were not to become entangled in the thicket of ethical viewpoints, would be like a bicycle brake on an intercontinental jet, considering the autonomization of technological development and its interconnections with economic interests. Moreover, we are concerned not merely with the ethics of research, but also with its logic and with the unity of culprits and judges (experts) of the engineering sciences in the technocracy of hazards.

An initial insight is central: in matters of hazards, no one is an expert – particularly not the experts. Predictions of risk contain a double fuzziness. First, they presume cultural acceptance and cannot produce it. There is no scientific bridge between destruction and protest or between destruction and acceptance. Acceptable risks are ultimately accepted risks. Second, new knowledge can turn normality into hazards overnight. Nuclear energy and the hole in the ozone layer are prominent examples. Therefore: the advancement of science refutes its original claims of safety. *It is the successes of science which sow the doubts as to its risk predictions.*

But conversely, it is also true that acute danger passes the monopoly of interpretation to those who caused it, of all people. In the shock of the catastrophe, people speak of rem, Becquerels or ethylene glycol as if they know what such words mean, and they must do so in order to find their way in the most everyday matters. This contradiction must be exposed. On the one hand, the engineering sciences involuntarily enact their own self-refutation in their contradictory risk diagnoses. On the other, they continue to administer the privilege handed down to them from the Kaiser's day, the right to determine according to their own internal standards the global social question of the most intensely political nature: how safe is safe enough?

The power of the hard sciences here rests on a simple social construct. They are granted the binding authority – binding for law and politics – to decide on the basis of their own standards what the 'state of technology' demands. But since this general clause is the legal standard for safety, private organizations and committees (for instance, the Society of German Engineers, the Institute for Standards) decide in Germany the amount of hazards to which everyone can be subjected (see Wolf, 1987). This is a situation that the Schröder government is going to change.

If one asks, for instance, what level of exposure to artificially produced radioactivity must be tolerated by the populace, that is, where the threshold of tolerance separating normality from hazardousness is situated, then the Atomic Energy Act gives the general answer that the necessary precautions are to correspond to 'the state of technology' (Sec. 7 II No. 3). This phrase is fleshed out in the 'Guidelines' of the Reactor Safety Commission – an 'advisory council' of the Ministry of the Environment in which representatives of engineering companies hold sway. When the Green Minister of the Environment, Jürgen Trittin, came to office in 1998, the first thing he did was to dismiss this commission, thus removing from the nuclear industry one of its major instruments of (no-)risk power definition.

In air pollution policy, noise protection and water policy one always finds the same pattern: laws prescribe the general programme. But anyone who wishes to know how large a continuing ration of standardized pollution citizens are expected to tolerate needs to consult the 'Ordinance on Large Combustion Facilities' or the 'Technical Instructions: Air Quality' and similar works for the (literally) 'irritating' details.

Even the classical instruments of political direction – statutes and administrative regulations – are empty in their central statements. They juggle with the 'state of technology', thus undercutting their own competence, and in its place they elevate 'scientific and technical expertise' to the throne of the civilization of threat.

This *monopoly of scientists and engineers in the diagnosis of hazards*, however, is simultaneously being called into question by the 'reality crisis' of the natural and engineering sciences in their dealings with the hazards they produce. It has not been true only since Chernobyl, but there it first became palpable to a broad public: safety and probable safety, seemingly so close, are worlds apart. The engineering sciences always have only probable safety at their command. Thus, even if two or three nuclear reactors blow up tomorrow, their statements remain true.

Wolf Häfele, the dean of the German reactor industry, wrote in 1974:

> It is precisely the interplay between theory and experiment or trial and error which is no longer possible for reactor technology. . . . Reactor engineers take account of this dilemma by dividing the problem of technical safety into sub-problems. But even the splitting of the problem can only serve to approximate ultimate safety. . . . The remaining 'residual risk' opens the door to the realm of the 'hypothetical'. . . . The interchange between theory and experiment, which leads to truth in the traditional sense, is no longer possible. . . . I believe it is this ultimate indecisiveness hidden in our plans which explains the particular sensitivities of public debates on the safety of nuclear reactors.
>
> (*Häfele, 1974: 247*)

What one hears here is nothing less than the contradiction between experimental logic and atomic peril. Just as sociologists cannot force society into a test tube, engineers cannot let people's reactors blow up all around them in order to test their safety, unless they turn the world into a laboratory. Theories of nuclear reactor safety are testable only after they are built, not beforehand. The expedient of testing partial systems amplifies the contingencies of their interaction, and thus contains sources of error which cannot themselves be controlled experimentally.

If one compares this with the logic of research that was originally agreed upon, this amounts to its sheer reversal. We no longer find the progression, first laboratory then application. Instead, testing comes after application and production precedes research. The dilemma into which the mega-hazards have plunged scientific logic applies across the board; that is, for nuclear, chemical and genetic experiments *science hovers blindly above the boundary of threats*. Test-tube babies must first be produced, genetically engineered artificial creatures released and reactors built, in order that their properties and safety can be studied. The question of safety, then, must be answered affirmatively before it can even be raised. The authority of the engineers is undermined by this 'safety circle'.

Through the anticipation of application before it has been fully explored, science has itself abolished the boundary between laboratory and society (Kohn and Weyer, 1989; Beck, 1995). Concomitantly, the conditions of freedom of research have shifted. Freedom of research implies freedom of application. Today, anyone who demands or grants only freedom of research abolishes research. The power of technology is based in its command of practice. Engineers can directly apply things, where politics must first advise, convince, vote and then push them through against resistance. This makes technology capable of conducting a policy of the *fait accompli*, which not only puts politicians and the public under constant pressure to react, but also puts them at the mercy of the engineers' judgement for assessment and avoidance of disaster. This power grows with the velocity of the innovations, the lack of clarity regarding their consequences and hazards, and it grows even though the credibility of technological promises of safety is thereby undermined.

Where the monopoly of technology becomes a monopoly on concealed social change, it must be called into question and cancelled by the principle of division of powers – like the earlier 'legal transcendence of the sovereign'. Internally, this implies a redistribution of the burdens of proof and, externally, the liberation of doubt (see Beck, 1995: ch. 8). In all central social issues and committees relative to technological development, systematic alternatives, dissenting voices, dissenting experts and an interdisciplinary diversity would have to be combined. The exposure of scientific uncertainty is the liberation of politics, law and the public sphere from their expert patronization by technocracy. Thus the public acknowledgement of uncertainty opens the space for democratization.

The Ecological Conflict in Society

If risk society does not mean only a technical challenge, then the question arises: what political dynamics, what social structure, what conflict scenarios arise from the legalization and normalization of global and uncontrollable systematic threats? To reduce things to an admittedly crude formula: hunger is hierarchical. Even following the Second World War, not everyone went hungry. Nuclear contamination, however, is egalitarian and in that sense 'democratic'. Nitrates in the ground water do not stop at the general director's water tap (see Beck, 1992: ch. 1).[9]

All suffering, all misery, all violence inflicted by people on other people to this point recognized the category of the Other – workers,

Jews, blacks, asylum-seekers, dissidents, and so forth – and those apparently unaffected could retreat behind this category. *The 'end of the Other', the end of all our carefully cultivated opportunities for distancing ourselves, is what we have become able to experience with the advent of nuclear and chemical contamination.* Misery can be marginalized, but that is no longer true of hazards in the age of nuclear, chemical and genetic technology. It is there that the peculiar and novel political force of those threats lies. Their power is the power of threat, which eliminates all the protective zones and social differentiations within and between nation-states.

It may be true that in the storm tide of threat 'we're all in the same boat', as the cliché goes. But, as is so often the case, here too there are captains, passengers, helmsmen, engineers, and men and women overboard. In other words, there are countries, sectors and enter-prises which *profit* from the production of risk, and others which find their economic existence threatened together with their physical well-being. If, for instance, the Adriatic or the North Sea dies or they are perceived socially as 'hazardous to health' – this difference is cancelled with respect to economic effects – then it is not just the North Sea or the Adriatic which die, along with the life those seas contain and make possible. The economic life in all the towns, sec-tors and coastal countries that live directly or indirectly from the commercialization of the sea is also extinguished. At the apex of the future, which reaches into the horizon of the present day, industrial civilization is transformed into a kind of 'world cup' of the global risk society. Destruction of nature and destruction of markets coincide here. It is not what one has or is able to do that determines one's social position and future, but rather where and from what one lives and to what extent others are permitted in a prearranged unaccountability to pollute one's possessions and abilities in the guise of 'environment'.

Even passionate denial, which can certainly count on full official support, has its limits. The revenge of the abstract expert dispute on hazards is its geographic concretion. One can dispute everything, operating the official whitewashing machinery in high gear. That does not prevent, but only accelerates, the destruction. In this way, 'toxin-absorbing regions' come into being, crossing national boundar-ies and old institutional lines of conflict, creating geographical posi-tions whose 'fate' coincides with the industrial destruction of nature (see Beck, 1995: ch. 6).

The greenhouse effect, for example, will raise temperatures and sea levels around the world through the melting of the polar icecaps. The period of warming will submerge entire coastal regions, turn farmland into desert, shift climatic zones in unpredictable ways and dramatically accelerate the extinction of species. *The poorest in the world will be hit the hardest.* They will be least able to adapt themselves to the changes in the environment. Those who find themselves deprived of the basis of their economic existence will flee the zone of misery. A veritable Exodus of eco-refugees and climatic asylum-seekers will flood across the wealthy North; crises in the Third and Fourth Worlds could escalate into wars. Even the climate of world politics will change at a faster pace than is imaginable today. So far, all these are just projections, but we must take them seriously. When they have become reality, it will already be too late to take action.

Many things would be easier here if those countries on the way to industrialization could be spared the mistakes of the highly industrialized countries. But the unchecked expansion of the industrial society is still considered the *via regia* that promises the mastery of many problems – not only those of poverty – so that the prevailing misery often displaces the abstract issues of environmental destruction.

'Threats to nature' are not only that; pointing them out also threatens property, capital, jobs, trade union power, the economic foundation of whole sectors and regions, and the structure of nation-states and global markets. So there are 'side-effects' to nature and 'side-effects of side-effects' within the basic institutions of first modernity.

Put another way: there is a major distinction between the conflict field of wealth production – '*goods*' – from which the nineteenth century derived the experience and premises of industrial and class society, and the conflict field of hazard production – '*bads*' – in the developed nuclear and chemical age, to which we are only just beginning to become sensitive in sociology. It probably lies in the fact that wealth production produced the antagonisms between capital and labour, while the systematic chemical, nuclear and genetic threats bring about polarizations between capital and capital – and thus also between labour and labour – cutting across the social order. If the social welfare state had to be forced through against the concerted resistance of the private investors, who were called on to pay in the form of wage and fringe-benefit costs, then *ecological threats split the business camp.* At first glance, it is impossible to discern where and how the boundary runs; or, more accurately, who receives the power, and from where, to cause the boundary to run in what way.

While it may still be possible to speak of the 'environment' on the level of an individual operation, this talk becomes simply fictitious on the level of the overall economy, because there a type of 'Russian roulette' is being played behind the increasingly thin walls of the 'environment'. If it is suddenly revealed and publicized in the mass media that certain products contain certain 'toxins' (information policy and mass media coverage is of key importance considering the fact that hazards are generally imperceptible in everyday life), then entire markets may collapse and invested capital and effort are instantly devalued.

No matter how abstract the threats may be, their concretizations are ultimately just as irreversible and regionally identifiable. What is denied collects itself into geographical positions, into 'loser regions' which have to pay the tab for the damage and its 'unaccountability' with their economic existence. In this 'ecological expropriation', we are facing the historical novelty of a devaluation of capital and achievement, while relationships of ownership and sometimes even the characteristics of the goods remain constant. Sectors that had nothing or very little causally to do with the production of the threat – agriculture, the food industry, tourism, fisheries, but also retail trade and parts of the service industry – are also among those most affected.

Where the (world) economy splits into risk winners and risk losers – in a manner difficult to define – this polarization will also make its mark upon the structure of employment. First, new types of antagonisms that are specific to countries, sectors and enterprises arise between groups of employees and correspondingly within and between trade union interest organizations. Second, these are, so to speak, third-hand antagonisms, derived from those between factions of capital, which turn the 'fate of workers' into 'fate' in a further and fundamental dimension. Third, with the intensified consciousness of the corresponding lines of conflict, a sector-specific alliance of the old 'class opponents', labour and capital, may arise. The consequence may be a confrontation between this union–management bloc and other mixed factions over and above the divisions of class differences which have been narrowed under the pressure of 'ecological politicization'.[10]

One has to wonder what an ecological labour movement would really mean. The production and definition of hazards aims largely at the level of products, which escapes almost completely from the influence of the works councils and workers' groups and falls completely under the jurisdiction of management. And this is still at the intra-organizational level. Hazards are produced by business operations, to be sure, but they are defined and evaluated socially – in the mass media, in the experts' debate, in the jungle of interpretations and jurisdictions, in courts or with strategic-intellectual dodges, in a milieu and in contexts, that is to say, to which the majority of workers are totally alien. We are dealing with 'scientific battles' waged over the heads of the workers, and fought out instead by intellectual strategies in intellectual milieux. The definition of hazards eludes the grasp of workers and even, as things stand, the approach of trade unions for the most part. Workers and unions are not even those primarily affected; that group consists of the enterprises and management. But as secondary targets they must count on losing their jobs if worst comes to worst.

Even a latent risk definition hits them in the centre of their pride in achievement, their promise of a usable commodity. Labour and labour power can no longer conceive of themselves only as the source of wealth, but must also be perceived socially as the motive force for threat and destruction. The labour society is not only running out of labour, the only thing which gives meaning and solidity to life, as Hannah Arendt puts it ironically, it is also losing even this residual meaning.

Somewhat crudely, one can say in conclusion: what is 'environment' for the polluting industry is the basis of economic existence for the affected loser regions and loser sectors. The consequence is: political systems in their architecture as nation-states, on the one hand, and large-scale ecological conflict positions, on the other, become mutually autonomous and create 'geopolitical' shifts which place the domestic and international structure of economic and military blocs under completely new stresses, but also offer new opportunities. *The phase of risk society politics which is beginning to make itself heard today in the arena of disarmament and detente in the East–West relationship can no longer be understood nationally, but only internationally, because the social mechanics of risk situations disregards the nation-state and its alliance systems.* In that sense, apparently iron-clad political, military and economic constellations are becoming mobile, and this forces or, better, permits, a new 'European global domestic policy' (Genscher).

Political Reflexivity: The Counterforce of Threat and the Opportunities for Influence by Social Movements

Risk conflict is certainly not the first conflict which modern societies have had to master, but it is one of the most fundamental. Class conflicts or revolutions change power relations and exchange elites, but they hold fast to the goals of techno-economic progress and clash over mutually recognized civil rights. The double face of 'self-annihilating progress', however, produces conflicts that cast doubt on the social basis of rationality – science, law, democracy. In that way, society is placed under permanent pressure to negotiate foundations without a foundation. It experiences an institutional destabilization, in which all decisions – from local government policy on speed limits and 'parking lots' to the manufacturing details of industrial goods to the fundamental issues of energy supply, law and technological development – can suddenly be sucked into fundamental political conflicts.

While the façades remain intact, quasi-governmental power positions arise in the research laboratories, nuclear power plants, genetic factories, editorial offices, courts, and so on, in the milieu of hazards dependent on definitions and publicity. Put another way: as the contradictions of the security- and safety-obligated state are stirred up, systems come to require action and become subject-dependent. The courageous Davids of this world get their chance, and so do social movements. The colossal interdependence of threat definitions – the collapse of markets, property rights, trade union power and political responsibility – brings about key positions and media of 'risk-definition' which cross the social and professional hierarchy.

One can use all one's powers of conviction to pile up arguments for the institutional non-existence of suicidal threats; one need not deny one iota of hope to the institutional hegemony; one can even draw on the distraction of the social movements and the limitations of their political effectiveness; and one must still recognize with equal realism that all this is countered by the opposing power of threat. It is constant and permanent, not tied to interpretations denying it, and even present in places demonstrators have long since abandoned. The probability of improbable accidents grows with time and the number of implemented mega-technologies. Every 'event' arouses memories of all the other ones, all over the world.

Different types of revolutions have been contrasted: coups d'état, the class struggle, civilian resistance, and so on. They all have in common the empowering and disempowering of social subjects. Revolution as an autonomized process, as a hidden, latent, permanent condition, in which conditions are involved against their own interests, while political structures or property and power relations remain unchanged – this is a possibility which so far, to my knowledge, has neither been taken into consideration nor thought through. But it is precisely this conceptual scheme into which the *social power of threat* fits (even if it is a social power only in relation to political movements that activate it). It is the product of the deed, requiring no political authorization and no authentication. Once in existence, public awareness of it endangers all institutions – from business to science, from law to politics – which have produced and legitimated it.

Everyone asks: from where will the opposing forces come? It is probably not very promising to place large or small ads for the missing 'revolutionary subject' in hip papers of the subculture. It feels good, of course, to appeal to reason with all the strictness at one's command, and it can do no harm, precisely because a realistic view of experience has shown that it leaves few traces behind. One could also found another circle for the solution of global problems. Certainly, it is to be hoped that political parties will catch on.

If all this does not suffice to stimulate alternative political action, however, then there remains the knowledge of the activatable political reflexivity of the hazard potential.[11] Three Mile Island, Chernobyl, Hanau, Biblis, Wackersdorf, and so forth: the global experiment of nuclear energy (toxic chemistry, genetic engineering, virtual reality machines, and so on) has by now taken over the roles of its own critics, perhaps even more convincingly and effectively than the political counter-movements could ever have managed on their own. This becomes clear not only in the world-wide, unpaid negative advertising at peak news times and on the front pages of papers, but also in the fact that everyone between the Alpine chalets and the North Sea mud flats now understands and speaks the language of the nuclear critics. Under the dictates of necessity, people have passed a kind of crash course in the contradictions of hazard administration in risk society: on the arbitrariness of acceptable levels and calculation procedures or the unimaginability of the long-term consequences and the possibilities of making them anonymous through statistics. They have learned more information, more vividly and more clearly than even the most critical critique could have ever taught them or demanded of them.

The most enduring, convincing and effective critics of nuclear energy (or the genetic industry and so forth) are not the demonstrators outside the fences or the critical public (no matter how important and indispensable they may be). The most influential opponent of the threat industry is the threat industry itself.

To put it differently, the power of the new social movements is based not only on themselves, but also on the quality and scope of the contradictions in which the hazard-producing and -administering industries are involved in risk society. Those contradictions become public and scandalous through the needling activities of the social movements. Thus, there is not only an autonomous process of the suppression of dangers, but there are also opposite tendencies to uncover this suppression, even though they are much less marked and always dependent on the civil courage of individuals and the vigilance of social movements. Catastrophes that touch the vital nerves of society in a context of highly developed bureaucratic safety and welfare arouse the sensationalist greed of the mass media, threaten markets, make sales prospects unpredictable, devalue capital and set streams of voters in motion. Thus the evening news ultimately exceeds even the fantasies of countercultural dissent; daily newspaper reading becomes an exercise in technology critique.

This oppositional power of the unintended revelation of hazards depends of course on overall social conditions, which have so far been fulfilled in only a few countries: parliamentary democracy, (relative) independence of the press, and advanced production of wealth in which the invisible threat of cancer is not overridden for the majority of the populace by acute undernourishment and famine.

In the cooperation from within and without over and above the boundary lines of the subsystems, there are also symptoms of strength, which have so far remained almost unnoticed. The socially most astonishing, most surprising and perhaps least understood phenomenon of the last twenty years, not only in Germany, is *individualization*, the unexpected renaissance of an 'enormous subjectivity' – inside and outside of the institutions (see Beck, 1992: part II; Beck and Beck-Gernsheim, 1995). In this sense it is not an exaggeration to say that *citizens' groups have taken the initiative thematically in this society*. It was they who put the themes of an endangered world on the social agenda, against the resistance of the established parties. Nowhere does this become so clear as in the spectre of the 'new unity' which is haunting Europe. The compulsion to perform ecological lip-service is universal. It unites the Christian Social Union with the Communists, and the chemical industry with its Green critics. All products, absolutely all products, are 'safe for the environment', to say the least. There are rumours that the chemical concerns plan to take out full-page ads announcing themselves as a registered conservation association.

Admittedly this is all just packaging, programmatic opportunism, and perhaps really intentional rethinking now and then. The actions and the points of origin of the facts are largely untouched by it. Yet it remains true: the themes of the future, which are now on everyone's lips, have not originated from the farsightedness of the rulers or from the struggle in parliament – and certainly not from the cathedrals of power in business, science and the state. They have been put on the social agenda against the concentrated resistance of this institutionalized ignorance by the entangled, moralizing groups and splinter groups fighting each other over the true path, split and plagued by doubts. *Democratic subversion has won a quite improbable thematic victory.* And this in Germany, breaking with an authoritarian everyday culture which, historically, has enabled all official nonsense and insanity with its anticipatory obedience.

The Utopia of Ecological Democracy

Europe is called to a new social project and has already set off on it. After the implosion of the East–West conflict and the emergence of states without enemies (Beck, 1998b), the international themes of the risk civilization are moving into the resulting vacuum. One sign of this is the pressure for global ecological politics and transnational arrangements which technology, science and business produce. Another is the dawning of the large and small, the creeping and the galloping suicidal hazards everywhere in the world, and a final sign comes from the elevated standards of promised safety and rationality in developed welfare state capitalism.

These are the horrendous opportunities that offer themselves to a European global domestic policy, not only in the foundation and building of the 'European house', but also by the highly industrialized countries assuming a large portion of the costs for the necessary corrective measures. In the place where the dynamic of industrial development had its origin, in Europe, enlightenment on and against industrial society could also begin. This project of an ecological enlightenment would have to be designed and fought for both on the macro and micro levels. Even in everyday life, because the threats overturn well-worn routine everywhere and represent a spectacular challenge for civil courage – at jobs in industry; in the practices of doctors where people come with their fears and questions; in research which can block off or reveal; in the courts; in the monitoring of the administration; and, not least, in the editorial offices of the mass media, where the invisible can be made culturally discernible. There are many concrete concerns in the relationship of the 'European house' to its neighbours on this planet. Among them is the impossibility of appearing any longer with the self-confidence of the donating wealthy, but rather admitting our destructive industrial role and correcting it in thought and action.

The technological project, the technological dogmatism of industrialism, must not simply be extended to the ecological crisis, lest an
ever more perfect technocracy result from the public dramatization
of the dangers. *Industrial society has produced a 'truncated democracy', in which questions of the technological change of society remain beyond the reach of political-parliamentary decision-making.*
As things stand, one can say 'no' to techno-economic progress, but
that will not change its course in any way. It is a blank cheque to be
honoured – beyond agreement or refusal. Even ethics, which everybody calls for, is, under these conditions, nothing but a bicycle brake
on an intercontinental aeroplane. We are living in an age of technological fatalism, an 'industrial middle ages', that must be overcome by
more democracy – the production of accountability, redistribution of
the burdens of proof, division of powers between the producers and the
evaluators of hazards, public disputes on technological alternatives.[12]
This in turn requires different organizational forms for science and
business, science and the public sphere, science and politics, technology
and law, and so forth.

The ecological extension of democracy then means: playing off the
concert of voices and powers, the development of the independence
of politics, law, the public sphere and daily life against the dangerous
and false security of a 'society conceived in the abstract'.

My suggestion contains two interlocking principles: first, carrying
out a division of powers and, second, the creation of a public sphere.
Only a strong, competent public debate, 'armed' with scientific arguments, is capable of separating the scientific wheat from the chaff
and allowing the institutions for directing technology – politics and
law – to reconquer the power of their own judgement.

The means: with regard to all issues that are central to society,
dissenting voices, alternative experts, an interdisciplinary variety and,
not least, alternatives to be developed systematically must always be
combined. The public sphere in cooperation with a kind of 'public
science' would act as a secondary body charged with the 'discursive
checking' of scientific laboratory results in the crossfire of opinions.
Their particular responsibility would comprise all issues that concern
the broad outlines and dangers of scientific civilization and are chron-
ically excluded in standard science. The public would have the role of
an 'open upper chamber'. It would be charged to apply the standard
'How do we wish to live?' to scientific plans, results and hazards.

That presupposes that research will fundamentally take account of
the public's questions and be addressed to them and not just multiply
our common problems in an economic short-circuit with industry.

Perhaps it would be possible that through these two steps – an opening of science from within and the filtering out of its limitations in a public test of its practice – politics and science could successively hone their direction-finding and self-monitoring instruments – instruments that are now largely inactive.

The cultural blindness of daily life in the civilization of threat can ultimately not be removed; but culture 'sees' in symbols. The images in the news of skeletal trees or of dying seals have opened people's eyes. Making the threats publicly visible and arousing attention in detail, in one's own living space – these are cultural eyes through which the 'blind *citoyens*' can perhaps win back the autonomy of their own judgement.

To conclude with a question: what would happen if radioactivity itched? Realists, also called cynics, will answer: people would invent something, perhaps a salve, to 'turn off' the itching. A profitable, never-ending business then. Certainly, explanations would soon arise and would enjoy great public acceptance: they would claim that the itching had no meaning, that it might be correlated to other factors besides radioactivity, and that it was innocuous in any case, unpleasant but demonstrably harmless. If everyone ran around scratching themselves and with rashes on their skin, and if photo sessions with fashion models as well as management meetings of the united denial institutes took place with all participants scratching themselves, it would have to be assumed that such explanations would have little chance of surviving. In that case, nuclear policy, as well as dealings with modern mega-hazards in general, would confront a completely changed situation: the object being disputed and negotiated would be culturally perceptible.[13]

That is precisely where the future of democracy is being decided: are we dependent in all the details of life-and-death issues on the judgement of experts, even dissenting experts, or will we win back the competence to make our own judgement through a culturally created perceptibility of the hazards? Is the only alternative still an authoritarian technocracy or a critical one? Or is there a way to counter the incapacitation and expropriation of daily life in the age of risk?

4

Risk Society and the Welfare State

If modernization is understood as a process of innovation which has become autonomous, then it must also be accepted that modernity itself ages. The other aspect of this ageing of industrial modernity is the emergence of risk society. This concept describes a phase of development of modern society in which the social, political, ecological and individual risks created by the momentum of innovation increasingly elude the control and protective institutions of industrial society.

Between Industrial Society and Risk Society

Two phases may be distinguished. The first is a stage in which consequences and self-endangerment are systematically produced, but are *not* the subject of public debate or at the centre of political conflict. This phase is dominated by the self-identity of industrial society, which simultaneously both intensifies and 'legitimates', as 'residual risks', hazards resulting from decisions made ('residual risk society').

A completely different situation arises when the hazards of industrial society dominate public, political and private debates. Now the institutions of industrial society produce and legitimate hazards which they cannot control. During this transition, property and power relationships remain *constant*. Industrial society sees and criticizes itself *as* risk society. On the one hand, the society *still* makes decisions and acts on the pattern of the old industrial society; on the other hand, debates and conflicts which originate in the dynamic of risk society are already being superimposed on interest organizations, the legal system and politics.

In view of these two stages and their sequence, the concept of 'reflexive modernization' may be introduced. (See on this: Lash, 1992; Merten and Olk, 1992; Rauschenbach, 1992; Zapf, 1992; Beck et al., 1994; Beck, 1997.) This precisely does *not* mean *reflection* (as the adjective 'reflexive' seems to suggest), but above all *self-confrontation*. The transition from the industrial to the risk epoch of modernity occurs *un*intentionally, *un*seen, compulsively, in the course of a dynamic of modernization which has made itself autonomous, on the pattern of *unintended consequences*. One can almost say that the constellations of risk society are created because the self-evident truths of industrial society (the consensus on progress, the abstraction from ecological consequences and hazards) dominate the thinking and behaviour of human beings and institutions. Risk society is *not an option* which could be chosen or rejected in the course of political debate. It arises through the automatic operation of autonomous modernization processes which are blind and deaf to consequences and dangers. In total, and latently, these produce hazards which call into question – indeed abolish – the basis of industrial society.

This kind of self-confrontation of the consequences of modernization with the basis of modernization should be clearly distinguished from the increase in knowledge and the penetration of all spheres of life by science and specialization in the sense of the self-reflection of modernization. If we call the autonomous, unintentional and unseen, *reflex*-like transition from industrial to risk society *reflexivity* – in distinction and opposition to *reflection* – then 'reflexive modernization' means self-confrontation with the consequences of risk society which cannot (adequately) be addressed and overcome in the system of industrial society (Beck, 1992) (that is, measured by industrial society's own institutionalized standards). At a second stage this constellation can, in turn, be made the object of (public, political and academic) reflection, but this must not cover up the unreflected, reflex-like 'mechanism' of the transition. This is produced and becomes real precisely through abstraction from risk society.

In risk society, conflicts over the distribution of the 'bads' produced by it are superimposed on the conflicts over the distribution of societal 'goods' (income, jobs, social security), which constituted the fundamental conflict of industrial society and led to attempts at solution in appropriate institutions. The former can be shown to be *conflicts of accountability.* They break out over the question of how the consequences of the risks accompanying commodity production – large-scale nuclear and chemical technology, genetic engineering, threats to the environment, the arms build-up and the increasing impoverishment of humanity living outside Western industrial society – can be distributed, averted, controlled and legitimated.

At any rate, the concept of risk society provides a term for this relationship of reflex and reflection. For a theory of society and for cultural diagnosis the concept describes a stage of modernity in which the hazards produced in the growth of industrial society become predominant. That both poses the question of the self-limitation of this development and sets the task of redefining previously attained standards (of responsibility, safety, control, damage limitation and distribution of the consequence of loss) with reference to potential dangers. These, however, elude not only sensory perception and the powers of the imagination, but also scientific determination. Modern societies are therefore confronted with the principles and limits of their own model precisely to the extent that they do *not* change themselves, do not reflect on the consequences, and pursue an industrial policy of more-of-the-same.

The concept of risk society takes this as its starting-point, in order to articulate systemic and epochal transformation in three areas. *First of all*, the relationship of modern industrial society to the resources of nature and culture, on whose existence it depends, but whose reserves are being used up in the course of an assertive modernization. This is true for nature external to human beings and human cultures as well as for cultural life-forms (such as the nuclear family and order of the sexes) and social labour assets (such as housewives' labour, which although it has still not been recognized as labour, nevertheless made men's paid labour possible).

Second, the relationship of society to the hazards and problems produced by it, which in turn *exceed the bases of societal conceptions of security*. As a result, they are, insofar as there is awareness of them, likely to upset the basic assumptions of the previously existing social order. This is true for all sectors of society – such as business, the law, academia – but becomes a problem above all in the area of political activity and decision-making.

Third, the exhaustion, dissolution and disenchantment of collective and group-specific sources of meaning (such as belief in progress, class consciousness) of the culture of industrial society (whose life-styles and ideas of security have also been fundamental to the Western democracies and economic societies until well into the twentieth century) lead to all the work of definition henceforth being expected of or imposed on individuals themselves. This is what the concept of 'individualizing process' means. Georg Simmel, Émile Durkheim and Max Weber shaped the theory of this process at the beginning of the century and investigated its various historical stages. The difference is that today human beings are being 'released' not from corporate, religious-transcendental securities into the world of industrial society, but *from* industrial society into the turbulence of world risk society. They are, not least, expected to live with the most diverse, contradictory global and personal risks.

At the same time, this release – at least in the highly developed welfare states of the West – occurs within the framework of the social state. It takes place, therefore, against a background of educational expansion, the high levels of mobility demanded by the labour market and an extended legal framework for working conditions. The individual is turned, however, into the bearer of rights (and duties) – but only as an individual. The opportunities, hazards and ambivalences of biography which once could be coped with in the family unit, in the village community, and by recourse to the social class or group, increasingly have to be grasped, interpreted and dealt with by the individual alone. These 'risky freedoms' (Beck and Beck-Gernsheim, 1994) are now imposed on individuals, without the latter being in a position, because of the great complexity of modern society, to make unavoidable decisions in a knowledgeable and responsible way; that is, with regard to possible consequences. At the same time the question as to the *we* that is able to bind and motivate the individualized individuals becomes urgent. If, after the end of the Cold War, even the national friendships and enmities of the East–West conflict disappear, then individuals in the networked media world, which compels not love-thy-neighbour, but love of whoever is far away, must repeatedly discover and justify even their own personal foreign policy in rapidly changing constellations.

The Welfare State and Risk Society

Risks always depend on decisions – that is, they presuppose decisions. They arise from the transformation of uncertainty and hazards into decisions (and compel the making of decisions, which in turn produce risks).[1] The incalculable threats of pre-industrial society (plague, famine, natural catastrophes, wars, but also magic, gods, demons) are transformed into calculable risks in the course of the development of instrumental rational control, which the process of modernization promotes in all spheres of life. This characterizes the situation and the conflicts in early, classical industrial and bourgeois society. In the course of its expansion it is true not only for the 'feasibility' of production capacities, tax revenues, the calculation of export risks and the consequences of war, but also for the vicissitudes of individual lives: accidents, illnesses, death, social insecurity and poverty. It leads, as François Ewald argues, to the emergence of diverse systems of insurance, to the extent that society as a whole comes to be understood as a risk group in insurers' terms – as a *provident state* and a *providing state* (Ewald, 1986). Consequently and simultaneously, more and more areas and concerns of society that have been considered to be natural (family size, questions of upbringing, choice of profession, mobility, relations between the sexes) are now made social and individual, are thereby held to be accountable and subject to decisions, and are so judged and condemned. This situation offers the possibility of autonomous creation and also involves the danger of wrong decisions, the risks of which are to be covered by the principle of provident after-care. For this purpose there exist accident scenarios, statistics, social research, technical planning and a great variety of safety measures.

The institutions of developing industrial society can and must also be understood from the point of view of how the self-produced consequences can be made socially calculable and accountable and their conflicts made controllable. The unpredictable is turned into something predictable; what has not-yet-occurred becomes the object of present (providential) action. The dialectic of risk and insurance calculation provides the cognitive and institutional apparatus. The process is not only theoretically, historically and philosophically of importance, but also of great political significance, because here a stage in the history of how early industrial society learned to cope with itself is opened up and investigated, and because this learning process can point the way to another modernity of self-limitation – especially at the end of the twentieth century, which is overshadowed by the ecological question.

As a result, the epochal difference that distinguishes the risks of industrial society and the bourgeois social order from the hazards and demands of risk society can also be grasped more clearly. The entry into risk society occurs at the moment when the hazards which are now decided and consequently produced by society *undermine and/or cancel the established safety systems of the welfare state's existing risk calculations.* In contrast to early industrial risks, nuclear, chemical, ecological and genetic engineering risks (a) can be limited in terms of neither time nor place, (b) are not accountable according to the established rules of causality, blame and liability, and (c) cannot be compensated for or insured against (Beck, 1994: 2). Or, to express it by reference to a single example: the injured of Chernobyl are today, years after the catastrophe, not even all *born* yet.

Anyone who inquires as to an operational criterion for this transition has it to hand here: *the absence of private insurance cover.* More than that, industrial technical-scientific projects are *not insurable.* This is a yardstick which no sociologist or any kind of artist needs to introduce to society from the outside. Society itself produces this standard and measures its own development by it. Industrial society, which has involuntarily mutated into risk society through its own systematically produced hazards, balances *beyond the insurance limit.* The rationality on which this judgement is based derives from the core rationality of this society: *economic* rationality. It is the private insurance companies which operate or mark the frontier barrier of risk society. With the logic of economic behaviour they contradict the protestations of safety made by the technicians and in the danger industries, because they say that in the case of 'low probability but high consequences risks' the technical risk may tend towards zero, while at the same time the economic risk is potentially infinite.[2] A simple mental experiment makes plain the extent of the normalized degeneration. Anyone who today demands private insurance cover – such as is taken for granted by every car owner – before an advanced and dangerous industrial production apparatus is allowed to get under way at all simultaneously proclaims the end for large sectors, above all of so-called 'industries of the future' and major research organizations, which all operate without any or without adequate insurance cover.

Hazards versus Providentiality: Environmental Crisis as Inner Crisis

The transformation of the unintended consequences of industrial production into global ecological trouble spots is therefore not at all a problem of the world surrounding us – not a so-called 'environmental problem' – but a far-reaching institutional crisis of industrial society itself. As long as these developments continue to be seen within the conceptual horizon of industrial society, then, as negative side-effects of seemingly accountable and calculable actions, their system-breaking consequences go unrecognized. Their central significance only emerges in the perspective and concepts of risk society, drawing attention to the need for reflexive self-definition and redefinition. In the phase of risk society, recognition of the incalculability of the hazards produced by technical-industrial development compels self-reflection on the foundations of the social context and a review of prevailing conventions and principles of 'rationality'. In the self-conception of risk society, society becomes *reflexive* (in the narrow sense of the word) – that is, becomes an issue and a problem to itself.

Industrial society, the bourgeois social order and, especially, the welfare and social state are subject to the demand that human lived relationships are made instrumentally rational, controllable, capable of being produced, available and (individually and legally) accountable. The ultimate deadlock of risk society, however, resides in the gap between knowledge and decision: there is no one who really knows the global outcome – at the level of positive knowledge, the situation is radically 'undecidable' – but we none the less *have to decide*. The risk epoch imposes on each of us the burden of making crucial decisions which may affect our very survival without any proper foundation in knowledge. All the panels of government experts, ethical committees, and so on, conceal this radical openness and manufactured uncertainty. And governments who still believe in and wait for scientific certainty do not understand our and their situation. The controversy surrounding the risks and unforeseeable consequences of genetically modified food is only one example of this move.

So risk society is provoking an obscene gamble, a kind of ironic reversal of predestination: I am held accountable for decisions which I was forced to make without proper knowledge of the situation. The freedom of decision enjoyed by the subject of risk society is the 'freedom' of someone who is compelled to make decisions without being aware of their consequences. It can correspondingly be shown that societal measures of organization, ethical and legal principles like responsibility, blame and the 'polluter-pays' principle (such as in the pursuance of damages), as well as political decision-making procedures (such as the majority-rule principle), are not suitable for grasping and/or legitimating the processes thereby set in motion. Analogously, social-scientific categories and methods no longer work when confronted by the complexity and ambiguity of the state of affairs to be described and understood. It is not only a matter of making decisions; more importantly, in the face of the unforeseeable and unaccountable consequences of large-scale technologies, it is necessary to redefine the rules and principles for decision-making, for areas of application and for critique. The reflexivity and incalculability of societal development therefore spreads to all sectors of society, breaking up regional, class-specific, national, political and scientific jurisdictions and boundaries. In the extreme case of the consequences of a nuclear disaster, there are no bystanders any more. Conversely, that also means that under this threat everyone is affected and involved and accordingly can speak in their own right.

Paradoxically, risk society is at the same time tendentially a *self-critical* society. Insurance experts contradict safety engineers. If the latter declare a zero risk, the former judge it non-insurable. Experts are relativized or dethroned by counter-experts. Politicians encounter the resistance of citizens' initiatives, industrial management that of consumer organizations. Bureaucracies are criticized by self-help groups. Ultimately, industries responsible for damage (for example, the chemical industry for marine pollution) must even expect resistance from other industries affected as a result (in this case fishing and the business dependent on coastal tourism). The former can be challenged by the latter, inspected, perhaps even corrected. Yes, the risk question even divides families and professional groups, from the skilled workers of the chemical industry right up to top management (Pries, 1991; Bogun et al., 1992; Heine, 1992), often even the individual: what the head wants, the mouth says, the hand is unable to carry out.

Reflexive Modernization as Theory of the Self-criticism of Society

Many say that with the collapse of really existing non-socialism the ground has been cut from under every critique of society. Just the opposite is true: the prospects for critique, including radical critique, have never been so favourable in Germany and elsewhere in Europe. With the end of the predominance of Marxian theory, the century-long petrification among Europe's intellectuals has been lifted. The father figure is dead. In fact, only now can the critique of society get its breath back and see more clearly.

The theory of risk society avoids the difficulties of a critical theory of society in which the theorists apply more or less well-justified standards to society and then judge and condemn accordingly (and often counter to the self-conception of those concerned). In a risk society which identifies itself as such, critique is *democratized*, as it were; that is, there arises a reciprocal critique of sectional rationalities and groups in society (see above). Thus a critical theory of society is replaced by a theory of *societal self-critique* and/or an analysis of the intersecting lines of conflict of a reflexive modernity. The uncovering of the immanent conflicts of institutions *still* programmed in terms of industrial society, which are *already* being reflected on and criticized from the perspective of the concept of the self-endangerment of risk society, allows norms, principles and practices in all society's fields of action to become contradictory – that is, measured by immanent rankings and claims. For example, risk calculations which are based on a (spatially, temporally and socially circumscribed) accident definition are supposed to estimate and legitimate the potential for catastrophe of modern large-scale technologies and industries. This, however, is precisely what they fail to do and so they are falsifications, and can be criticized and reformed in accordance with their own claims to rationality.

It is worth defining with conceptual precision the perspectives and conditions of societal self-criticism which the theory of risk society opens up. This is what the concept of reflexive modernization attempts to do. It contains two components (or dimensions of meaning). On the one hand, it refers to the automatic transition from industrial to risk society (argued with reference to this theme; the same could be demonstrated, for example, by way of the fulfilment of modernity beyond the limits of male–female duality or in the systematic self-doubt of the sciences through more and better knowledge and inter-rogation of the foundations and consequences of scientific distribution and decision-making). It is not the looking, or the looking away, which produces and accelerates the dynamic of world risk society. This 'mechanism' has its origin in the momentum of industry, which, alarmed at 'side-effects' of hazards, rescinds its own principles (of calculation).

On the other hand, if this is understood, experienced, enters general awareness, then a whole society is set in motion. What previously appeared 'functional' and 'rational' now becomes and appears to be a threat to life, and therefore produces and legitimates dysfunctional-ity and irrationality. If in addition professional *alternatives of self-control and self-limitation* arise and are propagated in contexts of activity, the institutions open themselves to the *political* right down to their foundations, and become malleable, dependent on subjects and coalitions.

This means that because the transition from industrial to risk society takes place unreflectingly, automatically, on the basis of industrial modernity's 'blindness to apocalypse' (Günther Anders), situations of danger establish themselves, which – having become the theme and centre of politics and public debates – lead to the questioning, the splitting of the centres of activity and decision-making of society. Within the horizon of the opposition between old routine and new awareness of consequences and dangers, society becomes self-critical. It is therefore the combination of reflex and reflections which, as long as the catastrophe itself fails to materialize, can set industrial modernity on the path to self-criticism and self-transformation.

Reflexive modernization contains both elements: the reflex-like threat to industrial society's own foundations through a successful further modernization which is blind to dangers, *and* the growth of awareness, the reflection on this situation. The difference between industrial and risk society is first of all a difference of knowledge – that is, of self-reflection on the dangers of developed industrial modernity. The political arises out of the growing awareness of the hazards dependent on decision-making, because at first property relations, social inequalities and the principles of the functioning of industrial society as a whole remain untouched by it. In this sense the theory of risk society is a *political theory of knowledge* of modernity becoming self-critical. At issue is that industrial society sees itself as risk society and how it criticizes and reforms itself.

Many candidates for the subject of the critique of society have appeared on (and departed) the stage of world history and the history of ideas: the working class, the critical intelligentsia, the public sphere, social movements of the most diverse tendencies and composition, women, subcultures, youth, lepers, self-organizing psychopaths and counter-experts. In the theory of reflexive modernization the basis of critique is first of all thought autonomously. Thanks to its momentum and its successes, industrial society is stumbling into the no man's land of uninsurable hazards. To the extent that this, briefly, is experienced, fatalistic industrial modernity can transform itself into a conflictual and self-critical risk society. Self-criticism in this context means that lines of conflict, which can be organized and are capable of coalitions, arise within and between the systems and institutions (and not only at the edges and areas of overlap of private lifeworlds).

The End of Linear Technology?

Even if the above does not allow any clear conclusions as to the nature, course and successes of conflicts and lines of conflict, one forecast at least seems justified: the decision-making centres and the 'objective laws' of scientific-technological progress are becoming political issues. That gives rise to a question: does the growing awareness of risk society coincide with the *invalidation of the linear models of technocracy* – models which, whether optimistic or pessimistic about progress, have fascinated society and its science for a hundred years?

In the 1960s Helmut Schelsky (drawing on Max Weber, Veblen, Gehlen and many others) had argued that, with ever-increasing automation and the penetration of science into all spheres of life, the modern state must internalize technology, as it were, in order to preserve and expand its power. Consequently, however, it pursues normative state goals less and less, and is determined solely by technological constraints – becomes the 'technological state'. In other words, the instrumental rationalization and the encroachment of technology exhaust the substance of an ever-modernizing society. It is increasingly the case that experts rule, even where politicians are nominally in charge. 'Technical-scientific decisions cannot be subject to any democratic informed opinion, otherwise they would become ineffective. If the political decisions of governments are made in accordance with scientifically determined objective laws, then the government has become an organ of the administration of objective necessity, the parliament a supervisory organ of the correctness of expert opinion' (Schelsky, 1965: 459).

Jost Halfmann points out that from a risk-sociological point of view, Schelsky assumes 'a development of society towards zero risk'. In other words, the explosive force of a modernity which transforms everything into decisions and therefore into risks remains completely unrecognized. '[High-]risk technologies directly contradict technocratic theoretical expectations. . . . The central position of the state in the material support and political regulation of technological progress has increasingly given political institutions an important role in the "liability" for the consequences of progress, with respect to society. Technological progress and its consequences have thereby assumed the character of collective goods.' Where society has become a laboratory (Krohn/Weyer), decisions about and control of technological progress become a collective problem.

> Science is no longer experimental activity without consequences, and technology is no longer low-risk application of secure knowledge. Science and technology produce risks in carrying out their experiments and thereby burden society as a whole with managing the risks. . . .

Depending on the risk culture quite different strategic consequences follow for dealing with risk. Industrialists assess risks according to cost–benefit principles; failure in the marketplace becomes the most important focus of risk avoidance. Bureaucracies judge risks according to hypothetical definitions of the common good and look for redistributive solutions in dealing with risks; here the principal problem is the institutional integrity of the administrative apparatus. Social movements measure risks by the potential for catastrophe involved and seek to avoid risks which could lead to a threat to present and future quality of life. The effective irreconcilability of these various risk assessments turns concrete decisions over acceptable risks into struggles for power. 'The issue is not risk, but power.'

　　　　(*Charles Perrow*) (*Halfmann, 1990: 21, 26, 28; Beck, 1994: 107ff*)

What is at stake in this new risk conflict, as Christoph Lau demonstrates, is not so much risk avoidance as the *distribution* of risk, which means that it is about the *architecture of risk definition* in the face of the growing competition between overlapping discourses of risk (such as nuclear power versus ozone hole):

Debates over risk definitions and their consequences for society take place essentially at the level of public (or partially public) discourses. They are conducted with the aid of scientific arguments and information, which serve, so to speak, as scarce resources of the collective actors. The scientifically penetrated public sphere then becomes the symbolic location of conflicts over distribution even if this is disguised by the objectified, scientistic autonomous logic of specialist argument about risk.

　　　　　　　　　　　　　(*Lau, 1991: 254*)

Such risk definitions impose boundaries on society, by attempting to determine factors such as the size, location and social characteristics of those responsible for and those affected by the risks involved. As such, they become the focus for contestation.

Whereas, within the framework of the 'old' distribution conflicts, the success of strategic behaviour can be designated and measured by distinct media (money, ownership of means of production, wage settlements, voting figures), such symbolic media which could unambiguously reflect risk gain and risk loss are hardly available. All attempts to establish risk yardsticks, such as probability estimates, threshold values and calculations of costs, founder, as far as late industrial risks are concerned, on the incommensurability of hazards and the problem of the subjective assessment of the probability of occurrence. This

explains why conflicts essentially break out at the level of knowledge around problems of definition and causal relationships. Primary
resources in this struggle over risk justice are not immediately strikes,
voting figures, political influence, but above all information, scientific
findings, assessments, arguments.

(*Lau, 1991: 254*)

Niklas Luhmann takes this pattern of risk conflict as his starting-
point. For him the distinction between risk and danger coincides with
the opposition between the situation of those *making* a decision and
those *affected* by the decision. Agreement between the two is difficult,
if not out of the question. At the same time neither do any clear lines of
conflict develop, because the confrontation between decision-makers
and those affected varies according to theme and situation.

We talk of risks if possible future injury is attributable to one's own
decision. If one does not enter an aeroplane, one cannot crash. In the
case of hazards, on the other hand, damage has an external source. If,
say, to stay with the given example, one is killed by falling aircraft
wreckage. . . . Familiar hazards – earthquakes and volcanic eruptions,
aquaplaning and marriages – become risks to the extent that the decisions by which it is possible to avoid exposing oneself to them become
known. But that illuminates only one half of the situation, since with
the decisions made, the hazards also increase once more, and, that is,
in the form of hazards which result from the decisions of others. . . .
Thus today the distinction between risk and hazard cuts through the
social order. One person's risk is another person's hazard. The smoker
may risk cancer, but for others it is a hazard. The car driver who takes
a chance when overtaking behaves in just the same way, the builder
and operator of nuclear power stations, genetic engineering research
– there is no lack of examples.

(*Luhmann, 1991: 81*)

The impossibility or at least the sheer insurmountability of the
barriers to agreement arises from the perception and assessment of
catastrophes. Here the yardstick of the 'rationality' of the probability
of occurrence is ineffective.

It may indeed be true that the danger which comes from a nearby
nuclear power station is no greater than the risk involved in the decision to drive an extra mile and a half per year. But who will be im-
pressed by an argument like that? The prospect of catastrophes sets a
limit to calculation. Under no circumstances whatsoever does one want
it – even if it is extremely improbable. But what is the catastrophe

threshold beyond which quantitative calculations are no longer convincing? Obviously, this question cannot be answered independently of other variables. It is different for rich and poor, for the independent and the dependent. . . . The really interesting question is what counts as a catastrophe. And that is presumably a question which will be answered very differently by decision-makers and victims.

(*Luhmann, 1991: 91; see also Luhmann, 1993*)

That may be, but it neglects and underestimates the systemic yardstick of economic insurance rationality. Risk society is *uncovered* society, in which insurance protection *decreases* with the scale of the danger – and this in the historic milieu of the 'welfare state', which encompasses all spheres of life, and of the fully comprehensive society. Only the two together – uncovered *and* comprehensively insured society – constitute the politically explosive force of risk society.

On the Antiquatedness of Pessimism about Progress

The ancestral line of profound and pitiless critics of modernity is long and includes many respected names. The best thinkers in Europe have been among them, even in the present century. Max Weber still tries to keep a cool head in the face of the grim consequence of his linear analyses (though repressed pessimism often bursts out between the lines and in the incidental and concluding remarks). In Horkheimer and Adorno's *Dialectic of Enlightenment* the judgement veers round. Here darkest darkness prevails (so that one sometimes asks oneself how the authors themselves were able to recognize what they believed they recognized). Subsequently, Günther Anders believed that the gulf between what rules our heads and what results from the labour of our hands was so great, so irrevocable, that to him all attempts to challenge it were embarrassing, if not unbearable. Karl Jaspers, Arnold Gehlen, Jacques Ellul or Hans Jonas, to whose analyses I am deeply indebted, also have to admit, when it comes to the point, that they do not know where the forces could come from which are to bring the superpower of technological progress to its knees or at least to admit contrition.

In these overpowering analyses one can read for oneself how the authors are spellbound by the automatic process they describe. Sometimes a hopeful little chapter is tacked on at the end, which bears the same relationship to the general hopelessness as a sigh to the end of the world, and then the writers make their exits, leaving their shattered readers behind in the vale of tears they have portrayed.

Certainly, hopelessness is ennobling and the advantages of wallowing in superiority, while at the same time being relieved of all responsibility for action, are not to be underestimated. However, if the theory sketched out here is correct, then the theorists of doom can begin to rejoice, because their theories are wrong or will become so!

In a discussion of the English edition of my *Risk Society*, Zygmunt Bauman once again summarized with breathtaking brilliance the arguments which encourage everyone to sit back and do nothing. The problem is not only that we are facing challenges on an undreamt of scale, but, more profoundly, that all attempts at solution bear in themselves the seed of new and more difficult problems. '[T]he most fearsome of disasters are those traceable to the past or present pursuits of rational solutions. Catastrophes most horrid are born – or are likely to be born – out of the war against catastrophes. . . . Dangers grow with our powers, and the one power we miss most is that which divines their arrival and sizes up their volume' (Bauman, 1992: 25).

But even where risks are picked up, it is always only the symptoms that are combated, never the causes, because the fight against the risks of unrestrained business activity has itself become

> a major business, offering a new lease of life to scientific/technological dreams of unlimited expansion. In our society, risk-fighting can be nothing else but business – the bigger it is, the more impressive and reassuring. The politics of fear lubricates the wheels of consumerism and helps to 'keep the economy going' and steers away from the 'bane of recession'. Ever more resources are to be consumed in order to repair the gruesome effects of yesterday's resource consumption. Individual fears beefed up by the exposure of yesterday's risks are deployed in the service of collective production of the unknown risks of tomorrow . . .
>
> *(Bauman, 1992: 25)*

Indeed, life and behaviour in risk society have become Kafkaesque – in the strict sense of the word (Beck, 1994: 77ff). Yet my principal argument comes from another angle. Even negative fatalism – it above all! – thinks of modernization in *linear* terms and so fails to recognize the ambivalences of a modernization of modernization, which revokes the principles of industrial society itself.

In fact Zygmunt Bauman explicitly takes up this idea of reflexive modernization:

> Beck has not lost hope (some would say illusion) that 'reflexivity' can accomplish what 'rationality' failed to do. . . . What amounts to another *apologia* for science (now boasting reflexivity as a weapon

more trustworthy than the rationality of yore and claiming the untried credentials of risk-anticipating instead of those of discredited problem-solving) can be upheld only as long as the role of science in the past and present plight of humanity is overstated and/or demonised. But it is only in the mind of the scientists and their hired or voluntary court-poets that knowledge (*their* knowledge) 'determines being'. And reflexivity, like rationality, is a double-edged sword. Servant as much as a master; healer as much as a hangman.

(Bauman, 1992: 25)

Bauman says 'reflexivity' but fails to recognize the peculiar relationship of reflex and reflection within risk society (see above). This does not exactly mean more of the same – science, research into effects, the controls on automatic. Rather, in reflexive modernity, the forms and principles of industrial society are dissolved. With the force, and as a consequence of its momentum, there arise unforeseen and also incalculable social situations and dynamics within, but also between, systems, organizations and (apparently) private spheres of life. These present new challenges for the social sciences, since their analysis requires new categories, theories and methods.

The theory of risk society suggests, therefore, that it is what cannot be foreseen that produces previously unknown situations (which are not for that reason by any means better, or closer to saving us!). If this becomes part of general awareness, society begins to move. Whether this is a good thing or simply accelerates the general decline can be left open for the time being.

At any rate, the theory of reflexive modernization contradicts the fundamental assumptions of negative fatalism. Proponents of the latter *know* that which from their own assumptions they cannot know at all: the outcome, the end, the hopelessness of everything. Negative fatalism is a twin to the belief in progress. If in the latter a momentum, thought in linear terms, becomes the source of a naïve belief in progress (according to the motto 'if we can't change it, let's welcome it'), with the former the incalculable is *foreseeably* incalculable. In fact, however, it is precisely the power of fatalism which makes fatalism wrong.

For example, it is because Günther Anders is right that the diagnosis of his *Die Antiquiertheit des Menschen* (The Antiquatedness of Human Beings) (1982) is antiquated. In the course of reflexive modernization new political lines of conflict of a high-revving industrial society, which understands and criticizes itself as risk society, arise. These may be better or worse, but are in any case *different*, and must first of all be perceived and decoded as such.

Similarly Zygmunt Bauman – the social theorist of ambivalence – thinks modernity in terms which are far too linear. The banal possibility that something unforeseeable emerges from the unforeseeable (and the more incalculable, the more surprising it is) is lost from sight. Yet it is with this adventure of decision-determined incalculability that the history of society begins anew at the end of the twentieth century.

Just as earlier generations lived in the age of the stagecoach, so we now and in future are living in the hazardous age of creeping catastrophe. What generations before us discovered despite resistance, and had to shout out loud at the world, we have come to take for granted: the impending 'suicide of the species' (Karl Jaspers). Perhaps fatalism is the *birth* mood of the risk epoch? Perhaps dominant yet still unspoken hopes inspire fatalism? Will the post-optimism of post-fatalism perhaps at last emerge, when the seriousness of the situation is really understood, and the situation has been accepted and understood as one's own situation? I am not playing with words. I know of no greater security and no deeper source of creativity than a pessimism which cannot be outbid. Where everything is at stake, everything can and must be rethought and re-examined.

Only the naïve, ontological pessimism of certainty commits one to pessimism. Whoever cultivates doubt can and must resaddle the stallions of inquiry.

Résumé and Prospects

A completely opposite picture of the historical evolution of society is often contrasted with the succession and overlapping of industrial and risk society presented here. According to this picture, the pre-industrial epochs and cultures were societies of *catastrophe*. In the course of industrialization these became and are becoming societies of *calculable risk*, while in the middle of Europe late industrial society has even perfected its technological and social welfare and security systems as *fully* comprehensively insured societies.

Here, however, it has been argued – drawing on François Ewald's systematic historical analyses – that risk society begins where industrial society's principles of calculation are submerged and annulled in the continuity of automatic and tempestuously successful modernization. Risk society negates the principles of its rationality. It has long ago left these behind, because it operates and balances beyond the insurance limit. This is only *one* indicator which demonstrates that an enterprise which began with the extension of calculability has slipped away into what is now decision-determined incalculability. The results are concrete reciprocal possibilities of critique and politicization within and between institutions, lifeworlds and organizations.

On the whole this represents only *one* special case of reflexive modernization. The concept combines the reflex of modernization threatening itself with reflection on this (self-)threat, whereby new conflicts and tensions between interests run through and split society. That, however, leads to further questions.

Does risk society already begin where the insurance limit has been crossed, but this is neither seen nor understood? How does this condition of industrial society, which by abstraction from the consequences and hazards actually exacerbates these, at the same time block out any insight into its threat to itself? Here the unsettling effects of risk society emerge and grow more significant, but they are not comprehended as such and are not at all made the object of political action and societal (self-)criticism. Are these disruptions of a modernization annulling its own principles thereby deflected and distorted into turbulences of every kind – from violence to right-wing extremism?

Or perhaps risk society only begins when the sound barrier of insurability has been broken *and* this has been understood, noted and made into the theme and conflict which is superimposed on everything. Do these turbulences of an industrial society which understands and criticizes itself *as* risk society now present a way out from the feeling that there is no way out? Or do the 'no exits' simply fork here, leaving no perspectives for action, but only a general paralysis and blockages which accelerate the catastrophe?

A third variant, involving both, would also be conceivable – first, the crossing of the insurance limit, leaving whole industries and areas of research hovering without a safety net in the weightless zone of non-insurability; and, second, the comprehension of this situation. These are certainly necessary but not sufficient conditions of risk society. It only begins where the discussion of the repair and reformation of industrial society becomes clearly defined. Does talk about risk society, therefore, only start to make full sense with the ecological reform of capitalism? Or does it already become less meaningful there, because, as a result, the politicizing dynamic of decision-determined hazards begins to fade away?

Are there not always first of all, and permanently, the distribution conflicts of an industrial society with a more or less encompassing welfare state? Whereas risk questions and conflicts are only superimposed on these as long as the latter appear tamed – that is, in periods of economic upturn, low unemployment, and so on?

All these questions require a new approach in order to be answered, which would be beyond the scope of this chapter. But I shall nevertheless make one point. The political confusions of risk society also arise (in contrast to the distribution conflicts of a society of lack) because institutional answers to the challenges of an uncovered (global) society of hazards in a comprehensively insured milieu have so far hardly been invented, still less tested and successfully realized. In other words, the contours of the social state are familiar. No one knows, however, how, whether and by what means it might be possible really to throttle back the self-endangering momentum of the global risk society. Talk of the nature state – by analogy with the social state – remains just as empty in this context as attempts to cure industrial society of its suicidal tendencies with more of the same: morality, technology and ecological markets. The necessary learning step still lies ahead of the global risk society on the threshold of the twenty-first century (see Beck, 1997).[3]

5
Subpolitics:
Ecology and the Disintegration of Institutional Power

The concept of the political in the nation-state has no clear boundaries between politics and non-politics. Politics exists and governs the political system. Outside of the officially classified political sphere – in business, science, technical laboratories, and in private life – there is a great deal of activity, arguing, bargaining, deception, separating, uniting, loving and betrayal, but none of that is done according to the legitimate rules of formal politics; there is no mandate, no party organization and no dependence on the consent of the governed. Even if the influence of the formal political system shrinks, politicians and political scientists continue to look for the political in the formal political system and only in that system. If it should turn out that for some reason no one holds power in that system and that even the most respected powers that be are only simulating power, then the diagnosis reads 'ungovernability' and we react accordingly.

But why can or should the political be at home or take place only in the political system? Who says that politics is possible only in the forms and terms of governmental, parliamentary and party politics? Perhaps the truly political disappears in and from the political system and reappears, changed and generalized, in a form that remains to be comprehended and developed, as *sub(system)politics* (Beck, 1992) in all the other fields of society.

My thesis is that opportunities for alternative action are opening up in all fields of activity – technology, medicine, law, the organization of work – under the pressure of changed challenges and fundamental convictions. The old industrial consensus built into the social system is encountering new and different fundamental convictions: ecological, feminist, and many others. Technocracy ends when alternatives erupt in the techno-economic process and polarize it. The ecological crisis is a case in point. As soon as some organizations take up what could be called 'ecological modernization', alternative lines of action become thinkable. When these alternatives become professional and profitable, dividing professions, founding careers and opening markets, possibly even on a global scale, thus dividing the power bloc of business, they permit and even require new types of conflicts and coalitions between and within institutions, parties, interest groups and publics of all types, and as this happens the image of the aloof self-referentiality of social systems breaks up. They become malleable. Just like social classes, social systems and unitary organizations fade away in the wake of reflexive modernization (Beck et al., 1994). Their existence comes to depend on decision-making and legitimation, and they become changeable. Alternative opportunities for action thus are the downfall of systems independent of individuals. This is not meant as a threat by any means, only as a diagnosis, perfectly value-free, even with a bit of regret over so much destruction.

To be sure, to the extent it behaves peacefully or can be kept peaceful, the political will continue to take place according to the democratic concept of industrial modernity that is exclusively a rules-directed struggle between parties for privileges and levers of power. The objectives of this industrial democracy are economic growth, full employment, social security and the succession of power in the sense of a change of parties or personnel. This is democracy and this is how it takes place and is implemented. Politics does not renovate or transform the government system by transferring decision-making powers to interest groups on the one hand and to global agents on the other. Politics in the structure and rules system of the nation-state amounts to keeping and protecting the established democratic and economic rules of the game, not setting off for a new land of political, even globally political, forces and a global risk society. The political is comprehended and operated as a rule-directed, rule-applying, but not a rule-changing, much less a rule-inventing, politics; it is a variation in the execution of politics but not a politics of politics.

Still, the ecological crisis and the growing awareness that we indeed live in a global risk society gives food for thought. Even if no one can sincerely say that he or she believes that the reformation of a natural economy of self-destruction into a global and democratic civilization is succeeding, it will still be possible quickly to reach agreement that the existing outmoded institutions simply will not do. If one no longer wishes to close one's eyes to this, then it is necessary to abandon the objectives of status quo politics, or at least to open, expand, rethink and recompose them. Then, one has already arrived at the 'reinvention of politics' (Beck, 1997).

At the turn of the nineteenth century Kant posed the question: how is knowledge possible? Today, two centuries later, the parallel question is: how is political design possible? It is no coincidence that this raises an overarching question that ties together art and politics. Beyond nature, God, altars, truth, causality, ego, id and superego begins the 'art of living', as the late Michel Foucault called it, or the art of the self-design or renaissance of politics as a fundamental universal condition of human existence. Without a doubt, no age of hope or paradise is dawning. Reflexive modernization is the age of uncertainty and ambivalence, which combines the constant threat of disasters on an entirely new scale with the possibility and necessity to reinvent our political institutions and invent new ways of conducting politics at social 'sites' that we previously considered unpolitical.

To make sense of this institutional crisis we should first examine the nature of our institutions. I will therefore first analyse the relationship between individual and system in some detail and then turn to consider the way in which the ecological issue challenges the traditional functioning of institutions.

The time has passed when it was possible to earn great credit or applause with extreme alternatives. This is not the time for discussing the liberation of the individual from the system. We all know too well that we constantly reproduce the social system with its successes and mistakes in our daily actions. Yet even if it is not the time for the great alternative scheme of action, perhaps it is the system of classification – which we use in our daily lives and in our organizations – that calls for explicit attention. Today, everything comes down to a mixture of the two standpoints of individual and system, and the controversies ignite over where the priorities should lie and how the issues of the opposing perspective appear or are suppressed in one's own argumentation. In the words of Mary Douglas (1987: 99–100):

> To know how to resist the classifying pressures of our institutions, we would like to start an independent classificatory exercise. Unfortunately, all the classifications that we have for thinking with are provided ready-made, along with our social life. For thinking about society we have at hand the categories we use as members of society speaking to each other about ourselves. These actor's categories work at every

possible level. At the top would be the most general, and at the bottom would be the most particular social rules. When we even try to assign items to this bottom level of least general social classifications, we may catch ourselves thinking of domestic situations and enumerating the roles of children, adults, males, and females. Starting at that point, we automatically reproduce the scheme of authority and the division of labor in the home, but it will be very different if an Indian or an American is thinking. . . . Or we may start by taking the roles least involved in social organization, say tramps, and move from the periphery towards the centers of influence. Or we may start with new babies and move up the age structure. In each case, we are adopting the categories used by our administrators for collecting taxes, making population censuses, and estimating the need for schools or prisons. Our minds are running on the old treadmill already. How can we possibly think of ourselves in society except by using the classifications established in our institutions? If we turn to the various social scientists, we find that their minds are still more deeply in thrall. Their professional subject matter is cast in administrative categories, art separated from science, affect from cognition, imagination from reasoning. For purposes of judicial and administrative control, we find persons neatly labeled according to levels of ability, and find thinking classed as rational, insane, criminal, and criminally insane. The work of classifying that is already done for us is performed as a service to instituted professions.

[But institutions do not just produce labels, the labels] stabilize the flux of social life and even create to some extent the realities to which they apply. . . . This process Hacking calls 'making up people' by labeling them 'the sheer proliferation of labels during the nineteenth century, may have engendered vastly more kinds of people than ever the world knew before.' . . . As fast as new medical categories (hitherto unimagined) were invented, or new criminal or sexual or moral categories, new kinds of people spontaneously came forward in hordes to accept the labels and to live accordingly. The responsiveness to new labels suggests extraordinary readiness to fall into new slots and to let selfhood be redefined . . . people are not merely re-labeled. . . . The new people behave differently than they ever did before.

'Thought strives to become deed, the word to become flesh,' wrote Heinrich Heine (1981: 95). 'The world is the signature of the word. Take note of this, you proud men of action. You are nothing but servants to the men of thought, who have often marked out all your deeds precisely for you even in their most humble silence.' Classifications are like institutions; this is a fundamental premise of functionalistic sociology, that the social must be explained from the social, not the individual, according to the classical formula in which Émile

Durkheim encapsulated this sociological method. Yet it must be asked whether this shaping and binding force of the social does not contradict precisely those things sociology has recognized and emphasized as the core of modernity: pluralization, individualization, construction, decidability, reflection and discursivity. After the large-group categories such as clan culture, estates and classes (the concepts with which modernity arose), the concept of the social system must be subjugated to the principles of modernity in a theory of reflexive modernization. I shall attempt this by turning around the question and inquiring once again into the social conditions for the rise and fall of the modern metaphysics of sovereign subject-free systems. The subject-oriented counter-question is: under what conditions do individuals create in their thought and action the social realities of systems that seem to be independent of individuals? And conversely: under what conditions do the predominance and hyper-reality of social systems become fictitious because the consensus forms and formulae that justified the supremacy of the systems over subjects are missing, or fail? In other words, the question of how systems make systems possible is replaced by the question of how individuals produce the fiction of a system. The presumption is that the autonomy of social systems presupposes consent to this autonomy, or, to put it more strongly, the production and reproduction of the independence of systems from individuals takes place in the thought and action of individuals. The question of the self-referentiality of systems is replaced by the question of the dependence of system realities and fictions on culture.

System formation is power formation, but without violent means. The associated questions did not arise so long as unquestioned consent to system formation was culturally available, or, more precisely, 'for sale' on the labour market as (religiously based) achievement consciousness (Calvinism, Protestant ethic, professional orientation, professional pride, motivation for social advancement, job orientation, and so on). Max Weber and Karl Marx developed two different arguments as to how this generation and use of cultural certainties can be protected for the autonomy of bureaucracies, organizations, industrial firms or capitalism in general.

Weber's famed study 'The Protestant Ethic and the Spirit of Capitalism' is a bridge from certain religious dogmas (specifically the inner-worldly asceticism of Calvinism) to the professional ethos (the reshaping of the world according to the maxims of calculability and economic profit). The 'methodical way of life', self-sacrifice and self-objectification become the living component of individual-independent systems. They have their basis in a certain religious concept of self and world. The technical transformation of the world and the accumulation of wealth become the direct method by which to struggle for and attain the unfathomable grace of God.

For Marx, on the other hand, the form of consensus that corresponds to the autonomous nature of capitalist exploitation is no longer, or at least not primarily, dependent on pre-capitalistic and religious traditions. Instead, capitalism itself produces orientation patterns in the form of the labour market that allow an (apparent or relative) individual-independence of industrial firms. Wage labour forces the individuals to develop a double and split relationship to themselves and their abilities. On the one hand, they must let their abilities shine in order to charm the purchasers on the labour market into a purchase of labour power, their commodity, at the most favourable possible prices; but, on the other, they must become indifferent to the use and effects of their labour power and their work. This coerced and learned indifference prepares and presents the form of consent to arbitrary purposes, of which the other side is the unquestioned power of self-referential systems.

It is necessary to go beyond Marx, however, to explain this. Not just abilities and capabilities are traded and acquired on the labour market but also consent to the shaping of human work processes and thus the material from which individual-independent organizations can be constructed. The labour agreement is also a consent agreement on the pattern of 'I, the entrepreneur, pay you and do not care what you do with your money in your leisure time, as long as you do not care what I do and produce with your labour power during the working hours that I pay you for.' The labour agreement is a power agreement; it indemnifies the worker, the owner and seller of labour power for the substance and the utility of work and directs them to leisure time to satisfy or assuage 'private' needs, wishes, hopes and fears. The conversion of labour power is ceded to the purchaser and organizer of the work. The consent to this exchange may be coerced and generated by the wage worker's financial distress, that is, unemployment; on the other hand, the system of hierarchical and fragmented industrial labour desensitizes workers to the substance and effects of their work. In other words, the cultural form of indifference from which self-referential systems are made is produced inside these systems and is inculcated over and over again. A worker in a jam factory need not like jam, in the flippant words of Niklas Luhmann. Power that functions is not perceived.

System formation is power formation in the overall conditions of the self-evident consent and the renewal of the consent according to the laws of supply and demand, hiring and firing, making a living and performing a role on the job. Self-referential systems thus rely on purchased consent; they are wage-dependent or hired organizations. The indifference of workers to the products, or the (ecological) effects and unseen consequences of their work, is the other side of the power that causes individuals to become, or, better, appear to become, one environment of the systems among others. To the extent that this indifference is cancelled (for whatever reasons) and replaced by substantive demands on labour, power begins to become questionable and to disintegrate. Management can no longer count on automatic consent. Instead, it is always compelled to generate consent in making its decisions. Of course, management can still transfer, discharge and promote employees and all the rest, but where this increases the probability of being unable to 'recruit' a blank cheque of consent is where power begins to deteriorate.

Below the surface of the labour contract a kind of balance of formal and informal power elements is coming into existence, and this balance is shifting towards the informal side as indifference diminishes and dependence on consent increases. The power of demands on the quality of work is usually not aware of itself because it is not presented strategically, but individually, individualized, infatuated, one could say, with the demands themselves. The continuing impotence of labour power suppliers as they become more substantively demanding is becoming evident to the opposing side, the purchasers of labour, as a deterioration of power or a power vacuum, and is the object of all sorts of exorcism activities: business ethics, corporate culture or corporate identity.

In a work-based society where everyone is contractually compelled to expend his or her own labour force to make a living, the systemic structure of power originates in and renews itself along with professional qualification, orientation, practice and identity. One can say that orientation to jobs and making a living, on the one hand, and relative system autonomy, on the other, are two sides of the same coin. To the extent, however, that the compulsion to work for a living is loosened by social protection, labour laws, higher education, two-earner families, and so on, the autonomy and the autonomous space for action allotted to self-referential systems disintegrate along with the indifference of employees.

Everything that extends into modernity and is favoured or compelled by it makes institutions more dependent on consent. This begins with universal suffrage, continues with the expansion of education and the achievements in social and legal protection, and is expressed not least importantly in the increasing dependence of all circumstances and decisions on science. If all of this results in a loosening of the imperative to work and an increased availability of alternatives (for support, work and identity), then we are involved with a latent democratization of corporate action, or, in other terms, with a disintegration or erosion of the power of institutions. Of course, this impotence of the institutions, growing with the uncertainty of a consensus, can itself remain latent so long as no one openly challenges it.

The environmental issue, which has entered and changed the consciousness of people active in companies, once again poses the question of power in companies, because traditional industrial policy has self-destructive effects, not just on the outside world, but also internally, in the company itself. It undermines the unquestioned consent that made the hierarchical autonomy of bureaucratic decision-making organizations possible in the first place.

The question as to what type of consent is at issue can be narrowed down. It is very possible for a high degree of general affirmation of the democratic institutions of the Western social system to go hand in hand with a withdrawal of consent in concrete issues, as the high potential for non-voters or protest voters in all industrial states clearly shows. Indeed, the consent to the basic principles of democracy and the character of its institutions may even be the basis for the withdrawal of consent in a concrete case. If one had inquired into the general agreement with socialism in the former GDR, the results would probably not have been too alarming to the regime, even though the general withdrawal of consent a few months later brought down the power system like a house of cards.

The theoretical assertion of self-referential systems must thus be reversed if it is not to lead straightaway to a late modern metaphysics. The systems do not reproduce themselves, but individuals in their indifference generate opportunities for control that appear to be self-referent of systems – temporarily. Whenever consent can no longer simply be bought but is made dependent on insight, foresight, objectives, side-effects, fun, thrills, reasons, discussions, recognition, identity, cooperation, and so on, that is, whenever it can be granted conditionally, then system autonomy loses its supporting pillars of consent, and two things happen. System formation becomes recognizable as power formation, and the disintegration of power opens up scope for subpolitical action.

The continuance of an institution is based on its social recognition as a permanent solution to a permanent problem. Agents who must perform institutionalized actions must, therefore, be systematically acquainted with the institutionalized meaning. This may occur in an appropriate education process – training, acquisition of competence, and application of the corresponding capabilities in the work process. On the other hand, a basic consensus is necessary regarding the means and ends with which these solutions can be produced and reproduced. This is precisely what expert knowledge and ability accomplish.

If the stability of autonomous systems, institutions and organizations is thus fundamentally based on the constancy and consistency of expert rationality, then this condition can also be reversed. Power becomes at risk in institutions when rival expert groups become independent of one another, compete substantively and confront one another. 'The confrontation of alternative symbolic universes implies a problem of power – which of the conflicting definitions of reality will be "made to stick" in the society. . . . Which of the two will win . . . will depend more on the power than on the theoretical ingenuity of the respective legitimators' (Berger and Luckmann, 1971: 126–7).

An essential role is certainly also played here by the question of the extent to which the emerging alternatives are conditioned randomly, morally or systematically; that is, in the further development of the objective rationality of the expert group itself. In other words, if the professions – the discoverers, protectors and creators of the new (new knowledge, diseases, medicines, and so on) – split up and create antagonistic opposing truths and realities, then that is exactly the extent to which the fictions or constructions of systems independent of individuals shatter.

So far this has been, or seemed to be, unthinkable, or at least not a concrete threat. Three conditions have changed this: the transition from simple to reflexive scientization, the environmental issue and the entry of feminist orientations and expectations into the various professions and fields of occupational activity.

Where the sciences and expert disciplines take up and examine their foundations, consequences and errors in reciprocal relationships, the same thing happens to expert rationality as happened to lay rationality in the triumph of science: its defects become recognizable, questionable and capable of arrangement and rearrangement. The environmental issue penetrates into all occupational fields and becomes concrete and manifest in substantive controversies regarding methods, orientations, calculation procedures, objectives, standards, plans, routines, and so on. In any case, the existence of ecological cleavages in occupational and expert groups is becoming an essential indicator and gauge of the stability with which the institutions of classical industrial society continue to be able to deceive themselves and others. The same goes in a somewhat different manner for the feminist critique of scholarly disciplines and professions. Whenever it is not satisfied with merely attacking the professional exclusion of woman, it criticizes the core, the professionally monopolized rationality and practice, and redefines and conceives of specialist competence with interprofessional acumen and methodology, not just individually, but organized in a coalition.

This is how an ideal is ruined. Experts are able – or so it is generally supposed – to solve differences of opinion by using their methodology and their scientific-technical standards. If one simply conducts research long enough, then the opposing arguments will fall silent and clarity and unanimity will prevail. The exact opposite could in fact occur. Research that inquires further and with more difficulty, even into its own preconditions, taking up and espousing all the objections to itself, would break up its own claims to non-ambiguity and monopoly; simultaneously, it heightens both the need to justify things and the uncertainty of all arguments.

The self-referentiality of subsystems in industrial society depends not only on these subsystems themselves but also on the cooperative structures and dependencies between the subsystems. The industrial agents in firms must rely on a basic conformity to modernization of the accompanying agencies of the administration, law, publicity, municipalities and citizen organizations. Conflicts are possible, but these must be able to be settled predictably in the designated arenas and with the designated procedures. This reliability includes the social acceptance of administrative acts and court judgments as well as monitoring administrative agencies that interpret the scope of action in the arena of conflict between opposing values and possible legal interpretations with a fundamental priority for calculable, inherently dynamic modernization.

The intersystemic consensus on modernization is endangered in all these aspects. To clarify this on the example of the environmental issue: the invasion of ecology into the economy opens it to politics. Industry and business become a political undertaking in the sense that the shaping of the enterprise itself – its organizational and personnel policies, range of products and production development, large-scale technical investments and organizational arrangements – can no longer be accomplished behind closed doors in the guise of objective and system constraints. Instead, all these activities are surrounded by alternatives, which means that other expectations, agents and considerations, as well as consumer consultation, have an effect on management groups that previously ruled alone and, therefore, 'unpolitically'. The unpolitical bourgeois of late capitalism as regulated by the welfare state is becoming a political bourgeois, who must 'rule' inside his/her economic sphere according to the standards of politics requiring legitimation. This political bourgeois should not be confused with the *citoyen*, or even an economic *citoyen*. This new type of open industrial politics remains quite distinguishable from the procedures and mechanisms of the political system. The entrepreneur or manager does not become an elected representative; the neutral indicators of wage and profit continue to decide on investments and the success of products and the organization, but the substantive 'how' becomes political, controversial, subject to codetermination, and capable of and even requiring consent. Trust becomes central; a trust capital that can be wasted by continuing to act out the old industrial scenario. That is the origin of the 'new piety' of business: environmental morality, ethics and responsibility, proclaimed for publicity in full-page ads and glossy pictures.

Reflexive modernization becomes discursive modernization. The 'communicative society' (Jürgen Habermas) is changing the general conditions of economic and technical activity, requiring not just a different 'communications style' but also different forms and forums of self-presentation. It also devalues previous organizational and strategic knowledge and requires new intraorganizational forms of action and legitimation.

The politicization that ecological and technological hazards bring to industry has two sides. First, organizational action thereby becomes dependent on publicity and industry on discourse. Second, the opportunities for external groups to exert influence grow, but so do those of the administration and parliamentary/governmental politics. The old unpolitical grand coalition of economic growth between the administration, the state, business, technology and science is no longer viable. It falls apart under public indictment of the hitherto accepted hazards. Increases in welfare and hazards condition one another. To the extent this reaches (public) awareness, the defenders of security are no longer in the same boat as the planners and producers of economic wealth. The coalition of technology and economy becomes fragile because technology does indeed enhance productivity but simultaneously places legitimacy at risk. The legal order no longer fosters peace because, along with the hazards, it sanctions and legitimates general disadvantage.

In other words, the powerlessness of official politics against the industrial bloc is powerlessness against the classical setting. It can be

overcome in a politics of politics that advances and develops its
opportunities in forging ecological alliances. In its dual function as
consumer and conscience, the public becomes the father confessor
for a sinful business sector. Things that had thus far existed only on
paper and had not been taken seriously by anyone – monitoring,
safety or protection of citizens and the environment from the destructive consequences of economic growth – suddenly become levers with
which the state, the public, citizens' groups and the administration
can plan and execute their intervention in the strongholds of business
and in the name of a new ecological crusade.

Losers generate winners. As industry loses its ecological innocence,
other business sectors build up their 'greening' livelihood. An economy
that becomes capable of learning ecological lessons will split. This
split in turn makes it possible to learn by political means. Just as
popes and emperors played one petty prince against another (and
vice versa), the distribution of winners and losers opens up a political
game involving sectors of industry, companies, taxes and monitoring, spiced up and prepared with 'scientific risk analyses' that pass
the buck back and forth or conceal it. This 'game', which originates
along with politics itself, makes it possible to forge coalitions of pro
and contra and to play them against one another in order to repoliticize
politics. In other words, it is possible to give tutoring to an environmental policy in the form of – to put it ironically – a pocket hand-
book of ecological Machiavellianism. This removes the technical and
naïve inflections from the slogan of an 'ecological renovation of industrial society' and equips it with political significance and a power
to act that are becoming necessary in the transition from ecological
morality to an ecological politics.

It is easy to object that these are all just speculations that are being
pushed aside by the hard imperatives of free-market success. These
are, many would say, fleeting opinions after all, affirmations that
can be taken away and given back again, but whose flags are mainly
blowing in the wind of the economic climate. A good hard recession
(no matter how regrettable it may be in detail) combined with mass
unemployment attacking the substance and self-confidence of the
populace will drive away these spectres and resurrect the principles
of classical industrial modernization in new splendour like the phoenix
from the ashes.

This objection may be valid under certain, early conditions of ecological criticism, but it applies less and less when business itself can
profit from the successes and hazards it has unleashed. If sectors arise
that build their existence and their markets on the recognition and

removal of the hazards, then even the centres of economic power are split into orthodox believers and reformists, reformers, environmental Protestants and ecological converts. If it becomes an established view that ecological solutions, as well as ecological competency and intelligence in all fields of society, are in tune not just with values but also with the market, in the long run perhaps even the world market, then trenches between losers and winners in the ecological competition for (economic) survival open up and deepen. Ecology becomes a hit, a self-seller – at least as cosmetics or packaging. The resistance of half of business and society faces a grand coalition of the alarmed public, ecoprofiteers and ecocareerists in industry, administration, science and politics. That means, however, that unthinking consent can no longer be purchased; alternatives open up; cooperation becomes uncertain; and coalitions must be forged, endured and fought out, which in turn causes further polarization. Precisely this accelerates disintegration of power in the institutions.

In systematic terms, environmental hazards constitute a field of conflict – there are always losers, but there are always winners as well. Polluter interests, victim interests and helper interests confront one another. As the danger and the general perception of this conflict increase, a highly legitimate interest in preventing and eliminating it grows at the same time. The ecological crisis produces and cultivates a cultural Red Cross consciousness. It transforms everyday trivial, unimportant things into tests of courage in which heroism can be exhibited. Far from intensifying and confirming the general pointlessness of modernity, environmental dangers create a substantive semantic horizon of avoidance, prevention and helping. This is a moral climate and milieu that intensifies with the size of the threat, in which the dramatic roles of heroes and villains achieve a new everyday meaning. Sisyphus legends spring up. Even negative fatalism – 'nothing works anymore, it's all too late' – is ultimately only a variant of the same idea. This is precisely the background against which the role of Cassandra can become a vocation or a career.

The environmental issue, the perception of the world in the coordinate system of ecological-industrial self-imperilment, turns morality, religion, fundamentalism, hopelessness, tragedy, suicide and death – always intermingled with the opposite, salvation or help – into a universal drama. In this real-life theatre, this continuing drama, this everyday horror comedy, business is free to take on the role of the villain and poisoner, or to slip into the role of the hero and helper and celebrate this publicly. The cultural stages on which the ecological issue is played out modernize archaism. There are dragons and dragon-slayers here, odysseys, gods and demons, except that these are now played, assigned and refused with shared roles in all spheres of action – in politics, law, the administration and, not least of all, in business. In the environmental issue, a postmodern, jaded, saturated, meaningless and fatalistic *pâté de foie gras* culture creates a Herculean task for itself that acts as a stimulus everywhere and splits business into villains and Robin Hoods.

In systematic terms, one can distinguish two constellations in the ecological conflict following the schema of Volker von Prittwitz (1990). The first constellation is confrontation, where polluter industries and affected groups face off against one another in spectacular fashion. This constellation begins to change only in a second constellation, in which (a) helper interests awaken and (b) the cover-up coalition between polluters and victims begins to crumble. This occurs as parts of business, and also of the professional intelligentsia (engineers, researchers, lawyers and judges), slip into the role of rescuer and helper; that is, they discover the environmental issue as a construction and expansion of power and markets. This in turn presupposes that industrial society becomes an industrial society with a bad conscience, that it understands and indicts itself as a risk society. Only in that way can helping and coping industries and careers develop themselves and their heroism, which both motivates and skims off profits. This presumes a turning away from mere criticism and a transition to the siege of the status quo by alternatives. The environmental issue must be broken down into other questions: technology, development, production arrangements, product policy, type of nutrition, lifestyles, legal norms, organizational and administrative forms, and so on.

Only a society that awakens from the pessimism of the confrontational constellation and conceives of the environmental issue as a providential gift for the universal self-reformation of a previously fatalistic industrial modernity can exploit the potential of the helping and heroic roles and gain impetus from them, not to conduct cosmetic ecology on a grand scale but actually to assure viability in the future.

On the international level as well, the activation of 'guardian angel industries' (the expansion of the waste management sector) is an important explanatory factor for expansive environmental policy:

> The internationalization process of environmental policy can be explained . . . from the effect of the helper, even the perpetrator industries. Countries in which a certain standard of environmental protection has

developed are interested in internationalizing this standard. One reason for this is that short-term comparative international price disadvantages versus other countries may arise (perpetrator interest), while on the other hand, if their standards become universal, due to the associated qualitative demands (such as demand for technology, spare parts and other services), new opportunities for sales, increasing profits and growing fame may result for them (helper interest).

(*Prittwitz, 1991: 185*)

In other words, the conditions for the deterioration of power that were sketched out above – the end of the East–West conflict, increased self-confidence among workers, substantive alternatives in professional fields of activity, intersystemic coalitions – are activated by the split in the institutions of business, professions and politics. The mills begin to grind, not contrary to business, but because business also profits from it.

Altogether, this implies that ecology abolishes the quasi-objective apoliticism of the economic sphere. The latter splits up in its sinfulness, all the way to its management, to the personality and the identity of the people on all levels of action. This splitting and susceptibility to division into the sinful and the redeemed permits a 'political sale of indulgences' and restores to politics the power instruments of 'papal jurisdiction and misjurisdiction', the public exhibition and self-castigation of the great industrial sinners, and even the public torture implements of an 'ecological inquisition'.

As an illustration of this, let me pick up the controversy about genetically modified food, which initially seems to contradict the subpoliticization thesis. It is first of all actually a good example of what Anthony Giddens and I are calling *manufactured uncertainties*: nobody, neither the experts nor the layperson, knows what the consequences will be. The victory of science once again imposes on us the burden of making crucial decisions which may affect our very survival without any proper foundations in knowledge. Thus this is a matter not of risk but of uncertainty. There is a pragmatic indication of this. If you ask 'Are genetically modified food industries privately (adequately) insured?' the answer is 'No'. Thus the industries and their experts say 'no risk', but the private insurance businesses say 'too risky, no (cheap) insurance'.

But this uncertainty is overruled by powerful forces. Globalized business, genetic advertisers and their fellow-travelling philosophers, stock market speculators and governments under the threat of unemployment have attempted to push through these radical and uncertain biotechnologies. They have chosen to ignore what all good scientists acknowledge – that the science of genetics is in its infancy. We do not even know the genetic alphabet completely, and have no idea how to speak the language.

Since the early 1970s the 'recombination' of DNA has enabled us to shift genes around – the technology that now allows us to modify crops and animals. Impressive as those advances are, their primary impact has been to reveal the depth of our uncertainty and ignorance. Even when, for example, we have the complete human sequence, it may be another century before we can unravel its place within the human anatomy. Medically, genetics has so far achieved almost nothing apart from providing more justifications for abortion (Beck-Gernsheim, 1995).

Genes have to be understood as parts of systems whose full complexity we are only now beginning to grasp. Genes with bad effects may also have good ones, and vice versa. Genes interact in ways that remain fundamentally unpredictable. And, out there in the real world, genetic change in one organism may have incalculable effects on the whole environment – or not. This complexity and acknowledged non-knowledge is the true context within which the genetically modified food debate should be viewed.

It is indeed very interesting to notice that at first there was a reflexive consensus among the leading scientists in the field about these uncertainties and potential threats. As a result of a conference at Asilomar, California, in 1975, American scientists effectively called a halt to their work. There were fears of a biological weapon more terrible than the atomic bomb and of rogue organisms escaping from the laboratory to infect humans or crops.

However, this academic and public brainstorming about the consequences of science and responsibilities of scientists in an age of revolutionary technologies subsided. There have been no accidents or catastrophes so far, the 'experts' now argued, therefore genetics appeared to be safe.

But suddenly, seemingly out of nowhere, the subpoliticization has begun. In February 1999, the British consumer, still terrified by the BSE crisis, was shocked by headlines proclaiming 'Frankenstein Food' – an approach which reached its climax on the front page of *The Daily Mirror*, a leading British newspaper. It featured a picture of Tony Blair, genetically modified to look like Boris Karloff, complete with green face and neckbolt, under the headline 'The Prime Monster'. This was the mass media's response to Blair's attempt to restore trust by demonstratively eating genetically modified food in public with his daughter.

Afterwards the normal chaos of risk conflict began: experts and counter-experts told the public their contradictory stories – with the foreseeable consequence of deepening consumers' doubts and therefore threatening the markets of the food industries. Instead of openly informing everybody, the industries ignored and neglected once again the severe uncertainties and fears of the consumer. They rejected and counteracted an information policy forcing industries to declare which food has been genetically modified and which not – thus again encouraging mistrust.

Underlying all this the question arose: who actually is governing our lives? Genetically modified food is a global business and anxiety about the unknown consequences and for the planet are a worldwide concern. Moreover, it is the globality of the phenomenon which explains why it is so hard to deal with. No single country can avoid genetically modified food and crops without bucking the system of free trade. If a government seeks to delay the introduction of genetically manipulated food it will face opposition from the food giants, who want uniform standards to apply across the world – that is, if those standards favour them. All this leaves serious questions about the sovereignty of national politics and its limits. Are Britons' post-BSE food scares beyond the reach of government when faced with global corporate opponents? Are consumers and voters powerless in the face of global financial powers?

In this ongoing global risk conflict we are again confronted with a biological hubris: now, we are told, genetics is on the brink of extending life, conquering disease, disseminating happiness and feeding the world. But this confidence is based on the false premise that it is as safe to shuffle genes in the world as it is in the lab. We do not know this to be the case because we know very little about the complex interactions of genes and the proteins for which they provide the blueprints.

At this moment, scientists must above all reflect, respect and confess their ignorance. It is up to them to make their uncertainties clear, whatever the professional, financial and political implications are. They should feel free to express their doubts in the broader public. There have been far too many attempts to evade this responsibility. This, of course, would not bring risk conflict to an end, but lead to a new one in which the relationship between science, the economy and democracy must be readjusted.

Conclusion

> In my opinion, the history of mankind, its endangerment,
> and its tragedy, is just beginning today. So far, there have
> been altars of saints and the signs of archangels behind it.
> Chalices and baptismal fonts bathed its weaknesses and
> wounds. Now the series of great insoluble disasters itself is
> beginning.
>
> *(Gottfried Benn)*

The history of nature is coming to an end, but the history of history
is just beginning. After the end of nature, history, society, nature, or
whatever the great bloated beast may be called, is finally reduced to
a history of humanity. Not only has modernity lost the 'altars of
saints' and the 'wings of archangels', the alter ego of nature and the
superego of the institutions are both dissolving into decision-making.
Shining through everywhere in its helplessness is the individual, to
which Adorno (1951: 251) referred in defensive melancholy:

> Among the standardized and administered humanity units, the indi-
> vidual continues to exist. It is even under protection and is achieving
> monopoly value. But in reality it is still the function of its uniqueness,
> like the deformed foetuses that were once stared at and laughed at by
> children. Since the individual no longer makes an independent economic
> living, his character comes into conflict with his objective social role.
> Precisely because of this contradiction, he is being tended in national
> parks and enjoyed in laborious contemplation.

The alternative, then, is the rethinking of government and politics
so as to create open governments and organizations, tendered by
much better-informed publics and socially aware firms, all brought
face to face with the consequences of their actions from which they
are at present largely divorced. Recent cases such as the political
turmoil over bovine spongiform encephalopathy (BSE) in Europe show
the extent to which the old methods of risk assessment have inflicted
an uncontrolled and uncontrollable experiment upon society. To
be sure, risk cannot be banned from modern life, but what we can
and indeed should achieve is the development of new institutional
arrangements that can better cope with the risks we are presently
facing; not with the idea in mind that we might be able to regain
full control, but much more with the idea in mind that we have to
find ways to deal democratically with the ambivalences of modern
life and decide democratically which risks we want to take.

6

Knowledge or Unawareness?
Two Perspectives on 'Reflexive Modernization'

Starting-Points: Institutional Reflection (Giddens), Reflexive Community (Lash), Unintended Consequences (Beck)

It is hard not to misunderstand 'reflexivity'. Anthony Giddens, Scott Lash and I (Beck et al., 1994) have understood and developed the concept and theory of reflexive modernization almost unconsciously with two distinguishable and yet overlapping meanings. In the first view (represented by Giddens, 1994a, and Lash, 1994), 'reflexive' modernization is bound in essence (in keeping with the literal meaning of the words) to *knowledge* (reflection) on foundations, consequences and problems of modernization processes, while in the second one represented by the present chapter, it is essentially tied to *unintended consequences* of modernization (thus deviating at first sight from the meaning of the words). In the former case, one could speak of *reflection* (*Reflexivität*, in the narrower sense) on modernization, and in the latter of the *reflexivity* (in the broader sense) of modernization. In the broader sense, this is true because, alongside reflection (knowledge), *Reflexivität* in German also includes *reflex* in the sense of the effect or preventive effect of *non*-knowing. Of course this terminology invites misunderstandings and is unfortunate in that sense.

A peculiarity and a difficulty of this distinction is that it is not really a sharp one. Thus, talk of a century of unintended consequences cannot appeal to absolute, only to relative, unawareness without contradicting itself, and the interesting issue is the type of this relativity: Who knows what, why and why not? How are knowledge and unawareness constructed, acknowledged, questioned, denied, asserted or ruled out? The concept of unintended consequences ultimately does not contradict the understanding of knowledge in reflexive modernization; instead it opens an expanded and more complex game involving various forms and constructions not just of knowledge, but also of unawareness (*Nicht-Wissen*). So, when I am explaining the concept of reflexive modernization in relation to Anthony Giddens and Scott Lash, I am also, to some extent, talking about my own idea of the concept at the same time. However, while all three of us include the knowledge aspect within our analysis, Giddens and Lash exclude the importance of unintended consequences and unawareness.

> Reflexive modernization says something about late modernity, reflecting on the limitations and difficulties of modernity itself. That relates to key problems of modern politics, because simple or linear modernization still predominates in some parts of the world, most notably in South-East Asia, at least up until recently. In the West and the developed industrial societies, there are conditions of reflexive modernization, with the key problem of modernization being what modernization itself is all about.
>
> (*Giddens and Pierson, 1998: 110*)

The approach to knowledge in reflexive modernization can be summarized, greatly oversimplified, as follows:

1 The more modern a society becomes, the more knowledge it creates about its foundations, structures, dynamics and conflicts.
2 The more knowledge it has available about itself and the more it applies this, the more emphatically a traditionally defined constellation of action within structures is broken up and replaced by a knowledge-dependent, scientifically mediated global reconstruction and restructuring of social structures and institutions.
3 Knowledge forces decisions and opens up contexts for action. Individuals are released from structures, and they must redefine their context of action under conditions of constructed insecurity in forms and strategies of 'reflected' modernization.

A difficulty with this approach to knowledge is that *whatever* form of knowledge, consciousness, reflection, communication or self-observation applies not only to all modern, but to all traditional societies as well. Indeed, as sociology has asserted in all its schools – from

Max Weber through Georg Simmel to Erving Goffman and Harold Garfinkel – it is a fundamental characteristic of every social interaction. There is a beautiful image for reflection, this cognitive image that has been so central ever since the Enlightenment: seeing yourself seeing it (Johann Gottlieb Fichte). This is the sense in which Alvin Gouldner speaks of 'reflexive sociology' and Jürgen Habermas of the 'communicative society'. In the talk of the 'self-referentiality of systems' (Niklas Luhmann), on the other hand, a quite different aspect of self-referentiality occupies the centre of attention. Measured on the contrast between consciousness and unconsciousness, Pierre Bourdieu occupies a mediating position: he conceives of 'reflexivity' as systematic reflection of the unconscious preconditions (categories) of our knowledge.

The generality of the concept of reflection poses a problem for any epistemological theory of reflexive modernization. Either one clings to an undifferentiated concept of reflection, in which case the talk of 'reflexive modernity' becomes a mere pleonasm, or at best a grandiose tautology; or one distinguishes different modes and types of knowledge and connects statements on late or reflexively modern society to particular types of knowledge and reflection. This second path is the one taken by Anthony Giddens and Scott Lash. This is the sense in which Giddens (1994a) speaks of 'institutional reflexivity'. He means the circulation of scientific and expert knowledge on the foundations of social action. This licensed knowledge leads to 'disembedding' and 're-embedding', that is to say, it is employed for changing structures and forms of social action. Let me give you an example: because of the reflexive appropriation of information, financial markets tend towards instability – markets can move in unexpected ways, become chaotic, can be influenced by 'bandwagon effects' and herd behaviour. As George Soros (1998) argues, global financial markets belong in the category of high-consequence global risks which are influenced by information and perceptions of it. You could even say: global reflection of those global financial risks is a main factor in the drive towards a total economic collapse.

> What we are finding now is that the world isn't quite as the Enlightenment thinkers assumed. Increasing our knowledge about the world, the drive to produce information, create new forms of risk for which we have little prior experience – and which can't be calculated on the basis of established time-series, for the data don't exist. Risk in financial markets is also problematic and complicated because it becomes more reflexive. . . . What I call 'manufactured uncertainty' is bound up more with the advance of knowledge than with its limitations. The economist

> Frank Knight made the distinction between risk and uncertainty. He argued that risk concerns future probabilities which can be calculated, uncertainty, ones that cannot be. But that distinction doesn't hold water: there are too many fuzzy areas in the middle. There isn't a tight distinction between risk and uncertainty.
>
> (*Giddens and Pierson, 1998: 104–5*)

'Manufactured uncertainty' means a mélange of risk, more knowledge, more unawareness and reflexivity, and *therefore* a new type of risk.

Giddens conceives of both expert rationality and money as symbolic media of global, not just national, validity. This results in differentiations of space and time which ultimately open up the horizon of social lifeworlds to global systems and dynamics. The question arises: is 'modernity' therefore just a synonym for industrialism in Giddens' view?

It certainly is not. The provocative aspect of his theory of modernization lies precisely in the emerging antithesis of modernity and capitalism (industrialism). In contrast to traditional social orders, according to Giddens' basic thesis, modernity is characterized by a type of highly nervous 'institutional reflexivity' that is to be understood in a double sense. People do not simply react reflexively to systemic processes, they also adjust their social practices over and over again to changed information and circumstances. The 'institutional reflection' of modernity is the cause of its enormous capabilities, but also of the threat to the autonomy of its functional systems and the destabilization of its institutional foundations.

So, in the information society, not only intervention in nature or production of technology, but also the social changes in the family are associated with reflexivity of manufactured risk.

> Consider marriage and family, for example. Up to even a generation ago, marriage was structured by established traditions. When people got married, they knew, as it were, what they were doing. Marriage was formed to a large degree in terms of traditional expectations of gender, sexuality and so forth. Now it is a much more open system with new forms of risk. Everyone who gets married is conscious of the fact that divorce rates are high, that woman demand greater equality than in the past. The very decision to get married is constitutively different from before. There has never been a high-divorce, high-marriage society before. No one knows, for example, what its consequences are for the future of the family or for the health of children.
>
> (*Giddens and Pierson, 1998: 105*)

The consequences of this high-divorce and high-marriage information society are enormous: families are becoming constellations of
different relationships. Take, for example, the way grandmothers and
grandfathers are being multiplied by divorce and remarriage (without genetic engineering). They get included and excluded without
any means of participating themselves in the decisions of their sons
and daughters. From the point of view of the grandchildren the meaning of grandparents has to be determined by individual decisions and
choices. Individuals must choose who is their main father, main mother
and their grandma and grandpa. We are entering *optional* relationships – optional parenthood and households – within families which
are very difficult to identify in an objective, empirical way because
they are a matter of subjective perspectives and decisions. And these
can change between men, women and children and between life phases
(Beck and Beck-Gernsheim, 1995).

Not only is the 'risk regime' changing and challenging families,
but new features of the reflexive modernization of work society are
emerging too (Beck, 1999b).

First, reflexivity is becoming a source of productivity. The outstanding characteristic of the new knowledge work in the information society
is the self-application of knowledge to knowledge as the central source
of productivity. It is this constant exchange between knowledge-based
technological innovations and the application of these technologies,
in order to create new knowledge-based technological and product
generations, which not only sets the productivity spiral of the information society in motion and keeps it spinning, but also accelerates it.

Second, the distinction between the industrial and the service
sector collapses. No new production sector is created in the transition
to the information society. Rather the knowledge-dependent increase
in productivity takes a hold of and changes *all* sectors of production
– agriculture, industry and services – and dissolves the distinction
between 'goods' and 'services'. All the talk of 'post-industrial' or 'service society' becomes just as much a myth and as untenable as the old
distinction between first, second and third sectors. Anyone who tries
to interpret the dynamics of the information economy in terms of the
assumptions and categories of the old work paradigm underestimates
its truly revolutionary potential. This is constituted by the possibility
of direct on-line communication between various kinds of activity –
development, production, management, application and distribution.
The consequence, however, is the dissolution of the old territorialized
paradigm of industrial society. At the same time there is a multiplication of options, which demand decisions and require standardization.

As a consequence, technological determinism is refuted by information technology.

Third, Fordism and the politics of Keynesianism were founded on the boundaries of the nation-state, that is, on an understanding of a national politics and society and of their regulatory potential. In the risk regime, however, this image of order disappears and is replaced by the compulsion to locate and assert oneself on the world market and in world risk society.

There can be no doubt that the risk regime determines and characterizes economic behaviour under the conditions of world-wide open markets and competition. Whether the dollar rate changes, interest rates rise or fall, the East Asian or South American banks and markets totter, whether Greenpeace intervenes and there is an ecological revolt by consumers, whether governments raise petrol prices and emission limits, whether companies market new products, merge, split or suddenly disappear – the order books, investment decisions, management strategies change from one year to the next, from one quarter to the next, often from one week to the next. The risk regime of the economy means, that, in principle, everything is possible and consequently nothing can be predicted and controlled. In this world of global risks the Fordist regime of standardized mass production on the basis of an inflexible, segmented, hierarchical division of labour becomes a decisive impediment to the utilization of capital. Where demand is unpredictable, in terms of both quantity and quality, where markets have diversified world-wide and are therefore uncontrollable, where information technologies simultaneously make possible new kinds of decentralized and global forms of production, then the bases of standardized production and work, as formulated in Taylor's 'scientific management' (and adopted by Lenin for the Soviet philosophy and organization of work), are no longer applicable, because the rigidity of the Fordist regime drives up costs.

Conversely the flexibilization of work becomes the central source of ongoing rationalization and rises in productivity, and in all three dimensions: work *time*, *place* of work and work *contract*. That means, however, that the risk regime, and with it the highly ambivalent model of 'precarious employment', encompasses and transforms ever-larger parts of human beings' work and living realities. This occurs not only in the area of low-skill employment, but also with jobs demanding high qualifications, as a glance at the rapidly increasing number of academic low-pay jobs in the United States shows, as well as the fact that the category of the well-paid 'permanently temporarily' is growing enormously in size precisely in the key areas of the information economy.

'Radicalized modernity', as seen by Giddens, is thus, in institution-alized reflexivity and uncertainty, the result of an 'autonomization of modern thought', which threatens to lose its powers to the extent it pushes out beyond its boundaries. Corresponding to the 'globalization of modernity', as can be observed in the global interlinking of eco-nomic, political and cultural processes, are crises and conflicts on the institutional level, in which Giddens includes the capitalist mode of production, the industrial rearrangement of nature, and the forms of social surveillance. The more strongly the interaction between the institutional dimensions is dominated by the 'reflexive appropriation of knowledge', the more uncontrollable the global interconnections become within a world that is fusing increasingly together into a planetary unit.

In this way, Giddens simultaneously keeps his distance from post-modern doom and gloom. Modern society, he says, can neither be captured with Weber's image of the 'iron cage' nor characterized directly as the monstrous crisis into which Marx made it; instead, argues Giddens, we are living in a 'run-away world'. For Giddens this is the name of an epoch that 'threatens to escape external con-trol', but over which we still have a certain power.

Giddens clarifies the relationship of inherent systemic dynamism and human exertion of influence with the concept of 'trust'. While the relationships between people and their environment in traditional social orders were determined by standardized rules of behaviour and activity, which guaranteed something like 'ontological security', the members of modern societies have nothing left except the hope that the functional systems might fulfil expectations. Lurking at the bottom, however, is the knowledge of their instability and endanger-ment, which grows with the reflexive dynamization of modernity.

Trust originally becomes generalized from some of the same contexts as risk, in commercial relationships. Its religious sources are less im-portant. The noun form of trust comes from that source as well, as when you talk about a bank as a trust, or holding things in trust and so on. If you think of trust as something relevant to the future rather than to the past, that's the basic difference. Previous forms of trust were much more deeply involved with more traditional forms of com-mitment and morality, such as kinship obligations. Trust involves a more directly future-oriented relationship with whomever or whatever you are trusting. . . . Trust has to be mutual to be effective, and it offers security in the face of future contingencies. That's why I relate it to the idea of basic security in personality, as well. . . . To survive in life at all you need a generalized notion of trust, and that's essentially something people get from their early emotional experiences. If you don't have that, you're in big trouble. But to repeat, to be effective trust is always reciprocal – it never rests upon blind faith.

(*Giddens and Pierson, 1998: 108–9*)

We are still living in an industrial society organized according to nation-states, to be sure, but we are already no longer living in it. 'Post-traditional trust', according to Giddens, is a blank cheque issued to the functionality of abstract systems of knowledge and experts. This is how concrete, everyday actions are tied into a system of impenetrable global connections. A more or less successful mediation of 'anthropological certainty' in abstract systems in the corresponding socialization processes makes this 're-embedding' in global dependencies possible. The decisive point, according to Giddens, is the extent to which post-traditional trust can be converted to *active* trust. Active trust cannot be called up, but must be won. It should not be confused with duty, but instead requires equality, discursiveness, reciprocity, substantiation. Ultimately, Giddens is concerned with the figure of the '*reflexive citizen*', for whom individual autonomy and responsibility must be readjusted to fit his vision and scope of activity. This figure also provides late modernity with a 'realistic utopia' that can give direction and impetus to a policy of reform.

Scott Lash (1994) also identifies reflexive modernization with modernization of *knowledge*, with questions of the distribution, circulation, consumption and enhancement of the substance and forms of knowledge, as well as the resulting conflicts. In his eyes, reflexive modernization is a modernization of knowledge, through which the foundations of social action and life (and thus the foundations of sociological thinking and research as well) become questionable, reorganizable and restructurable. More than Giddens, however, Lash sees new types of conflict coming about through different types of knowledge, which are simultaneously types of certainty. He distinguishes (connecting up with Kant) between *cognitive, moral* and *aesthetic* reflection. His attention lies on the emotional particularities of '*aesthetic* reflection' which cannot be resolved emotionally, cognitively and morally and which create '*reflexive communities*'. Connected with this is the objection to Giddens and myself that our arguments are based on a cognitivistically foreshortened understanding of reflection (and thus of reflexive modernization). Against the background of advanced individualization and in the line of Anglo-American cultural theory and tendencies towards 'new communitarianism', Lash considers the central issue to be 'reflexive communities'. These are understood in essence as a second and selectable naturalness of aesthetic symbolic worlds. These interconnect global markets, mobility, modes of consumption and local symbolisms and lifeworlds and at the same time allow what had seemed to be out of the question: social, personal and global identities that are mobile, interchangeable, decidable as well as rigid, and suited to be lived out in a standardized manner.

Yet Scott Lash goes a step further (in collaboration with John Urry: Lash and Urry, 1994); he also inquires into the new forms of social inequality which this society based on science, communication and information is generating as the dark side of its knowledge-dependence. The distribution of information and opportunities for access to information networks do not just compel and enable the reorganization of production, circulation, capital accumulation and consumption by means of knowledge. At the same time, they present or, more accurately, construct, elevated prerequisites of achievement and access that can lead to a radicalization of social inequality, all the way to the new fate of the 'outcasts', the 'drop-outs' or the 'homeless', who slip through all the safety nets.

Thus Lash, unlike Giddens, poses the question of the *selectivity* of knowledge and *unawareness* which is becoming central to future society as knowledge is modernized. He inquires, of course, not into the role of unawareness in reflexive modernity, but rather into the possible new class formations in 'reflexive' society. For him this means science and expert society, but also information and communications society, subject to the tension between 'communicative rationality' (Habermas) and 'discursive power' (Foucault). That is, for Lash, 'reflexive' modernity is a modernity in which – on the basis of contentious cognitive, moral and aesthetic horizons of knowledge, consumption and identity – new rules of inside and outside, inclusion and exclusion are negotiated and established.[1]

The outstanding aspect of Scott Lash's article is how radically he poses the inquiry into the conditions that make community formation and commitment possible in contexts that Giddens calls 'post-traditional' and 'cosmopolitan' (and I call the second modernity). Here is where the controversy is situated for him, and probably for Giddens and me as well, and it is difficult initially to resist the spell of his arguments. 'Community', Lash (1994: 148–9) writes,

> in whatever form, as 'we', as a national identity or as some other collective identity, does not require any kind of hermeneutics of suspicion, but does need a 'hermeneutics of recovery' which, in contrast to

the masters of suspicion (and their present-day colleagues), is not constantly eliminating prerequisites, but makes the attempt to uncover the ontological bases for Being-in-the-World as a community.

Lash wishes to discover or uncover what predominantly holds people together under conditions of advanced individualization, now that this opposing factor is no longer a consensus on religion, status, class, male and female identities, and the like.

In his extraordinarily well-informed search for an answer, he first eliminates everything that remains abstract and cognitivistic in light of his concept of post-traditional community and everything that resists the pre-reflexively known everyday practice of Being-in-the-World with others. For him, all types of rational explanation, expert knowledge and interests miss this reality level of a commitment to the social which precedes any individualization. The categories of aesthetic modernity, such as allegory, mimesis and deconstruction, are equally unable to help.

For Lash this type of trans-individual counter-individualization forms within the horizon of *shared significance*, not in reflexive interpretation; in *active experience* and sympathy, not politically mediated experience; in *self-assured life praxis*, not political and ideological programmes of action, and so on. In a conceptually very subtle manner, Lash thus distils what is at stake for him: not to sacrifice the social too soon and uncritically to a universalized and internally contradictory theory of individualization that leaves its own prerequisites behind in the dark.

Lash, the constructivist of the first water, one of the outstanding thinkers in Anglo-American cultural theory, is thus attempting an 'anti-constructivistic constructivism'. His real opponent is not (only) the theory of individualization, but (also) those varieties of radical constructivism that decode collective identities as mere 'imaginary communities' and thereby (in Lash's opinion) ultimately tend to dissolve them. Taking recourse in Heidegger's 'workshop model' from *Being and Time* (Heidegger, 1986), Lash attempts to free himself from constructivism by turning it against itself, at least to the extent that a concept of 'reflexive community' becomes possible. This is equidistant from pre-ordained traditions and from identities that are only socially constructed. It has its basis in (individualized) contexts of practical action in life, in which the *limits* of individualization are experienced and suffered, but likewise in outbursts of violence and recollected terror that inculcate cultural *differences* over and over again.

It is unfortunate that Lash does not also discuss Weber's concept of the *'political* community' in this context. This is based after all, similarly to the way Lash sees things, not in cognitive knowledge or the ferment of interests of social activity, but in suffered or inflicted *violence*, particularly, state and military violence (wars). In a political kind of 'concrete constructivism', this violence and the cultivated recollection of it continually create and inculcate, according to Weber, national and ethnic identities which are not grounded at all in anything original and natural (in fact, Weber argued vehemently against this). This supplementation is meant to show that I find Scott Lash's indefatigable and undaunted search for a simultaneously post-essentialist and post-constructivist foundation of individualized social action extremely important and stimulating, but am not really convinced of his results. It may simply be that Lash breaks off too early. Why is it not true that a number of different and contradictory social identities overlap in what Giddens and I call a 'reflexive bio-graphy'? But then how are we to understand the concept of 'collective identity'? What role do *political freedoms* play as a source of social commitments? (See chapter 1 above.)

Conversely, Lash's (1994) argumentation misses my point, namely the upsetting and transformation of the foundations of industrial modernization by unintended consequences, understood as a conflict over unawareness, more specifically, the construction, circulation and destruction of knowledge and unawareness.

What distinguishes my concept of reflexive modernization from those of Giddens and Lash? To put it briefly and pointedly: *the 'medium' of reflexive modernization is not knowledge, but – more or less reflexive – unawareness*. It is this aspect of the distribution and defence of unawareness (*Nicht-Wissen*) that opens the horizon of inquiry for *non*-linear theories (of reflexive modernization). We live in the age of unintended consequences, and it is this state of affairs that must be decoded and shaped methodologically and theoretically, in everyday life and politically.

How can the theory of reflexive modernization be understood and formulated as a theory of knowledge/unawareness? Stated in simplified form as theses:

1   The more modern a society becomes, the more unintended con-sequences it produces, and as these become known and acknowledged, they call the foundations of industrial modernization into question.

2   Unintended consequences are also part of knowledge. The only question is: who knows them and on what basis? Even the concept of

'*latent* unintended consequence' does not mean *no* knowledge at all but *one* knowledge whose claims are *controversial*. The talk of 'unintended consequences' thus denotes a conflict of knowledge, a conflict of rationality. The claims of different expert groups collide with one another, as well as with the claims of ordinary knowledge and of the knowledge of social movements. The latter may well have been developed by experts, but according to the hierarchy of social credibility, it is not considered to be expert knowledge and consequently is not perceived and valued as such in the key institutions of law, business and politics. The knowledge of side-effects thus opens up a *battleground of pluralistic rationality claims*. This involves knowledge of the consequences of industrial modernization even on the lowest rungs of the ladder of social recognition.

3   This conflict does *not* run along clear and unambiguous associations of knowledge and unawareness, either in the sense of expert rationality or in the expert critique from activist movements. The characteristic is that, in the interplay of claim on *all* sides, knowledge and unawareness, limitations, selectivities, other relevances, rationalities, 'rationalizations' and dogmatism emerge (usually involuntarily) – quite in the spirit of Karl Popper's 'critical rationalism' as expanded by the ruse of public reason. This conflict of rationalities implies that there is an enlarged (possibly difficult-to-delimit) horizon of competing agents, producers and interested parties for knowledge, in which the established linear associations of knowledge and unawareness become dubious.

4   As diffuse as this conflict is, it flares up over an objective. What is at stake is the defence or overcoming of institutional expert constructions of the inability of others (persons, groups, institutions, subsystems, countries, continents) to have knowledge regarding the unintended consequences of organizational action. The question is: can the dams constructed around the unawareness of the foundation-endangering and foundation-changing consequences of industrial modernization be upheld, or will the recognition in its own centres of the consequences of knowledge-based industrial modernization change the basis of business, the social contract of industrial modernization, so that modernity becomes political? That is to say, the foundations and basic norms in business, science, politics and the family must be renegotiated and re-established.

5   In that sense, what is at stake in this conflict scenario (of a 'negative-sum game' of self-endangerment [Offe]) is essentially the 'preventive effect of unawareness' (Heinrich Popitz): prevailing constructions of unintended consequences, no matter what foundation in knowledge they are built upon or questioned from, allow us to

look the other way. They are constructions of (ir)relevance in an anticipatory defence against uncomfortable challenges (the moral and economic costs of liability or changes in politics and lifestyle) which intrude along with the recognition of the consequences and thus the responsibility for them.

Types of Unawareness

In this sketch of an argument, the (terminologically unfortunate) distinction between reflection (knowledge) and reflexivity ('unintended consequence') of industrial modernization is replaced by the distinction between knowledge and unawareness. However, this could simply mean replacing one unclear concept with an even larger one. The concept of 'unawareness' (as well as the overlap and possible potentiation of forms of knowledge and unawareness), after all, opens up not only new horizons of questions, but an unexplored jungle of meanings and misunderstandings as well. Unawareness can be known or not known, concrete or theoretical, unwillingness to know or inability to know, and so on. Of course it is out of the question to be able even to pose and elaborate all these questions of the analysis of unawareness in cognitive sociology in the context of a closing argument in a debate. Therefore, only a few aspects that play a part in the conflict of rationalities over 'unintended consequences' will be taken up here.

In his book, *But Is It True? The Relationship Between Knowledge and Action in the Great Environmental and Safety Issues of Our Time* (1994), Aaron Wildavsky demonstrated (on the basis of empirical studies) shortly before his death that the knowledge of the 'unintended consequences' of natural destruction and health risks which upsets the public also contains much unawareness – wilful omissions, mistakes, errors, exaggerations, dogmatisms:

> Looking back at the array of environmental and safety issues, many of which, like Love Canal and global warming, have become imprinted on the public consciousness, we can discern a clear pattern: the more that is known, the less reason there is to fear the worrisome object and the weaker the rationale for preventive measures. The one partial exception is CFCs leading to ozone depletion.
>
> (*Wildavsky, 1994: 24*)

Wildavsky and his colleagues draw this conclusion from an analysis in which they compared scientific results and their presentation in public (television, newspapers) for a number of issues of 'environmentalism' or 'health risks'. The authors often demonstrate 'bad reporting practices' (limitation to *one* source of knowledge, for instance) or the mere allegation of the 'existence' of risks, which evidently are not considered to require any further substantiation. The exploration of risks, according to the authors, is obviously only a necessary but definitely not a sufficient condition for informing people about 'hazardous unintended consequences' of industrial activity. In addition there is the necessity to set up and practise appropriate ways of giving information and active ways of reacting to and processing this information on the part of the 'active citizen' (to put it in Giddens' terms).

In their informative question 'but is it true?', however, it is striking that even Wildavsky et al. still proceed from a clear, unambiguous distinction between knowledge and unawareness. For them this is defined by expert rationality. They do not inquire into forms of (involuntary) self-discreditation of expert knowledge, for instance by risk diagnoses that change from one point in time, institute, methodological approach and work context to the next. 'Unawareness', in the sense of distortions of expert knowledge by public media and 'translators', is therefore only *one* dimension of the key question 'but is it true?', but one which becomes central in the conflict of rationalities in reflexive modernization. The unwanted and involuntary revelation of half-knowledge, unawareness, repressed unawareness and the corresponding limitations in expert knowledge itself must be accepted (see Beck, 1992: ch. 7).

In general terms, at least the following aspects or dimensions of unawareness must be distinguished with regard to hazardous unintended consequences: (a) *selective reception and transmission* of the knowledge of risk – 'falsification' in Wildavsky's sense (on all sides in public, of course, among social movements, but also among the various experts and organizations); (b) *uncertainty* of knowledge (in a concrete and a theoretical sense); (c) *mistakes and errors*; (d) *inability* to know (which may in turn be known or repressed); and (e) *unwillingness* to know.

Wildavsky once again notes, very selectively, 'much of recent environmental and safety alarms are false, mostly false, or unproven' (Wildavsky 1994: 142). This remark not only trivializes the 'knowledge' that has been worked out and is available on, for instance, the global effects of industrialization. More significantly, its seemingly clear distinction between knowledge and lack of knowledge conceals the central problem: the decision-making in uncertainty on all sides, which is becoming characteristic of the second, reflexive, phase of modernity.

'Many of the essays in this volume', writes Albert Reiss (1992: 29) in a chapter entitled 'Institutionalization of Risk', 'are about how decision makers struggle with uncertainty, rather than risk, even when many risks (as in the case of the space shuttle) appear to be calculable. Decisions under conditions of both uncertainty and risk are, of course, subject to error. What is at stake is the acceptability of the error' (see also Bonß, 1995).

Wildavsky's central fear is that the rejection of error probabilities in the calculus of risk may lead to an overestimation of the hazards and thus ultimately to an overreaction and overregulation of all spheres of social activity in the sense of a preventive policy of risk avoidance. His demand is therefore: 'Reject the Cautionary Principle, Reverse the Environmentalist Paradigm, Stop Regulating Small Causes with Tiny Effects!' That is certainly worth considering, but once again it very selectively follows the progressivistic idea that the greatest and most frequent errors are to be found not in the realm of the experts, but among their critics – a unilateral attribution of errors and mistakes that is at war not just with the history of the sciences, but with the history of those concrete controversies over the destruction of nature and health hazards with which Wildavsky is concerned.

Corresponding to the dogmatization of expert knowledge to which Wildavsky succumbs is a dogmatization of anti-expert knowledge to which many social movements succumb (with the 'good intention' of politicizing topics and circumstances). Uncertainties in one's own (risk) knowledge, it seems to many activists, block political action: 'Effective management of highly publicized risks such as nuclear power and storing nuclear wastes, global warming and the greenhouse effect depends heavily on public trust in science, in technology and in managing institutions. . . . Institutional legitimacy rests to a considerable extent on trust' (Short and Clarke, 1992: 12). This indicates that, in the horizon of modernity, unawareness is viewed as a shortcoming or a failure.

Alfred Schütz, Thomas Luckmann and Robert Zaner distinguish various types of unawareness in their book *The Structures of the Lifeworld* (1979): 'The lifeworld is apprehended not only in that which it is, but also in that which it is not.' The elements of knowledge are structured according to 'cores of meaning, by degrees of familiarity, definiteness and credibility. . . . Even without theoretical reflection, we know that we do not know everything.' The authors conceive of unawareness (insofar as it does not relate to the fundamental lack of clarity of the lifeworld) as *potential* knowledge. It consists of 'reconstructable knowledge', which was forgotten, but can in principle be recalled, and 'achievable knowledge', of which it is known that one can learn it in certain ways (from a reference work or from education) (Schütz et al., 1979: 214–17).

In this conceptual frame of reference of an ultimately unbroken certainty of knowledge of the lifeworld, unawareness is predominantly conceived of as *not-yet* knowledge or *no-longer* knowledge, that is to say, *potential* knowledge. The problems of unawareness are understood from its antithesis, the knowledge, indeed the (unspoken) certainty, in which the lifeworld resides. By contrast to that, the *inability* to know is gaining in importance in reflexive modernization, as Anthony Giddens and Scott Lash stress. This is not the expression of selective standpoints, momentary forgetting or underdeveloped expertise, but precisely the product of highly developed expert rationality. Thus, for instance, the calculus of probability can never completely rule out a particular event. Or specialists in risk may question one another's detailed results, while other experts demystify the foundations of expert activity with their inborn thoroughness.

Against this background the question of deciding comes up again in a radical way. If we cannot (yet) know anything about the consequences of industrial research, activity and production (as is overwhelmingly the case today in fields of genetic engineering and human genetics), if, that is, neither the optimism of the protagonists nor the pessimism of their critics is based on knowledge, then which rule applies: Is there a green light or a red light for large-scale utilization of technology in industry? Is the inability to know therefore a licence for action or grounds for *slowing down* action, for moratoria or perhaps not acting at all? How can maxims of acting and not being permitted to act be justified by the inability to know?

It is interesting in this sense that Wildavsky advises a kind of pragmatic scepticism in dealing with risks and information about risk: 'Nihilism is not the point. Distrusting everyone and everything, especially one's own judgment, is self-destructive. Instead, the citizen risk detective should learn to recognize patterns of misperception so as to avoid being controlled by them' (Wildavsky, 1994).[2] In other terms, reflected doubt, 'effective distrust' (Wildavsky) definitely presents opportunities for a better public understanding in dealing with the (in many respects) 'uncertain' knowledge of risk.

Linear and Non-linear Theories of Knowledge

One can and must therefore distinguish between *linear* and *non-linear* theories of knowledge of 'reflexive' modernization, with the ability to locate this distinction essentially on the question as to the distribution and defence of unawareness. This distinction cannot be mapped unambiguously onto Giddens, Lash and myself; it runs across us:

1   Linear theories imply (usually tacitly as the other side of their central assumption) that unawareness is *not* relevant (central) to reflexive modernization. Non-linear theories assert the opposite: types, constructs and consequences of unawareness of risks are *the* key problem in the transition to a second, reflexive modernity.

2   While linear theories of knowledge assume (more or less) *closed* circles of formally responsible expert groups and people who act on knowledge, non-linear theories see an open, *multiple* field of competitors acting on knowledge. In the limiting case, two scenarios confront one another here: the expert-monopoly or the *technocratic* decision model, on the one hand, and, on the other, the late-modern 'palaver model', in which it is unclear who is *not* allowed to participate in the discussion. In the zone where the two models overlap, this problem arises: how can rules of admission and procedure be agreed upon and practised with consensus and dissent simultaneously?[3]

3   Linearity means knowledge based on the *consensus of experts*, limited numbers of recognized and licensed practitioners inside research institutes and organizations and the corresponding explicit, cooperatively interlinked sites for producing, acknowledging and implementing knowledge. Non-linearity means *dissent* and conflicts over rationality, and hence principles, that is to say, unclear, uncooperative and oppositely polarized networks of people and coalitions acting on knowledge (Hajer, 1995). They play out conflicts with antagonistic strategies and complementary chances for success in subsidiary public spheres over (in the limiting case) *contradictory certainties* (images of nature and humankind).

4   The distinction between and distribution of knowledge and unawareness is thus based on a social structure, a power gradient between individuals, groups, authorities, monopolies and resources (institutes, research funding, and so on) on one side and, on the other, those who call them into question. This distinction, turned concrete and sociological, is the correlative of a rationalization conflict which is very difficult to delimit. The talk of 'unintended consequences' signals a stage in the conflict in which homogeneous expert groups are *still* capable of excluding other forms of knowledge and people using it as unawareness. To the extent they can no longer manage this, linear modernization ends and non-linear modernization ('reflexive' in *my* sense) begins.

5   The criterion for this is therefore: closed versus open; consensual versus dissenting networks of agents, questions, methods, governing hypotheses, scenarios, assessments and evaluations of risk and danger. Why is this distinction so central? Because the issues of unawareness (in the double meaning *of inability* and *unwillingness* to know) erupt there *for everybody*; moreover, that very state of affairs brings about a compulsion to open oneself to 'outside knowledge', the outsider perspective. This is how the foundations of the oblivious monorationality (economic, technical, political, scientific, and so on) characteristic of linear modernization are shattered; this same monorationality is being exaggerated even today in the form of systems theory (with the insinuation that functionality and autonomy depend precisely on screening out the outsider perspective). Both factors – the inquiry into our *own* inability to know and the ability to empathize with outside rationalities – mark the transition to the second modernity of (self-)uncertainty which is both constructed by civilization and known. Only then does the question gradually arise of how these antagonisms and differences in *known unawareness* can be related to one another, worked out and joined into procedures for reaching decisions in new forms and forums.

Both approaches to reflexive modernization, knowledge and unintended consequences, have a number of points in common:

* They are opposed to theories of postmodernism, for instance.
* They emphasize the key significance of knowledge for the reorganization of modern societies.
* They explicitly see that reflexive modernization must not be confused with *Enlightened* modernization and certainly not with *self-controlled* modernization; on the contrary, both viewpoints agree in emphasizing the central importance of constructed uncertainty, that is, self-generated risks and dangers, in modernity as it becomes inwardly and outwardly globalized.
* They also do not see the motor of reflexive modernization in something new, but rather in the familiar crisis-wracked production cycle of capital, technology, labour, science and the state.

Unawareness, Unintended Consequences and Self-endangerment

Yet the following distinctions (beyond what has already been said) worth noting and discussing:

1 If one demonstrates 'reflexive modernization' (as I do) not on the distribution of knowledge, but on the distribution of unawareness of unintended consequences, then one cannot ascribe the adjective 'reflexive' either to traditional societies or to classical industrial modernity. This concept of 'reflexivity' is, after all, formulated much more narrowly than the difficult-to-delimit concept of 'reflection'. It only seems paradoxical that known, repressed, maintained and attacked or recognized and admitted *un*awareness marks the dividing line from 'reflexive' modernization.

2 The approach to knowledge in reflexive modernization (as represented by Giddens and Lash in different variants) seems at first sight to be supported by the fundamental cognitive-sociological insight of modern constructivistic epistemologies that all phenomena are constructed in knowledge, while the 'unintended consequence' approach seems to become entangled in the contradiction between 'seen and unseen'. In fact, the concept of 'unintended consequence' only raises the programme of cognitive sociology to a more complex level. The distribution and circulation of knowledge is simultaneously undermined, parried and supplemented by the distribution and circulation of unawareness. As mentioned above, this opens access to reflexive modernization's non-linear (negative) theories of knowledge, the possibilities of which cannot be exhausted in this chapter. The introduction of unawareness as the key conflict in 'reflexive' modernization forces distinctions.

(a) So far everyone has always spoken of the opening of the knowledge agenda by conflicts over *selective inference*, which attempts to move up the ladder of credibility from unawareness to knowledge.

(b) *Reflected unawareness*, however, must be distinguished from this. This follows the pattern that one knows that one does not know and what one does not know. Thus knowledge and unawareness are separated within knowledge.

(c) This brings about regions and zones of known inability to know. The issue of how knowledge of the *inability* to know is to be evaluated, whether it means, for instance, a green light or a red light for technological development, is hotly contentious in the insecurities of self-imperilling modernity.

(d) On the other hand, repressed or *unknown unawareness* ultimately means ignorance. One is unaware of what one does not know. This is found among experts and counter-experts, as well as in the hysterias of new (and old) religious and social movements.

3   The concept of unintended consequence does of course reveal a certain combination of knowledge and unawareness. It is generally known (independently of the gradations of knowledge and unawareness in the concrete case) that unseen, screened-out 'unintended consequences' do not erase the self-imperilment they signify, they intensify it. This is related, among other things, to the fact that 'unintended consequences' presuppose *actions*, and thus subjects, practices and institutions as well. The latter do not stop functioning because of the unawareness of the unintended consequences, but are in fact favoured by it. Knowledge of unintended consequences has an inhibitory effect on presumed routines of action, which becomes unnecessary as the unintended consequences become better known. The theoretical knowledge of unintended consequences thus also contains the implication of the paradoxical *intensification* effect of unintended consequences *because* they are not known. This effect is very closely tied to definite (more or less verifiable) items of knowledge (hypotheses), such as the assumption of causal attribution contained in the metaphor of the 'dying forests' (*Waldsterben*). The prerequisite is that there be knowledge of unintended consequences – the 'dying forests' in this case – and that this knowledge be acknowledged. Then the active desire not to know does not halt the death of forests and the extinction of species, it *accelerates* them by not stopping or correcting the dynamics of industrial self-endangerment.

4   'Unintended consequences' are thus a paradoxical (negative) cognitive image, in which (under certain circumstances) unawareness is *known* as an intensification of self-endangerment, presuming that there is a believed knowledge of the unintended consequences, whatever its basis in specific cases. The power of social movements and a public inspired by science to make alternative definitions is based on this fact: the more emphatically the believed knowledge of industrial self-endangerment is negated, the more threatening the 'actual' potential for endangerment becomes (behind the façades of unwillingness to know). The knowledge contained in the knowledge of industrial unintended consequences allows, or perhaps forces, a distinction to be made between *known* and *actual* ('objective') endangerment. In pointed terms, it rests on the cognitive construction of an '*in-itself*', an 'objective' active world of constructed dangers of civilization independent of our knowledge or unawareness of them. In fact, it even contains a built-in hypothesis of amplification and exacerbation (independent

of knowledge of the concrete case). Active unawareness – ignoring and hushing things up, that is – *intensifies* the 'actual' dynamic of the routine self-endangerment in industrial modernity, which is practised independently of our knowledge of it. In that sense, the inquiry into the types of unawareness enlarges the narrow, linear perspective of cognitive sociology by the immanent distinction between the known and unknown, but thereby intensified dynamism of action of industrial self-endangerment.

5 This social construction of a knowledge-independent and thus 'objective' endangerment, however, is not true in and of itself. Instead, it needs focused investigations and the appropriate indicators. The question arises of the *social construction* (and sociological reconstruction) of 'objective' indicators of hazard and destruction. My answer is based on two considerations: the 'objective' indication of self-endangerment is tied back into the mutual criticism of social agents. The presumption is that, wherever established expert rationalities come into contradiction, there are indicators of an *institutionally constructivistic* 'objectivity' of the hazard indicators.

The central example of this, in my view, is the *principle of private insurance*. It proclaims that private insurance enterprises man the border-crossing between the risks of industrial society (still considered socially controllable) and the self-constructed threats of risk society (*no longer* considered controllable, because they render even the institutionalized bases of calculation and control inoperative). With their verdicts 'uninsured' or (more radically) 'uninsurable', the insurers contradict the engineers, scientists and industrial executives who appeal to technical calculations of risk as they brush aside any reservations of a concerned public with gestures of innocence and attribute (virtually) *zero* or vestigial risk to uninsured and uninsurable forms of production, products and technologies.

'Vestigial risk' means: 'we don't know, we can't know'. This inability to know is of course not really ever expressed, but generally distorted into a certainty. 'Vestigial risk' is the language of repressed uncertainty within the horizon of putative (cognitive) certainty – no more than high-flown claims to perfection and control. The phrase 'vestigial risk' *negates* the knowledge of unawareness. But it refers to it and announces it. The knowledge of not knowing (or being able to know) is, one could say, relegated to the irrelevance of a footnote. Thus the main characteristic of world risk society is neglected, where, in a Kafkaesque scenario, we are guilty but do not even know what we are guilty of.

6 This erosion of technical, scientific and industrial controllability
   subpoliticizes modernity, not only within the officially labelled
   political system, but also in business, in organizations, even in
   private life. In this sense, congestion has become a metaphor for
   the involuntary politicization of modernity. It symbolizes the forced
   utopia of self-limitation. Congestion means the involuntary sit-
   down strike of everyone against everyone else, technically imposed mass Buddhism, an egalitarian forced meditation for drivers
   of all classes of cars. 'You're not caught in the congestion, you
   are the congestion' is written in large letters in a tunnel. Thus
   congestion becomes the quality of an entire culture. This does not
   mean just traffic congestion, but the infarction of modernization
   in general. The linear modernity of 'bigger, faster, more' is at risk
   of infarction everywhere. This applies, as we have found out by
   now, to the ecological infarction, but also the infarction of the
   welfare state, wage labour society, the transportation system, the
   pension system, and so on. The implacable 'more' and 'faster' of
   primary modernity collides everywhere with the problems, erosion
   and obstructions it generates: destroyed nature, empty coffers,
   more demands and fewer jobs despite, or perhaps because of, the
   economic upswing and economic growth. This is how politics
   becomes *unbound*, while the established political institutions are
   becoming *zombies* – the living-dead institutions.

Summary: Points in Dispute

What, then, are the points in dispute? More than anyone else, Anthony
Giddens (1994a) confronts the question of what is being broken up
with the question of what is being created. He uncovers the dependencies of global expert systems, emphasizes the role of 'institutional
reflexivity' and inquires into the possibilities of 'active trust', which
cannot simply be called upon, but must be created and won. That is
how he describes in progressively clearer strokes the 'reflexive citizen', who must master and define politically and biographically the
emerging uncertainties of the de-traditionalized order on a cosmopolitan scale.

   Yet, in equating reflexive and *expert-determined* modernization,
Giddens underestimates the *pluralization* of rationalities and agents
of knowledge and the key role of known and repressed types of
*un*awareness, which constitute and establish the discontinuity of

'reflexive' modernization in the first place. Giddens thus misunderstands the questioning of the foundations of expert-determined modernization as well as the various efforts to create forms and forums of debate inside and outside of organizations in order at least to tie these contradicting rationality claims into a discursive context and a consensus on procedure. Of course, there is no guarantee that the democratization of decision-making in the crucial areas of potential hazards will necessarily improve the quality of decisions and thus effectively lessen global risks.

Even where this democratization does not happen, the question is: how does one deal with the competing rationality claims, that is, with the creatures of unawareness that are flourishing in the shade of a self-endangering modernity? To repress or to acknowledge (on *all* sides), that is, the Hamlet question which is being posed on the dividing line of the second, non-linear modernity.

In contrast, a double construction of unawareness characterizes linear modernization. First, *other* forms of knowledge are blocked out and rejected, and, second, we deny our own *inability* to know. This applies not just to experts, but to activist movements as well. The former stand with their backs to the future and operate in the false self-assurance that comes from having denied their unawareness. The latter dogmatize their (un)awareness for purposes of political intervention. It is precisely this admitted uncertainty which opens the context of action for industrial modernity. Both groups would have to look at themselves from the outside, so to speak, in order to understand and shape reflexive modernity's horizon of uncertainty in constructive political terms.

Both issues of the second modernity – the deliberate acknowledgement of outside perspectives and rationalities, on the one hand, and the explicit working out and processing of unawareness, on the other – have not really become an issue so far.

We must agree with Scott Lash (1994) that aesthetic reflexivity is also a key issue of reflexive modernization, and one which I have woefully neglected. His inquiry into the conditions and possibilities of 'reflexive community' is equally deserving of attention and urgent action. This inquiry is, after all, situated at the intersection of debates in social philosophy, ethics, sociology and politics regarding the bases for cohesion in self-endangering modernity. But Scott Lash must face the question as to how he distinguishes between communities that are 'reflexive', in his sense, and those which are *countermodern*.[4]

To pick out only one example standing for many: particularly in the United States, it is more and more common – and thoroughly reflexive – for only self-representation to be asserted and accepted as a legitimate form for representing a group.[5] Any representation by others (for instance, the representation of blacks by whites, women by men or gays by straights) is considered to be 'racist' and 'sexist' by definition. It is easy to understand how this negation of the universalistic exchange of viewpoints and perspectives comes about, namely as a defence against repression and as a reaction to pluralization and individualization. It is completely obvious to me that Scott Lash does *not* mean this type of, one could almost say, 'post-modern racism'. But what remains to be clarified is how this can be spelled out in the context of his inquiry into the intra-modern sources of commitment in individualized lifeworlds.

The crucial issue of reflexive modernization, however, is this: how do 'we' (experts, social movements, ordinary people, politicians, not to forget sociologists) deal with our unawareness (or inability to know)? How do we *decide* in and between manufactured uncertainties?

7

Risk Society Revisited:
Theory, Politics, Critiques and Research Programmes

Living in an age of constructivism, the attempt to draw a line between modernity (or, as I would prefer to say, first industrial modernity) and world risk society (or second reflexive modernity) seems to be naïve or even contradictory. Within a constructivist framework, no one is able to define or declare what really 'is' or 'is not'. Yet, this does not square with my experience. I cannot understand how anyone can make use of the frameworks of reference developed in the eighteenth and nineteenth centuries in order to understand the transformation into the post-traditional cosmopolitan world we live in today. Max Weber's 'iron cage' – in which he thought humanity was condemned to live for the foreseeable future – is to me a prison *of categories and basic assumptions* of classical sociology (and the cultural, social and political sciences). We have to free ourselves from these categories in order to find out about the unknown post-Cold-War world. Don't get me wrong. I do not consider most of the philosophies and theories (sociologies) of so-called 'postmodernity' to fare any better since they cannot answer very basic questions about how and in what ways everyday lives and professional fields are being transformed. Conventional social sciences, I therefore want to argue, even if they are conducting highly sophisticated theoretical and empirical research programmes, are caught up in a circular argument. By using the old categories (like class, family, gender roles, industry, technology, science, nation-state, and so on), they take for granted what they actually try to demonstrate: that we still live, act and die in the normal world of nation-state modernity.

Some critiques of my book *Risk Society* (Beck, 1992) accuse me of being a 'realist'. But this is the result of a misinterpretation of my arguments. What strikes me about them is the inability of constructivist thinking to criticize and renew the frameworks of modern and post-modern sociology. Let me explain. I consider realism and constructivism to be neither an either–or option nor a mere matter of belief. We should not have to swear allegiance to any particular view or theoretical perspective. The decision whether to take a realist or a constructivist approach is for me a rather *pragmatic* one, a matter of choosing the appropriate means for a desired goal. If I have to be a realist (for the moment) in order to open up the social sciences for the new and contradictory experiences of the global age of global risks, then I have no qualms about adopting the guise and language of a ('reflexive') 'realist'. If constructivism makes a (positive) problem shift possible and if it allows us to raise important questions that realists do not ask, then I am content (for that moment at least) to be a constructivist. Having grown up with the constructivist philosophies of thinkers such as Kant, Fichte and Hegel, I find it insufficient today, especially in the area of sociology of risk, to restrict my analysis to one perspective or conceptual dogma only: I can be both a realist and constructivist, using realism *and* constructivism as far as those meta-narratives are useful for the purpose of understanding the complex and ambivalent 'nature' of risk in the world risk society we live in.[1]

Let us consider for a moment the current state of European intellectual thought. In 1989 a whole world order broke down. What an opportunity for venturing into uncharted terrain, exploring new intellectual horizons. This opportunity has not been seized. Instead the vast majority of theorists are still holding on to the same old concepts. Reversal rather than revision seems to be the order of the day: radical socialism, Giddens (1994b) suggests, has become conservative, and conservatism has become radical. Little has changed: the script of modernity is yet be rewritten, redefined, reinvented. This is what the theory of world risk society is all about.

At this point, I should emphasize that I do not believe that 'everything goes'. I feel strongly that we have to be imaginative yet disciplined if we are to break out of the iron cage of conventional and orthodox social science and politics. We need a new sociological imagination which is sensitive to the concrete paradoxes and challenges of reflexive modernity and which at the same time is thoughtful and strong enough to open up the walls of abstraction in which the academic routines are captured.

In this chapter I would like to accomplish three main tasks. First, once again, I wish briefly to reiterate my argument of why the notion of risk society can be introduced as a new conception of a 'non-industrial' society, to ask 'what are "risks"?', and to inquire about the reality status of risks using 'constructivism' and 'realism' as a matter of pragmatic choice. Second, I want to address the views of some of my critics and in the process offer the reader a discussion of what I see as the theoretical issues which now limit the development of my ideas on global risk. Finally, I will highlight some of the theoretical and political avenues I would like to see explored in the near future and identify some issues for comparative study at a European level and beyond.

Elements of a Theory of Risk Society

In the first part of this chapter I would like to gather up into a coherent whole arguments that are dispersed throughout my work on the sociological concept of risk and risk society. In so doing, I also hope to illustrate, indirectly, what I have learned from the existing criticisms of my earlier work.[2] I have structured these issues into eight major points.

1   Risks do not refer to damages incurred. They are not the same as destruction. If they were, all insurance companies would be made bankrupt. However, risks do threaten destruction. The discourse of risk begins where our trust in our security ends and ceases to be relevant when the potential catastrophe occurs. The concept of risk thus characterizes a peculiar, intermediate state between security and destruction, where the *perception* of threatening risks determines thought and action. As a result, I find it difficult to distinguish any great difference between Scott Lash's (1999) conception of 'risk culture' and my concept of 'risk society'. I do, however, find Lash's discussion valuable in that he has highlighted the radicalization of the cultural framework of risk by cultural theory and cultural studies. Yet, it seems to me that the 'relation of definition' (Marx) in the age of culturally defined risks still makes the notion of 'risk society' necessary (see discussion below). So ultimately: *it is cultural perception and definition that constitute risk*. 'Risk' and the '(public) definition of risk' are one and the same.

This peculiar reality status of 'no-longer-but-not-yet' – no longer trust/security, not yet destruction/disaster – is what the concept of risk expresses and what makes it a public frame of reference. The sociology of risk is a science of potentialities and judgements about probabilities – what Max Weber (1991) called '*Möglichkeitsurteile*'. So risks 'are' a type of *virtual reality*, real virtuality. Risks are only a small step away from what Joost van Loon (1998) calls 'virtual risks in an age of cybernetic reproduction', and I wholeheartedly agree with his assessment when he writes: 'Only by thinking of risk in terms of reality, or better, a *becoming-real* (a virtuality) can social materialization be understood. Only by thinking risk in terms of a construction can we understand its indefinable "essence". Risks cannot be understood outside their materialisation in particular mediations, be they scientific, political, economic or popular' (van Loon, 1999). I believe this is the way in which the notions of constructivism and realism, although seemingly incompatible, can complement each other. The electronic media involved in the BSE crisis connect science, politics and popular consumer culture. In so doing, they render the invisibility of risk, for example the mutating prions of BSE, visible. They bring them into being through digitalized imagery. We, the consumers of such images, have no means of testing the adequacy of such representations, nor do we have to. Their origin is fabricated, manufactured in laboratories under microscopes and further enhanced by computer simulations. Their sources are truly cybertechnological, connecting chemistry, molecular biology and medicine with computer graphics and television broadcasts. Rendering the prion visible as a computer simulation has allowed news broadcasts to begin to interpret the uninterpretable (for instance, to tell us what BSE and CJD actually 'are') and to explain the unexplainable (how a normal prion – whatever that might be – could become 'pathological'). The mere possibility that the pathogenesis might be linked to the banal practice of consuming beef further illustrates the force of Benjamin's (1968) claim that in an age of mechanical reproduction, all aesthetic experiences may become politicized.

The 'becoming-real' of the risk of BSE is directly related to its mediation. Now that 'we' know that there 'are' possible risks, 'we' face a responsibility. This responsibility takes the form of a *decision* whether to eat beef and other bovine products or not. Therefore, CJD is no longer exclusively a hazard, as a strain has been identified that can be linked to BSE. Although the calculability of this risk has remained problematic, as a virtuality, it operates in exactly the same way. The sudden accessibility of the 'knowledge' regarding the possible relationship between BSE and CJD has thus transformed a hazard into a risk:

we now have a decision to make with consequences for ourselves, our loved ones and possibly the rest of our world (van Loon, 1999).[3]

The sociology of risk reconstructs a techno-social event of its (im)materiality. Where risks are believed to be real, the foundations of business, politics, science and everyday life are in flux. Accordingly, the concept of risk, when considered scientifically (risk = accident × probability), takes the form of the calculus of probability, which we know can never rule out the worst case (see Prior, 1999). This becomes important in view of the socially very relevant distinction between risk *decision-makers* and those who have to deal with the consequences of the decisions of *others*. In this respect, Niklas Luhmann's (1993) differentiation between risk and danger pointed to the sociologically crucial problem of the acceptance of risk decisions. However, this leaves the central question unanswered: What does the calculus of probability and the social difference between decision-makers (risks) and the affected parties, encompassing ever larger social groups (dangers), mean for dealing with disasters? Who has the legitimate right to make decisions in such cases? Or, more generally, how will decisions on hazardous technologies become capable of legitimation in the future?

Closely associated with this issue is the question of what the 'objectivity' and 'subjectivity' of risks would mean in the first place in the context of 'virtual risk realities'. What is 'rational' and what is 'irrational'? This is certainly one point where a sociology of risk and risk society differs fundamentally from technical and scientific risk assessment (more on this later).

2   The concept of risk reverses the relationship of past, present and future. The past loses its power to determine the present. Its place as the cause of present-day experience and action is taken by the future, that is to say, something non-existent, constructed and fictitious. We are discussing and arguing about something which is *not* the case, but *could* happen if we continue to steer the same course as we have been.

Believed risks are the whip used to keep the present day moving along at a gallop. The more threatening the shadows that fall on the present day from a terrible future looming in the distance, the more compelling the shock that can be provoked by dramatizing risk today. This can be demonstrated not only with the discourse on the environmental crisis, but also, and perhaps even more emphatically, with the example of the discourse on globalization. For instance, the globalization of paid labour does not (as yet) exist to a large degree; it threatens or, more accurately, transnational management threatens us with it. The exchange of (expensive) labour in Europe for (cheap) labour in India or Korea, after all, amounts to at most 10 per cent (in Germany) and primarily affects the lower wage and skilled groups (Kommission für Zukunftsfragen, 1997: ch. 7). The brilliantly staged *risk* of globalization, however, has already become an instrument for reopening the issue of power in society. By invoking the horrors of globalization, everything can be called into question: trade unions, of course, but also the welfare state, maxims of national policy and, it goes without saying, welfare assistance. Moreover, all of this is done with an expression of regret that it is – unfortunately – necessary to terminate Christian compassion for the sake of Christian compassion.

Established risk definitions are thus a magic wand with which a stagnant society can terrify itself and thereby activate its political centres and become politicized from within. The public (mass media) dramatization of risk is in this sense an antidote to current narrow-minded 'more-of-the-same' attitudes. A society that conceives of itself as a risk society is, to use a Catholic metaphor, in the position of the sinner who confesses his or her sins in order to be able to contemplate the possibility and desirability of a 'better' life in harmony with nature and the world's conscience. However, few sinners actually want to repent and instigate a change. Most prefer for nothing to happen whilst complaining about that very fact, because then everything is possible. Profession of sins and the identification with the risk society allow us simultaneously to enjoy both the bad good life and the threats to it.

3   Are risks factual statements? Are risks value statements? Risk statements are neither only factual nor only value statements. Instead, they are either both at the same time or something in between, a 'mathematicized morality' as it were. As mathematical calculations (probability computations or accident scenarios), risks are related directly and indirectly to cultural definitions and standards of a tolerable or intolerable life. So in a risk society the question we must ask ourselves is: how do we want to live? This means, among other things, that risk statements are by nature statements that can be deciphered only in an interdisciplinary (competitive) relationship, because they assume in equal measure insight into technical know-how and familiarity with cultural perceptions and norms.

What, then, is the source of the peculiarity in our political dynamics that allows risk statements to develop as a hybrid of evaluations in the intermediate realm of real virtuality and non-existent future which none the less activates present action? This political explosiveness derives, primarily, from two sources: the first one relates to the cultural importance of the universal value of survival. Thus Thomas Hobbes, the conservative theorist of the state and society, recognized as a citizen's right the right to resist where the state threatens the life or survival of its citizens (characteristically enough, he uses phrases such as 'poisoned air and poisoned foodstuffs' which seem to anticipate ecological issues in this regard). The second source is tied to the attribution of the dangers to the producers and guarantors of the social order (business, politics, law, science), that is, to the suspicion that those who endanger the public well-being and those charged to protect it may well be identical.

4   In their (difficult-to-localize) early stage, risks and risk perception are 'unintended consequences' of the *logic of control* which dominates modernity. Politically and sociologically, modernity is a project of social and technological control by the nation-state. Above all others, it was Talcott Parsons who conceptualized modern society as an enterprise for constructing order and control. In this way, consequences – risks – are generated that call this very assertion of control by the nation-state into question, not only because of the globality of the risks (climatic disasters or the ozone hole) but also through the inherent indeterminacies and uncertainties of risk diagnosis. It is interesting to note that Max Weber (1968) does indeed discuss the concept of 'unintended consequences' in a crucial context, and not least of all because that concept remains related in structure to the dominance of instrumental rationality. However, Weber does *not* recognize or discuss the concept of 'risk', one of whose peculiarities is to have lost precisely this relationship between intention and outcome, instrumental rationality and control.

The construction of security and control of the type that dominated (social) thought and (political) action in the first stage of modernity is becoming fictitious in global risk society. The more we attempt to 'colonize' the future with the aid of the category of risk, the more it slips out of our control. It is no longer possible to externalize risks in the world risk society. That is what makes the issue of risk so 'political' (in a subversive meaning). In this paradox lies an essential basis for an important distinction between two stages or forms of the concept of risk (which, I feel, should answer some of the questions Scott Lash (1999) raises with his concept of 'determinate judgement' in opposition to 'reflexive judgement'). In the first stage of modernity (essentially the period from the beginning of industrial modernity in the seventeenth and eighteenth centuries to the early twentieth century), risk essentially signifies a way of calculating unpredictable consequences (industrial decisions). As François Ewald (1986) argues, the calculus of risk develops forms and methods for making the *unpredictable predictable*. This is what Lash means by 'determinant judgement'. The corresponding repertoire of methods includes statistical representations, accident probabilities and scenarios, actuarial calculations, as well as standards and organizations for anticipatory care. This meaning of the concept of risk refers to a world in which most things, including external nature and the ways of life as determined and coordinated by tradition, continue to be considered preordained (fate).

To the extent that nature becomes industrialized and traditions become optional, new types of uncertainties arise which Anthony Giddens and I call *'manufactured uncertainties'*. These types of internal risks and dangers presume a threefold participation of scientific experts, in the roles of producers, analysts and profiteers from risk definitions. Under these conditions, many attempts to confine and control risks turn into a broadening of the uncertainties and dangers.

5   So the contemporary concept of risk associated with risk society and manufactured uncertainty refers to a peculiar *synthesis of knowledge and unawareness*. To be precise, two meanings, namely risk assessment based on empirical knowledge (automobile accidents, for instance), on the one hand, and making decisions and acting on risk in indefinite uncertainty, that is, indeterminacy, on the other, are being conflated here. In this sense the concept of 'manufactured uncertainties' has a double reference. First, more and better knowledge, which most people assess in unreservedly positive terms, is becoming the source of new risks. Because we know more and more about brain function, we now know that a person who is 'brain-dead' may very well be alive in some other sense (because the heart is still beating, for instance). By opening more and more new spheres of action, science creates new types of risks as well. The current examples are again the advances in human genetics, which make it possible to blur the boundary between ill people and healthy people because more and more congenital diseases can be diagnosed, even those affecting people who consider themselves healthy based on their own experience (Beck-Gernsheim, 1993). Second, however, the opposite is also true: risks come from and consist of unawareness (non-knowledge). What are we to understand by 'unawareness'? In the unbroken security of a lifeworld, unawareness is often understood as being *not yet* aware or no longer aware, that is to say, as *potential* knowledge. The problems of unawareness are understood here from its opposite, from knowledge and the (unspoken) certainty in which the lifeworld resides.

In contrast to that, the inability to know is becoming ever more important in this second phase of modernity. I am not referring here to the expression of selective viewpoints, momentary forgetting or underdeveloped expertise, but, on the contrary, to highly developed expert rationality. Thus, for instance, the calculus of probability can never rule out a given event, or risk specialists may call each other's detailed results into question because they quite sensibly start from different assumptions. (See chapter 6 above.)

This is how a society based on knowledge, information and risk opens up a threatening sphere of possibilities. Everything falls under an imperative of avoidance. Everyday life thus becomes an involuntary lottery of misfortune. The probability of a 'winner' here is probably no higher than in the weekly lottery, but it has become almost impossible *not* to take part in this raffle of evils where the 'winner' gets sick and may even die. Politicians such as the British ex-Prime Minister John Major, who complained about the 'hysteria' of consumers in reaction to the debate over BSE in Europe and the resulting collapse in the beef market, yet encouraged people to take part in the national lottery, render a particular service to the credibility of politics. At the extreme end of the spectrum two strategies for dealing with 'manufactured uncertainties' are conceivable: if one embraces the view of John Major that only certain knowledge can compel us to act, then one must accept that the denial of risks causes them to grow immeasurably and uncontrollably. There is no better humus for risks than denying them. If one selects the opposite strategy and makes presumed (lack of) knowledge the foundation of action against risks, then this opens the flood-gates of fear and everything becomes risky.

Risks only suggest what should *not* be done, not what *should* be done. To the extent that risks become the all-embracing background for perceiving the world, the alarm they provoke creates an atmosphere of powerlessness and paralysis. Doing nothing and demanding too much both transform the world into a series of indomitable risks. This could be called the *risk trap*, which is what the world can turn into in the perceptual form of risk. There is no prescription for how to act in the risk trap, but there are very antithetical cultural reactions (within and outside Europe). Within different boundaries and times, indifference and alarmed agitation often alternate abruptly and radically.

One thing is clear: how one acts in this situation is no longer something that can be decided by experts. Risks pointed out (or obscured) by experts at the same time disarm these experts, because they force everyone to decide for themselves: what is still tolerable and what no longer? They require a decision about whether or not and when and where to protest, even if this only takes the form of an organized, intercultural consumer boycott. These issues raise questions about the authority of the public, cultural definitions, the citizenry, parliaments, politicians, ethics and self-organization.

6   Even the antithesis of globality and locality is short-circuited by risks. The new types of risks are simultaneously local and global, or 'glocal' (Robertson, 1992). Thus it was the fundamental experience that environmental dangers 'know no boundaries', that they are universalized by the air, the wind, the water and food chains, which justified the global environmental movement everywhere and brought up gobal risks for discussion.

This 'time-space distantiation' (Harvey, 1989) of the hazards of choices between local and global risks confirms the diagnosis of the global risk society. The global threats have led to a world in which the foundations of the established risk logic are undermined and invalidated, in which there are only difficult-to-control dangers instead of calculable risks. The new dangers destroy the pillars of the conventional calculus of security: damages can scarcely still be attributed to definite perpetrators, so that the polluter-pays principle loses acuity; damages can no longer be compensated financially – it makes no sense to insure oneself against the worst-case ramifications of the global spiral of threat. Accordingly, there are no plans for follow-up care in case the worst case should occur. In the world of risk society the logic of control collapses from within. So, risk society is a (latent) *political* society.

World risk society theory does not plead for or encourage (as some assume) a return to a logic of control in an age of risk and manufactured uncertainties – that was the solution of the first and simple modernity. On the contrary, in the world risk society the logic of control is questioned fundamentally and not only from a sociological point of view but by ongoing modernization itself. Here is one of the reasons why risk societies can become *self-critical* societies. Different agencies and actors – for example managers of chemical industries and insurance experts – contradict each other. Technicians argue that: 'There is no risk', whilst the insurers refuse insurance because risks are too high. A similar debate is currently taking place within the realm of genetically engineered food.

In order to speak of the world risk *society,* it is also necessary for the global hazards to begin to shape *actions* and facilitate the creation of *international institutions.* That there are indeed such impulses can be seen from the fact that the majority of the international environmental agreements were concluded during the past two decades. This border-transcending dynamism of the new risks does not only apply internationally, but also exists inside nation-states, implying that system boundaries no longer function properly either. This can be seen from the fact that risks are a kind of 'involuntary, negative currency'. No one wants to accept them or admit them, but they are present and active everywhere, resistant to all attempts to repress them. A characteristic of the global risk society is a metamorphosis of danger which is difficult to delineate or monitor: markets collapse and there is shortage in the midst of surplus. Medical treatments fail. Constructs of economic rationality wobble. Governments are forced to resign. The taken-for-granted rules of everyday life are turned upside-down. Almost everyone is defenceless against the threats of nature as re-created by industry. Dangers are integral to normal consumption habits. And yet they are and remain essentially knowledge-dependent and tied to cultural perception, whether they are manifested as alarm, tolerance or cynicism.

7   Let us now return to the realism–constructivism debate and concentrate on the distinction between *knowledge* and *impact*, as suggested by Barbara Adam (1998) in her latest book.[4] This distinction is important for understanding the second degree of 'uncertain global risks' faced by the world risk society, because the point of impact is not obviously tied to the point of origin. At the same time the transmissions and movements of hazards are often latent and immanent, that is, invisible and untrackable to everyday perceptions. This social invisibility means that, unlike many other political issues, risks must clearly be brought to consciousness; only then can it be said that they constitute an actual threat, and this includes cultural values and symbols ('the dying woods' or '*Le Waldsterben*') as well as scientific arguments. At the same time we know, at least in principle, that the *impacts* of risk grow precisely *because* nobody knows or wants to know about them. A case in point is the environmental devastation of Eastern Europe under the communist regime.

So – once again – risks are at the same time 'real' *and* constituted by social perception and construction. Their reality springs from '*impacts*' that are rooted in the ongoing industrial and scientific production and research routines. Knowledge about the risks, in contrast, is tied to the history and symbols of one's culture (the understanding of nature, for example) and the social fabric of knowledge. This is one of the reasons why the same risk is perceived and handled politically so differently throughout Europe and other parts of the globe. Moreover, there are interesting relations between those two dimensions of risk. Thus, the enormous spatial disjuncture between knowledge and impact: perception is always and necessarily contextual and locally constituted. This local contextuality is only extendible in the imagination and with the aid of such technologies as television, computers and the mass media. The impact of the industrial way of life, in contrast, is spatially and temporarily open and tends to extend across the globe, on the one hand, and to the stratosphere and the universe, on the other. Radiation, synthetic chemicals and genetically engineered organisms are pertinent cases in point.

Many other examples can be used to highlight the unbridgeable temporal gap between actions and their impacts. Contemporary environmental hazards such as ozone depletion, damage to the reproductive and immune system of species or BSE have not arisen as symptoms until years after they began their impact as invisible effects of specific actions. Thus, for example, some of the Britons who died from the new variant of CJD had been vegetarians for the last ten years or so, which suggests a latent impact-period of at least that time. Other hazards externalize as symptoms only after they have combined to form a critical mass. That is to say, the impact is temporarily open-ended and becomes perceivable as symptomatic (thus knowable) only after it materializes into a visible 'cultural' phenomenon at some time and some place. This gap between source and perceivable symptom is one of the main conflict matters of social and expert construction: pesticides in foods, radiation and chemical damage to the unborn, and global warming are just a few illustrations of this temporal disjuncture.

This in turn links back to an issue I raised before and to the recognition that *the less risks are publicly recognized, the more risks are produced* (not only because of high industrialization but because of functional differentiation too). This might be an interesting 'law' of the risk society with particular relevance to the insurance business. The neglect of risk, in the first instance, would seem to serve the interests of the insurer, not those of the potential victims. Basic to the risk society is the self-transformation of risk from technical to economic risks, market risk, health risk, political risk, and so on. Important to the insurer is the *time gap* between the insurance contract and the emergence of the risk through nature and culture. So the insurer (or the insurer of the insurer) has to pay for it when this time bomb explodes. The problems that befell Lloyd's of London illustrate this case nicely. Several elements of this case are worthy of additional attention:

- Insurers are not in the same boat as manufacturers. Instead, insurers find themselves in a 'natural coalition' with the potential victims. This means that in order to act in their business' interest, they have to trust socio-scientific risk definitions, even rumours, and they have to find out about them during early stages of technological and industrial development.
- The neglect of risk information facilitates the growth and spread of risks. Asbestos is a case in point. During the Second World War the use of this material was expanding fast because it was seen as effective, durable and, above all, cheap, whilst the attendant risks were ignored.
- Commercial success and freedom from litigation result in complacency. Even worse, manufacturers turn their back on medical evidence of the link between their products and ill health. Just as the tobacco manufacturers did not – and still do not – want to know the health consequences of smoking, so the asbestos industries preferred to ignore warnings.
- Consequently, risk industries and insurance businesses get captured in the 'time cage' between ignored impact and growing risk, on the one hand, and between risk knowledge and cultural sensitivity, on the other. This is the very normal way in which the manufactured uncertainties of hazards are becoming internalized by industries and are transformed into potential *economic* disasters.

8   Finally, the notion of world risk society is pertinent to a world which can be characterized by the *loss of clear distinction between nature and culture*. Today if we talk about nature we talk about culture, and if we talk about culture we talk about nature. Our conception of a separation of worlds into nature and culture, which is intimately bound to modernist thought, fails to recognize that we are building, acting and living in a constructed artificial world of civilization whose characteristics are beyond these distinctions, which still dominate our thinking. The loss of boundaries between these realms is not only brought about by the industrialization of nature and culture but also by the hazards that endanger humans, animals and plants alike. Whether we think of the ozone hole, pollution or food scares, nature is inescapably contaminated by human activity. That is to say, the common danger has a levelling effect that whittles away some of the carefully erected boundaries between classes, nations, humans and the rest of nature, between creators of culture and creatures of instinct, or, to use an earlier distinction, between beings with and those without a soul (Adam, 1998: 24). Faced with the threat

people have the experience that they breathe like plants, and live *from* water as the fish live *in* water. The toxic threat makes them sense that they participate with their bodies in things – 'a metabolic process with consciousness and morality' – and consequently that they can be eroded like the stones and the trees in the acid rain (Schütz, 1984, quoted in Beck, 1992: 74).

That we live in a *hybrid* world which transcends our dichotic framework of thought has convincingly been argued by Bruno Latour (1995). I totally agree with him. Both of us see that the hybrid world we live in and constantly produce is at the same time a matter of cultural perception, moral judgement, politics and technology, which have been constructed in actor-networks and have been made hard facts by 'black boxing'. Yet the notion of a 'hybrid' world is necessary but insufficient to understand the new. 'Hybrid' is more of a negative than a positive concept. It somehow says what it is not – *not* nature and *not* society and so on – but it does not really say what it is. I want to suggest that we have to overcome the 'nots', 'beyonds' and 'posts' which dominate our thinking. But if you ask what begins where the ends end, my answer is: the notion of risk and risk society. So risks are *man-made hybrids*. They include and combine politics, ethics, mathematics, mass media, technologies, cultural definitions and perception; and – most important of all – you cannot separate these aspects and realities, if you want to understand the cultural and political dynamics of the world risk society. So 'risk' is not only a notion which is used in a central matter by very different disciplines, it is the way the 'hybrid society' watches, describes, values, criticizes its own hybridity.

This complex 'and', which resists thinking in either–or categories, is what constitutes the cultural and political dynamism of global risk society and makes it so difficult to comprehend (for more detail on this, see Beck, 1999a). A society that perceives itself as a risk society becomes *reflexive*, that is to say, the foundations of its activity and its objectives become the object of public scientific and political controversies. One could say that there is a naïvely realistic misapprehension in the talk of risk society and this can culminate in a type of 'neo-Spenglerism'. Equally possible and rational, however, is a reflexive understanding of risks, as developed here in the eight theses above. The concept of risk and the concept of world risk society are concepts of ambivalence, meaning that they destroy distinctions and reconnect antitheses. Accordingly, as stated above, the concept of (world) risk (society) means:

1   neither destruction nor trust/security but real virtuality;
2   a threatening future, (still) contrary to fact, becomes the parameter of influence for current action;
3   both a factual and a value statement, it combines in mathematicized morality;
4   control and lack of control as expressed in manufactured uncertainty;
5   knowledge or unawareness realized in conflicts of (re)cognition;
6   simultaneously global and local reconstituted as the 'glocality' of risks;
7   the distinction between knowledge, latent impact and symptomatic consequences;
8   a man-made hybrid world which has lost the dualism between nature and culture.

Many social theories (including those of Michel Foucault and those of the Frankfurt School of Max Horkheimer and Theodor Adorno) paint modern society as a technocratic prison of bureaucratic institutions and expert knowledge in which people are mere wheels in the giant machine of technocratic and bureaucratic rationality. The picture of modernity drawn by the theory of world risk society contrasts sharply with these images. After all, one of the most important characteristics of the theory of risk society, so far scarcely understood in science or politics, is to open up – at least intellectually – the seemingly rigid circumstances and to set them in motion. Unlike most theories of modern societies, the theory of risk society develops an image that makes the circumstances of modernity contingent, ambivalent and (involuntarily) susceptible to political rearrangement.

Due to this often unseen and undesired self-discreditation ('reflexive modernization') which is provoked everywhere by the discourse of risk, something ultimately happens which sociologists loyal to Max Weber would consider impossible: *institutions begin to change.* As we know, Max Weber's diagnosis is that modernity transforms into an iron cage in which people must sacrifice to the altars of rationality like the fellahim of ancient Egypt. The theory of world risk society elaborates the antithesis: *the cage of modernity opens up* (see also Beck et al., 1994, and chapter 2 above). So there is a utopia built into risk society and risk society theory – the utopia of a *responsible* modernity, the utopia of *another* modernity, *many* modernities to be invented and experienced in different cultures and parts of the globe (see below). Anyone who is simply focused on the risk potential of the industrial society fails to understand that risks are a matter not just of unintended consequences – the 'toxin of the week' – but also of the unintended consequences of unintended consequences *in* the institutions. Using the case of BSE, one could say that it is not just cows, but also governing parties, agencies, markets for meat and consumers who are affected and thus implicated in the madness.

Organized Irresponsibility and the Power Game of Risk Definitions

In the second part of this chapter I want to engage with some of the critiques formulated in Adam et al. (1999) and elsewhere. First, that there is a Germanocentrism, even 'Bavariancentrism' (Alan Scott), to my vision that risk society is identical with the '*Le Waldsterben*-society'. If this were the case, would it mean that Great Britain, even after BSE, is *not* part of world risk society?

Maybe there is a German background to risk society theory. Being 'green' is undoubtedly part of the German national identity. Testing atomic weapons may be part of the French national identity – I don't know. And the cultural significance of 'British (Sunday lunch) beef' may be an important backdrop to the BSE crisis. Yet the conflicts that arise from these national issues cannot be confined within national boundaries. People, expert groups, cultures, nations, are getting involved involuntarily at every level of social organization: a European public is born unintentionally and involuntarily from the conflict over British beef.

In all my books I try to demonstrate that the return to the theoretical and political philosophy of industrial modernity in the age of global risk is doomed to failure. Those orthodox theories and politics remain tied to notions of progress and valorization of technological change. As such, they perpetuate the belief that the environmental hazards we face today can still be captured by nineteenth-century, scientific models of risk assessment and industrial assumptions about danger and safety. Simultaneously, they maintain the illusion that the disintegrating institutions of industrial modernity – nuclear families, stable labour markets, segregated gender roles, social classes, nation-state – can be shored up and buttressed against the waves of reflexive modernization sweeping across the West. This attempt to apply nineteenth-century ideas to the late twentieth century is the pervasive *category mistake* of social theory, social sciences and politics I am addressing in my writings. In risk society theory 'environmental' problems are no longer conceived as external problems. Instead they are theorized at the centre of institutions. This immanence has been recognized by the legal science in Germany (with a debate on manufactured risks and uncertainties in public law), but *not* as yet clearly by the sociology of risk in either Great Britain or Germany.

At this point it is pertinent briefly to outline some of the core notions of the hazards of risk society: *organized irresponsibility, relations of definition, social explosiveness of hazards*, and to summarize the arguments of the *welfare state*. To me these concepts combine arguments why it is necessary not only to talk in terms of 'risk *culture*' (Scott Lash, 1999), which lacks the institutional dimension of risk and power, but also to theorize risk society with its cultural focus on the institutional base of contemporary globalized industrial society.

The concept of 'organized irresponsibility' helps to explain how and why the institutions of modern society must unavoidably acknowledge the reality of catastrophe while simultaneously denying its existence, hiding its origins and precluding compensation or control. To put it in another way, risk societies are characterized by the paradox of more and more environmental degradation – perceived and possible – coupled with an expansion of environmental law and regulation. Yet at the same time, no individual or institution seems to be held specifically accountable for anything. How can this be? To me the key to explaining this state of affairs is the mismatch that exists in the risk society between the character of hazards or manufactured uncertainties produced by late industrialism and the prevalent *relations of definition* which date in their construction and content from an earlier and qualitatively different epoch.

In risk society we must conceive of *relations of definition* analogous to Karl Marx's *relations of production*. Risk society's relations of definition include the specific rules, institutions and capacities that structure the identification and assessment of risk in a specific cultural context. They are the legal, epistemological and cultural power-matrix in which risk politics is conducted. The relations of definition I focus on can be identified with reference to four clusters of questions (see Beck, 1996):

1   Who is to define and determine the harmfulness of products, the danger, the risks? Where does the responsibility lie – with those who generate the risks, those who benefit from them, those who are potentially affected by them or with public agencies?

2 What kind of knowledge or non-knowledge about the causes, dimensions, actors, and so on, is involved? To whom have evidence and 'proof' to be submitted?
3 What is to count as sufficient proof in a world where knowledge about environmental risks is necessarily contested and probabilistic?
4 Who is to decide on compensation for the afflicted, and what constitute appropriate forms of future damage limitation control and regulation?

In relation to each of these questions, risk societies are currently trapped in a vocabulary that is singularly inappropriate not only for modern catastrophes, but also for the challenges constituted by manufactured insecurities. Consequently we face the paradox that at the very time when threats and hazards are seen to become more dangerous and more obvious, they become increasingly inaccessible to attempts to establish proof, attributions and compensation by scientific legal and political means.

Of course, there is the question about the identity of the political subject of risk society. Despite my extensive discussions on this subject, however, my answer to this question eludes critics as long as they read my texts from within the dualistic frames of Enlightenment thought: to argue that nobody and everybody is the subject. So it should not surprise us that this answer gets lost. But there is more to it, and my argument here is close to Bruno Latour's theory of quasi-objects. In my work, hazards are quasi-subjects, whose acting-active quality is produced by risk societies' institutional contradictions. Moreover, risk society is *not* about a 'dystopian warning'. I use the metaphor of the *social explosiveness of hazard* to explain the politicizing effects of risk (definition) conflicts. I explore the ways in which the virtuality, the 'becoming real' (van Loon, 1999) of large-scale hazards, risks and manufactured uncertainties set off a dynamic of cultural and political change that undermines state bureaucracies, challenges the dominance of science, and redraws the boundaries and battle-lines of contemporary politics. So hazards, understood as socially constructed and produced 'quasi-subjects', are a powerful, uncontrollable 'actor' that delegitimates and destabilizes state institutions with responsibilities for pollution control, in particular, and public safety, in general.

Hazards themselves sweep away the attempts of institutional elites and experts to control them. The 'risk assessment bureaucracies', of course, have well-worn routines of denial. By utilizing the gap between impact and knowledge, data can be hidden, denied and

distorted. Counter-arguments can be mobilized. Maximum permiss-
ible levels of acceptance can be raised. Human error rather than
system risk can be cast as villain of the piece. However, these are
battles where victories are temporary and defeat is probable or at
least possible because they are fought with nineteenth-century pledges
of security in a world risk society where such promises are hollow
and have lost their purchase. No longer the preserve of scientists and
experts, the nature of hazards is demonstrated everywhere and for
everyone willing and interested to see.

My political description and vision is close to François Ewald's
idea of *safety* and the *welfare state*. Ewald's theory marks a significant shift in the interpretation of the welfare state. While the
majority of social scientists have sought to explain the origins and
constructions of the welfare state in terms of class interests, the main-
tenance of social order or the enhancement of national productivity
and military power, Ewald's argument underlines the provision of
services (health care), the creation of insurance schemes (pensions
and unemployment insurance), and the regulation of the economy
and the environment in terms of the *creation of security*. In relation
to industries and technologies, of course, technical experts play a
central role in answering the question: how safe is safe enough? We
need to appreciate, however, that this model of the welfare state is
most closely correlated with the institutions and procedures of contin-
ental Western Europe and much less with either Anglo-American
capitalism or the social-democratic states of Scandinavia.

Outlook: Opportunities of Risk

What follows from this for the future of sociology of risk and risk
society? In this final section of the chapter I will offer a discussion of
two possible implications.

First, as I said earlier, I admire the work of Bruno Latour, but with
respect to the global risk society I disagree with his idea that 'We
have never been modern'. Of course, the sun is rising as it has always
done since ancient times. But – and this is a significant proviso – this
similarity is only a surface one. If you take the issue of risk beyond its
cultural definition and explore instead the details of the management
of risks in modern *institutions*, the contemporary paradoxes and
dilemmas come to the fore and it becomes apparent that the global
risk society and its cultural and political contradictions cannot be
understood and explained in terms of pre-modern management of

dangers and threats. This is not to deny, of course, that politicians as well as technical and legal experts could learn from the high priests of previous ages how to handle the demons of socially explosive hazards.

Second, risk society theory is *not* about exploding nuclear submarines; it is *not* one more expression of 'German Angst' at the millennium. On the contrary, I am working on a new and optimistic model for understanding our times. My argument interprets what others see as the development of a postmodern order in terms of a stage of *radicalized* (second phase) modernity, a stage where the dynamics of individualization, globalization and risk undermine the first phase of industrial nation-state modernity and its foundations. Modernity becomes *reflexive*, which means concerned with its unintended consequences, risks and their implications for its foundations. Where most postmodern theorists are critical of grand narratives, general theory and humanity, I remain committed to all of these, but in a new sense. To me the Enlightenment is *not* a historical notion and set of ideas but a process and dynamics where criticism, self-criticism, irony and humanity play a central role. Where for many philosophers and sociologists 'rationality' means 'discourse' and 'cultural relativism', my notion of 'second reflexive modernity' implies that we do not have *enough* reason (*Vernunft*) in a new postmodern meaning to live and act in a Global Age (Albrow) of manufactured uncertainties.

Many theories and theorists do not recognize the *opportunities* of the risk society, the opportunities of the 'bads'. I argue for the opening up to democratic scrutiny of the previously depoliticized realms of decision-making and for the need to recognize the ways in which contemporary debates of this sort are constrained by the epistemological and legal systems within which they are conducted. This, then, is one of the themes I would like to see explored further, preferably on a comparative transnational, transcultural, potential global level (see *Korean Journal of Sociology*, 1998). It would entail that we reconstruct social definitions of risks and risk management in different cultural framings; that we find out about the (negative) power of risk conflicts and definition where people who do not want to communicate with each other are forced together into a 'community' of shared (global) risks; and thus that we clarify the questions of *organized irresponsibility* and *relations of definition* in different cultural-political settings. This, it seems to me, would be a new worthwhile conceptual and political social science.

Notes

Chapter 1   Introduction: The Cosmopolitan Manifesto

1   For a critique of global capitalism in this respect, see Gray (1998); and Beck (1999).
2   See Beck (1992), where an account is given of risk as a biographical dimension, as a consequence of work relations, and so on. For the debate on and a broadening of the concept of risk society, see also Rustin (1994), Beck-Gernsheim (1995), Goldblatt (1996), Lash et al. (1996), Ericson and Haggerty (1997), Jacobs (1997), Dressel and Wynne (1998), Franklin (1998), Giddens (1998), *Korean Journal of Sociology* (1998) and Adam et al. (1999).
3   This was already considered in chapter 6 of my *Risk Society* (1992), first published in German in 1986. If *Freiheit* became vulnerable in the quest of the first modernity for safety, security and certainty, then *Sicherheit* is the principal victim of risk society and its career of individual freedom. With the end of risk-free choices, the world itself is increasingly perceived as a risk. At the same time, a 'protectionist reflex' has become apparent. For in an ever more unsafe or insecure world, withdrawal into the safe haven of territoriality becomes an intense temptation.
4   It would be more precise to speak here of (second-order) 'danger', because the word 'risk' suggests calculable uncertainty, whereas (second-order) danger evokes incalculable uncertainty stemming from the decisions of a civilization. See chapter 7 (endnotes).
5   For a proposed reform of the welfare state, see Giddens (1998a).
6   I thus agree with David Held (1995: 24) when he writes: 'Cosmopolitan democracy involves the development of administrative capacity and

independent political resources at regional and global levels, as a necessary complement to those in local and national politics.'

Chapter 2　World Risk Society as Cosmopolitan Society? Ecological Questions in a Framework of Manufactured Uncertainties

1　See the historical-theoretical account of the basic conceptions of nature and the concept of 'nature after the end of nature' in Böhme (1991); a culture-theory approach to the (perhaps at once universal and subculturally specific) images of nature among environmental activists, industrial managers, and so on, in Schwarz and Thompson (1990); and on the general images of nature in modern society, Hitzler (1991) and van den Daele (1992).

2　This is bringing to an end a long period in which sociology – in strict accordance with its founding division of labour with the natural sciences – could abstract from 'nature' as the other, the environment, the already given. This disregarding of nature fully corresponded to a certain relationship to it. Comte said as much without disguising it. He explicitly wanted the relationship of national conquest to be replaced with one of natural conquest by the rising bourgeois-industrial society, so that the teeth of intra-social conflicts would be drawn. (Right up to the present day this theme has lost none of its significance.) Abstraction from nature thus presupposes domination over nature.

　　In this way, the 'process of consuming nature' – which is how Marx understood the labour and production process – could be driven onward. When people talk today of 'ecological citizenship', arguing that basic rights must be extended to animals, plants, and so on, they are precisely expressing the break-up of this subordination-abstraction relationship into its polar opposite.

3　Margit Eichler has reported a little reading-experiment that she conducted as a sociologist, in order to track the social content of environmental questions. After a whole semester of systematically reading and analysing the *Globe and Mail* and a number of other papers, she noted that they were awash with largely natural-scientific reports of various dangers. Their general picture was of a world deep in a huge ecological crisis. 'I concluded that we, as an insider-community of scientists, wilfully construct barriers to knowledge that appears too terrifying or overwhelming and places too many demands on us to rethink not only our private life but also our professional activity' (Eichler, 1993: 372).

4　It is, moreover, difficult to square the claims of cultural theory to transhistorical context-independence with its interest in contextual precision, relativity and cultural construction. In which context-culture does this almost unthinking universalism originate? It is hard to give an answer without making some reference to Eurocentrism.

5　Anthony Tucker (1996: 12) writes:

The world had much to learn from the meltdown of its most notorious nuclear reactor. Ten years on, poor organization, underfunding and political expediency have combined to hide the real horrors of Chernobyl. But at last the truth is beginning to emerge. . . . The lives and livelihoods of around 10 million people have already been affected by the disaster. Half a million people have been displaced. Predictably, the abandoned villages and forests of the 30-kilometre exclusion zone around Chernobyl have become the wild, sinister no-go haunt of criminal and bandit communities. But in Belarus, in the Russian Federation and in the Ukraine, where weather-determined fallout was greatest, agriculture is corrupted by contamination, there is massive social and industrial dislocation, and humanitarian, health and economic problems are of such immensity and complexity that they are far beyond available resources. These are conditions that are perhaps comparable only to the aftermath of civil war.

6   'In the 1970s local claims were made by ordinary people living near the Sellafield nuclear reprocessing complex, that excess childhood leukemias were occurring in that area. . . . The issue came to the attention of TV researchers, and a national documentary programme was eventually broadcast in 1983.' In the end, however, the excess cancers around Sellafield 'were almost routinely referred to as having been *discovered* by the Black Committee' (Wynne, 1966a: 49).

7   Latour's *We Have Never Been Modern* (1995) is, however, one of the most outstanding and challenging to have appeared for years on the sociology of technology.

8   'Politics is a process of the creation of discourse-coalitions based on a shared definition of reality. We suggested that credibility, acceptability, and trust determine the extent to which this process of world-making is successful. This implies, first of all, that if one seeks to design reflexive institutional arrangements, one should take into consideration the socio-cognitive basis of discourse-coalitions. For instance, the fact that Third World platforms refute the new construct of global environmental problems seems not so much due to a scientific doubt about the importance of global threats. It is more likely that it was the result of the complete lack of trust on their part towards supranational institutions such as the World Bank that were given a central role in the implementation of Agenda 21. . . . Reflexive institutional arrangements can therefore never be based on pre-conceived problem definitions. Indeed, reflexive practices should in large part be oriented towards constructing the social problem' (Hajer, 1996: 280, 287; see also Bonß, 1995).

9   In a review of my *The Reinvention of Politics* (1997; originally published in German in 1993), Wolfgang van den Daele (1995) has also taken issue with this key criterion. He writes:

> It is true that in many cases [the model: the operating authority of a nuclear power station], liability for all the consequences of a technological disaster will exceed the capacity of the private-sector insurance system. However, in individual cover for such accidents or other new threats,

there are no discernible limits to private insurance. Even for someone living next to a nuclear power station or a chemicals plant, life assurance will be offered for sale.

This is an interesting mistake. For in fact the opposite is the case: individuals in the vicinity of nuclear power stations have considerable difficulty in taking out life assurance.

Van den Daele continues: 'If, as a result of climate change, storm damage dramatically increases in our part of the world, the premiums will rise to the level that today applies to regions often ravaged by whirlwinds or earthquakes.' This has now increased so much that whole regions are becoming 'no-insurance' areas, and insurance companies are facing crises everywhere in the world. 'Furthermore,' he writes, 'limits of insurability are not simply the sociological correlate of in-creasing objective risk. They also derive from *change in risk inclusion.*' Obviously! Because:

> The consequences of an oil-tanker disaster exceed the limits of insurabil-ity, once coastal cleaning, seabird deaths and tourism losses can be counted as damage for which the shipping company has liability. The actual effects (apart from liability) are not, however, greater than they used to be when they went down as a disaster to be borne by those affected or by the community at large. Meanwhile, in some states of the USA, mid-wifery risks are 'beyond insurability' because the courts award arbitrarily high compensation in cases involving professional error. Unlimited risk cover for unknown dangers, regardless of blame, would mean unin-surability for many classes of action. That such liability is demanded for the introduction of new technology (in genetic engineering, for example) says more about the degree of political rejection of technology than about its objective risk potential.

This is a distinction that I cannot share; both attitudes are part of what I called above a 'realist–constructivist' view.

Van den Daele draws the following conclusion.

> Limits of insurability are not an unambiguous indicator; it does not dis-tinguish whether the risk has become greater or the risk perception sharper. That may be all the same politically, insofar as both factors produce an awareness of living in a risk-filled world. Sociologically, however, import-ant questions are bound up with this distinction. Why does the virulence of certain risks and uncertainties differ from country to country? Why is Germany visibly advancing along the road to the 'risk society', whereas most atomic power stations in France are turned on and most genetically engineered organisms in the United States are being set loose? What role is played by a country's history and legal system, the porousness of its political decision-making hierarchy, and so on?

I too consider these questions important. They do not constitute objec-tions, however, but are points of view indicating that 'further research is necessary'. Characteristically, van den Daele's whole argument is within the framework of a national risk society; the dynamic of global threats in a world risk society does not figure at all in what he writes.

10   An example of these new negotiation-constraints is the open-ended 'motor-car consensus' reached between industrialists and politicians in the summer of 1995:

> With a wide palette of special measures of their own plus promises of political support, the motor producers Volkswagen, BMW, Mercedes-Benz and Porsche are making sure that Germany remains the production site for cars. In a paper issued jointly with the 'native lands' of Lower Saxony, Bavaria and Baden-Württemberg, they committed themselves to further improvements in production, especially as far as environmental interests are concerned. They also set themselves the goal of stable employment conditions. The condition is the setting of a clear political framework, with no additional tax or social-wage burdens, and no general speed limits for drivers. Three-litre cars should be on the market by the year 2000 at the latest.
>
> (Frankfurter Allgemeine Zeitung, *12 August 1995*)

11   Ernst Ulrich von Weizsäcker has pointed out that there have in the past also been armed conflicts over natural resources, but that today and in the future these will centre on wider and even global goods and challenges:

> For some years now, there have been regular reports in the Argentinian and Chilean press about the Antarctic *ozone hole*, mainly caused by the industrial North, which has become an acute threat to people and animals in the tip of South America. Since the Second Conference on World Climate, held in Geneva in 1990, low-lying island states have established their own diplomatic group (AOSIS) which, fearing the enhanced greenhouse effect, has protested against the possibility of a sudden and uncontrollable rise in the *sea-level*. *Over-fishing of the oceans*, especially by Japanese and Russian vessels, has brought into action not only environmental activists but also many of the countries dependent upon small-scale fishing. And already in the run-up to the Rio 'earth summit' of June 1992, the whole debate over protection of the tropical forests – with ideas such as a boycott of tropical wood – caused sharp diplomatic tension between industrialized countries and tropical countries rich in forest.
>
> No end is in sight to these new-style ecological conflicts. With the growing threat to the world climate, species diversity, ozone protection and water resources (including the oceans), and with the ever-rising population density, those most affected are becoming increasingly on edge. The issues in the new ecological conflicts are thus general environmental goods, and not so much natural resources belonging to the sovereign territory of individual states. International law has long been in difficulty over these general goods. It cannot be excluded that tensions over these ecological disputes will grow to such an extent that a major war – even a Third World War – could be unleashed.
>
> (*Weizsäcker, 1995: 57*)

12   Article by Martin Merz and Christian Wernicke, *Die Zeit*, 25 August 1995: 9ff.

Chapter 3   From Industrial Society to Risk Society

1   Niklas Luhmann (1993) has pointed out the difference between *risk*, the result of decision, and *danger*, relating to those many persons or groups which are affected and afflicted by risks others take (and can avoid). Here Luhmann, the systems theorist, ascribes the decisions exclusively to individuals, who otherwise are never presented as within organizations and bureaucracies in his theory.

2   This occurs in a historical amalgam of nature and society, where even natural catastrophes such as floods, landslides, and so on, which are apparently externally caused, appear to be caused by human beings (see Beck, 1995: ch. 2).

3   This idea was first elaborated in case studies of major accidents by Lagadec (1987), deepened by Perrow (1984) and Ewald (1986); the argument was also developed in the field of German linguistics by Evers and Nowotny (1987). For details, see Lau (1989) and Beck (1995).

4   In this respect the disputes over so-called 'catastrophic medicine' have an exemplary character.

5   Reported in *Der Spiegel*, 46, 1986: 32ff.

6   The debate over the duties and function of law in risk societies has increased accordingly in recent years. See Calliess (1981); Blanke (1986); Ritter (1987); Bruggemeier (1988); and Heinz and Meinberg (1988).

7   Later we will not be concerned only, nor primarily, with issues of a new ethics of civilizational action, but with the fact that the established categories and criteria for institutional action stem from a different world.

8   Until Chernobyl, protection against catastrophes, for example, was planned only within a radius of 29 km around a power plant; foreign accidents were officially excluded (cf. Czada and Drexler, 1988; Gottweis, 1988).

9   The conflicts and crises of first industrial modernity have not ended after all, so that, realistically, overlaps will occur between the social structure and conflict dynamics of industrial and risk society. These are excluded here.

10   'That there are symptoms of such a bloc-formation is seen in the West German nuclear industry following Chernobyl: works councils and employers' representatives jointly defended prevailing West German energy policy against any change of course' (Schumann, 1987). Contrary to the prevailing assumptions, Heine and Mautz, in a corresponding study on 'industrial workers contra environmentalism', reach the conclusion: 'With the trend to professionalization of production work in the chemical industry, chemical workers could in future constitute a growing potential of ecologically vigilant production workers, who are capable of reflecting critically upon the ecological conditions and consequences of their own labour, and represent a supporting force for ecologically motivated political interventions' (Heine and Mautz, 1989: 187).

11   This view is based generally on the theoretical distinction between

simple and reflexive modernization, which has not yet been adequately developed. To put it crudely, simple modernization runs within the framework of categories and principles of industrial society. In the second case, however, we are concerned with a phase of social transformation in which, by dint of its own dynamics, modernization changes its foundations, basic assumptions. Class, stratum, occupation, sex roles, businesses, sectoral structure and in general the presuppositions and the course of 'natural' techno-economic progress are being questioned. The world of classical industrial society is becoming just as much a tradition to be run over and demystified as, in the nineteenth century, industrial modernization ran over and demystified status-based feudal society. Unconsciously, acting against its own plan, modernization is undercutting modernization. In that way, however, restratifications in social structures arise, along with power shifts, new lines of conflict, possibilities and constraints for coalitions. Social movements, the public sphere, ethics, the civil disobedience of individuals and the networks of differential politics get their chances to exert historical influence.

12 The arguments developed in Beck (1995) are often misunderstood as suggested political solutions, whereas they actually aim to stimulate institutional relearning by political means.

13 In figurative terms: making radioactivity itch is a central task of political education in the risk society (cf. Claussen, 1989).

Chapter 4   Risk Society and the Welfare State

1 There is now a consensus on this: see Perrow (1984); Ewald (1986); Evers and Nowotny (1987); Lagadec (1987); Halfmann (1990), as well as the other essays collected in this volume; Prittwitz (1991); Bonß (1991); Brock (1991); Lau (1991); Beck (1992, 1995); Hahn et al. (1992); Japp (1992); and Luhmann (1993).

2 Recently, the insured but increasingly incalculable hazards which have driven many insurance companies to the brink of ruin have been added to what cannot be insured. The international insurance trade is feeling the devastating consequences of the greenhouse effect. This encourages tornadoes, which, for example, in 1992 in Florida alone, caused insurance losses of $20 billion. Nine insurance companies went bankrupt because of the hurricanes in Florida and Hawaii, according to Greenpeace. The result is that insurance companies drop risks. Today, new house owners in Hawaii can no longer get any insurance cover. The same could soon also be true for Florida and the US Gulf Coast, reports *Süddeutsche Zeitung* (3 February 1993: 12).

3 A step in this direction was taken with the switch of the Federal German Environmental Liability Law from liability for damage caused by intentional and negligent acts to absolute liability. Under this law (changed in 1991 following the major fire in a warehouse belonging to Sandoz, the Basle chemical company) companies are liable – without proof of fault – for damage up to a level of DM160 million each for injury to persons

and to property. A *suspicion of cause* is sufficient (para. 6, Environmental Commercial Code): simply, if the 'plant is likely, given the circumstances of the particular case, to cause the injuries arising, then it is presumed that the injury has been caused by this plant'. In other words, the burden of proof is no longer on the injured party, who, as a rule, cannot offer proof, but on the (potential) injurer. Para. 19, appendix 2, requires, for especially high-risk production plants, a 'cover provision', which – under given conditions – can effectively only be provided by an environmental liability insurance. According to an insurance model for environmental risks developed by the liability insurers, the 'legal liability under civil law is insured for injuries to persons and property which have been caused by an "environmental effect" on ground, air or water' (Jörrissen). Uninsured and uninsurable in principle are thereby injuries to the plant itself, and contaminated sites. Here the limit of *economically* incalculable hazards has quite evidently been reached and/or crossed, because the international reinsurance market does not make any provision for these environmental risks either. The result is that 'hundreds of thousands of companies will have to take good care' (cf. *Süddeutsche Zeitung*, 13–14 February 1993: 24).

Chapter 6   Knowledge or Unawareness? Two Perspectives on 'Reflexive Modernization'

1 The fact that the distinctions inside/outside and inclusion/exclusion – alongside secure/insecure (knowledge/unawareness) and political/ unpolitical – are intended to describe and comprehend the conflict lines of second modernity is presented in chapter 1 above.
2 For extensive discussion of this point, see Beck (1997: ch. 6).
3 This has been worked out, in particular, by Brian Wynne (1991, 1996a) in numerous publications; see also Hajer (1995).
4 On the concept of 'countermodern', see Beck (1997: ch. 2).
5 On this point, see Heller (1994).

Chapter 7   Risk Society Revisited: Theory, Politics, Critiques and Research Programmes

1 For the realism–constructivism debate, see chapter 2, pp. 23ff. above.
2 In addition to authors and papers in Adam et al. (1999), I owe a number of suggestions to Lau (1989), Giddens (1990, 1994), Bonß (1991, 1995), Beck-Gernsheim (1995), Goldblatt (1996), Lash et al. (1996) and Franklin (1998).
3 Van Loon (1999) perhaps offers a different view on Alan Scott's (1999) very sophisticated distinction between Mary Douglas' and my version of 'constructed' and 'real risks'.
4 I am using Barbara Adam's arguments here.

References

Adam, B. (1995) *Timewatch: The Social Analysis of Time.* Cambridge: Polity.

Adam, B. (1996) 'Re-Vision: The Centrality of Time for an Ecological Social Science Perspective', in S. Lash, B. Szerszynski and B. Wynne (eds), *Risk, Environment and Modernity: Towards a New Ecology.* London: Sage.

Adam, B. (1998) *Timescapes of Modernity: The Environment and Invisible Hazards.* London: Routledge.

Adam, B., Beck, U. and van Loon, J. (eds) (1999) *Repositioning Risk.* London: Sage.

Adorno, T.W. (1981) *Minima Moralia.* Frankfurt am Main: Suhrkamp. (English edn: *Minima Moralia: Reflections from Damaged Life.* London: Verso, 1978.)

Albrow, G. (1986) *The Global Age.* Cambridge: Polity.

Anders, G. (1982) *Die Antiquiertheit des Menschen* (7th edn). Munich: Beck.

Archibuggi, D. and Held, D. (eds) (1995) *Cosmopolitan Democracy.* Cambridge: Polity.

Bauman, Z. (1992) 'The Solution as Problem', *The Times Higher Education Supplement,* 13 November: 25.

Bauman, Z. (1999) *In Search of Public Space.* Cambridge: Polity.

Beck, U. (1992) *Risk Society: Towards a New Modernity.* London: Sage.

Beck, U. (1994) *Ecological Enlightenment: Essays on the Politics of the Risk Society.* Atlantic Highlands, NJ: Humanities Press.

Beck, U. (1995) *Ecological Politics in an Age of Risk.* Cambridge: Polity.

Beck, U. (1997) *The Reinvention of Politics.* Cambridge: Polity.

Beck, U. (1998a) 'Freedom's Children', in *Democracy without Enemies.* Cambridge: Polity.

Beck, U. (1998b) *Democracy without Enemies*. Cambridge: Polity.

Beck, U. (1999a) *What Is Globalization?* Cambridge: Polity.

Beck, U. (1999b) *Schöne neue Arbeitswelt*. Frankfurt am Main: Campus. (English edn forthcoming from Polity in 2000.)

Beck, U. and Beck-Gernsheim, E. (eds) (1994) *Risikante Freiheiten – Individualisierung in der modernen Gesellschaft*. Frankfurt am Main: Suhrkamp.

Beck, U. and Beck-Gernsheim, E. (1995) *The Normal Chaos of Love*. Cambridge: Polity.

Beck, U., Giddens, A. and Lash, S. (1994) *Reflexive Modernization: Politics, Tradition and Aesthetics in the Modern Social Order*. Cambridge: Polity.

Becker, E. (1990) 'Transformation und kulturelle Hülle', *Prokla*, 79: 12–27.

Beck-Gernsheim, E. (ed.) (1993) *Welche Gesundheit wollen wir?* Frankfurt am Main: Suhrkamp.

Beck-Gernsheim, E. (1995) *The Social Implications of Bioengineering*. Atlantic Highlands, NJ: Humanities Press.

Benjamin, W. (1968) 'The Work of Art in the Age of Mechanical Reproduction', in *Illuminations*. New York: Harcourt, Brace and World.

Benn, G. (1986) *Das Gottfried Benn Brevier*. Munich: Fischer.

Berger, P.L. and Luckmann, T. (1971) *The Social Construction of Reality: A Treatise on the Sociology of Knowledge*. London: Penguin.

Blanke, T. (1986) 'Autonomie und Demokratie', *Kritische Justiz*, 4: 406–22.

Bogun, R., Osterland, M. and Warsewa, G. (1992) 'Arbeit und Umwelt im Risikobewußtsein', *Soziale Welt*, 2: 237–45.

Böhme, G. (1991) 'Die Natur im Zeitalter ihrer technischen Reproduzierbarkeit', in *Die Natur im Zeitalter ihrer technischen Reproduzierbarkeit*. Frankfurt am Main: Suhrkamp.

Böhret, C. (ed.) (1987) *Herausforderungen an die Innovationskraft der Verwaltung*. Opladen: Leske und Budrich.

Bonß, W. (1991) 'Unsicherheit und Gesellschaft – Argumente für eine soziologische Risikoforschung', *Soziale Welt*, 42: 258–77.

Bonß, W. (1995) *Vom Risiko: Unsicherheit und Ungewißheit in der Moderne*. Hamburg: Bund.

Brock, D. (1991) 'Die Risikogesellschaft und das Risiko soziologischer Zuspitzung', *Zeitschrift für Soziologie*, 1: 12–24.

Bruggemeier, G. (1988) 'Umwelthaftsrecht: Ein Betrag zum Recht in der "Risikogesellschaft"', *Kritische Justiz*, 2: 209–30.

Calliess, R.-P. (1981) 'Strafzweck und Strafrecht. 40 Jahre Grundgesetz – Entwicklungstendenzen vom freiheitlichen zum sozial-autoritären Rechtsstaat?', *Neue Juristische Wochenschrift*, 21: 1338–43.

Claussen, B. (1989) 'Politische Bildung in der Risikogesellschaft', *Aus Politik und Zeitgeschichte*, 36: 231–7.

Czada, R. and Drexler, A. (1988) 'Konturen einer politischen Risikoverwaltung', *Österreichische Zeitschrift für Politikwissenschaft*, 1: 52–67.

Doubiago, S. (1989) 'Mama Coyote Talks to the Boys', in J. Plant (ed.), *Healing the Wounds: The Promise of Ecofeminism*. Philadelphia: Green Print.

Douglas, M. (1987) *How Institutions Think*. London: Routledge & Kegan Paul.
Douglas, M. and Wildavsky, A. (1982) *Risk and Culture*. Berkeley: University of California Press.
Dressel, K. and Wynne, B. (1998) 'Anglo-German Comparison of Modern Risk Political Cultures: The BSE Case'. Unpublished manuscript, Centre for the Study of Environmental Change, Lancaster University.
Eade, J. (ed.) (1997) *Living the Global City*. London and New York: Routledge.
Eichler, M. (1993) ' "Umwelt" als soziologisches Problem', *Das Argument*, 205: 359–76.
Elkins, D.J. (1995) *Beyond Sovereignty*. Toronto: University of Toronto Press.
Ericson, R.V. and Haggerty, K.D. (1997) *Policing the Risk Society*. Oxford: Clarendon Press.
Evers, A. and Nowotny, H. (1987) *Über den Umgang mit Unsicherheit*. Frankfurt am Main: Suhrkamp.
Ewald, F. (1986) *L'État Providence*. Paris: Édition Grasser & Fasquell.
Ewald, F. (1991) 'Die Versicherungsgesellschaft', in U. Beck (ed.), *Politik in der Risikogesellschaft*. Frankfurt am Main: Suhrkamp.
Falk, R. (1994) 'The Making of Global Citizenship', in B. van Steenbergen (ed.), *The Conditions of Citizenship*. London: Sage.
Fischer, J. (1989) *Der Umbau der Industriegesellschaft*. Berlin: Rowohlt.
Frankenfeld, P.J. (1992) 'Technological Citizenship: A Normative Framework for Risk Studies', *Science, Technology and Human Values*, 17: 459–84.
Franklin, J. (ed.) (1998) *The Politics of Risk Society*. Cambridge: Polity.
Giddens, A. (1990) *The Consequences of Modernity*. Cambridge: Polity,
Giddens, A. (1994a) 'Living in a Post-Traditional Society', in U. Beck, A. Giddens and S. Lash, *Reflexive Modernization: Politics, Tradition and Aesthetics in the Modern Social Order*. Cambridge: Polity.
Giddens, A. (1994b) *Beyond Left and Right*. Cambridge: Polity.
Giddens, A. (1998) *The Third Way*. Cambridge: Polity.
Giddens, A. and Pierson, C. (1998) *Conversations with Anthony Giddens: Making Sense of Modernity*. Cambridge: Polity.
Goldblatt, D. (1996) *Social Theory and the Environment*. Cambridge: Polity.
Gottweis, H. (1988) 'Politik in der Risikogesellschaft', *Österreichische Zeitschrift für Politikwissenschaft*, 1: 3–18.
Gray, J. (1998) *False Dawn*. London: Granta.
Häfele, W. (1974) 'Hypotheticality and the New Challenges: The Pathfinder Role of Nuclear Energy', *Minerva*, 12(1): 313–21.
Hahn, A., Eimbter, W.H. and Jacob, R. (1992) 'Aids: Risiko oder Gefahr?', *Soziale Welt*, 4: 404–21.
Hajer, M. (1995) *The Politics of Environmental Discourse: Ecological Modernization and the Policy Process*. Oxford: Clarendon Press.
Halfmann, J. (1990) 'Technik und soziale Organisation im Widerspruch', in J. Halfmann and K.P. Japp (eds), *Riskante Entscheidungen und Katastrophenpotentiale*. Opladen: Budderich.

Haraway, D. (1991) *Simians, Cyborgs and Women: The Reinvention of Nature*. London: Free Association Books.

Harvey, D. (1989) *The Conditions of Postmodernity*. Oxford: Blackwell.

Heidegger, M. (1986) *Being and Time*. Oxford: Blackwell.

Heine, H. (1992) 'Das Verhältnis der Naturwissenschaftler und Ingenieure in der Großchemie zur ökologischen Industriekritik', *Soziale Welt*, 2: 246–55.

Heine, H. and Mautz, R. (1989) *Industriearbeiter contra Umweltschutz*. Frankfurt am Main: Campus.

Heine, Heinrich (1981) 'Zur Geschichte der Religion und der Philosophie in Deutschland', in *Gesammelte Werke*, Vol. 5. Weimar: Klassiker.

Heinz, G. and Meinberg, U. (1988) 'Empfehlen sich Änderungen im strafrechtlichen Umweltschutz, insbes. in Verbindung mit dem Verwaltungsrecht. Gutachten D für den 57. Juristentag', in Ständige Deputation des Dt. Juristentages (ed.), *Verhandlungen des 57. Dt. Juristentages in Mainz*. Vol. I, Part D.

Held, D. (1995) 'Democracy and Globalization', in D. Archibuggi, D. Held and M. Köhler (eds), *Reimagining Political Community*. Cambridge: Polity.

Heller, A. (1994) 'Zerstörung der Privatsphäre durch die Zivilgesellschaft', in *Ästhetik und Kommunikation*. Berlin: Links.

Hildebrandt, E., Gerhardt, U., Kühleis, C., Schenk, S. and Zimpelmann, B. (1994) 'Politisierung und Entgrenzung – Am Beispiel ökologisch erweiterter Arbeitspolitik', *Soziale Welt*, Special Issue 9: 429–44.

Hitzler, R. (1991) 'Zur gesellschaftlichen Konstruktion von Natur', *Wechselwirkung*, 50: 58–75.

Hobbes, T. (1968) *Leviathan*. Harmondsworth: Penguin.

Jacobs, M. (ed.) (1997) *Greening the Millennium? The New Politics of the Environment*. Special Issue of *The Political Quarterly*. Oxford: Blackwell.

Japp, K.P. (1992) 'Selbstverstärkungseffekte riskanter Entscheidungen', *Zeitschrift für Soziologie*, 1: 33–50.

King, Y. (1989) 'The Ecology of Feminism and the Feminism of Ecology', in J. Plant (ed.), *Healing the Wounds: The Promise of Ecofeminism*. Philadelphia: Green Print.

Kohn, W. and Weyer, J. (1989) 'Gesellschaft als Labor', *Soziale Welt*, 3: 349–73.

Kommission für Zukunftsfragen (1997) *Arbeitsmarktentwicklungen*, Bericht Teil II. Bonn: Bayerisite Staatsregierung.

Korean Journal of Sociology (1998) 39(1), Spring, special issue on *Korea: A 'Risk Society'*.

Lagadec, P. (1987) *Das große Risiko*. Nördlingen: Greno.

Lash, S. (1992) 'Reflexive Modernization: The Aesthetic Dimension', *Theory, Culture & Society*, 10(1): 1–23.

Lash, S. (1994) 'Reflexivity and its Doubles: Structure, Aesthetics, Community', in U. Beck, A. Giddens and S. Lash, *Reflexive Modernization: Politics, Tradition and Aesthetics in the Modern Social Order*. Cambridge: Polity.

Lash, S. (1999) 'Risk Culture', in B. Adam, U. Beck and J. van Loon (eds), *Positioning Risk*. London: Sage.

Lash, S. and Urry, J. (1994) *Economy of Time and Space*. London: Sage.

Lash, S., Szerszynski, B. and Wynne, B. (eds) (1996) *Risk, Environment and Modernity: Towards a New Ecology*. London: Sage.

Latour, B. (1995) *We Have Never Been Modern*. Cambridge, MA: Harvard University Press.

Lau, C.H. (1989) 'Risikodiskurse', *Soziale Welt*, 3: 271–92.

Lau, C.H. (1991) 'Neue Risiken und gesellschaftliche Konflikte', in U. Beck (ed.), *Politik in der Risikogesellschaft*. Frankfurt am Main: Suhrkamp.

Luhmann, N. (1991) 'Verständigung über Risiken und Gefahren', *Die politische Meinung*, 4: pp. 217–28.

Luhmann, N. (1993) *Risk: A Sociological Theory*. New York: Aldine de Gruyter.

Merten, R. and Olk, T. (1992) 'Wenn Sozialarbeit sich selbst zum Problem wird – Strategien reflexiver Modernisierung', in T. Rauschenbach and H. Gängler (eds), *Soziale Arbeit und Erziehung in der Risikogesellschaft*. Berlin: Neuwied.

Nelkin, D. (ed.) (1992) *Controversy: Politics of Technical Decisions* (3rd edn). London: Sage.

Oechsle, M. (1988) *Der ökologische Naturalismus*. Frankfurt am Main: Suhrkamp.

Perrow, C. (1984) *Normal Accidents: Living with High-Risk Technologies*. New York: Basic Books.

Pries, L. (1991) *Betrieblicher Wandel in der Risikogesellschaft*. Opladen: Westdeutscher.

Prior, L. (1999) 'Repositioning Risk' in B. Adam, U. Beck and J. van Loon (eds), *Repositioning Risk*. London: Sage.

Prittwitz, V. von (1991) *Das Katastrophen-Paradox*. Opladen: Westdeutscher.

Rammert, W. (1993) 'Wer oder was steuert den technischen Fortschritt?', in *Technik aus soziologischer Perspektive*. Opladen: Westdeutscher.

Rauschenbach, T. (1992) 'Soziale Arbeit und soziales Risiko', in T. Rauschenbach and H. Gängler (eds), *Soziale Arbeit und Erziehung in der Risikogesellschaft*. Berlin: Neuwied.

Reiss, A.J. (1992) 'The Institutionalization of Risk', in J.F. Short and L. Clarke (eds), *Organization, Uncertainty and Risk*. Boulder, CO: Westview Press.

Ritter, E.H. (1987) 'Umweltpolitik und Rechtsentwicklung', *Neue Zeitschrift für Verwaltungsrecht*, 11: 929–38.

Robertson, R. (1992) *Globalization: Social Theory and Global Culture*. London: Sage.

Rustin, M. (1994) 'Incomplete Modernity: Ulrich Beck's Risk Society', *Radical Philosophy*, 67: 1–12.

Scharping, M. and Görg, C. (1994) 'Natur in der Soziologie', in C. Görg and M. Scharping (eds), *Gesellschaft im Übergang*. Darmstadt: Wissenschaftliche Buchgesellschaft.

Schelsky, H. (1965) 'Der Mensch in der wissenschaftlichen Zivilisation', in *Auf der Suche nach Wirklichkeit*. Düsseldorf: Schöningen.

Schumann, M. (1987) 'Industrielle Produzenten in der ökologischen Herausforderung', research proposal, Göttingen.

Schütz. A. (1984) 'Ökologische Aspekte einer naturphilosophischen Ethik'. Unpublished manuscript, Bamberg.

Schütz, A., Luckmann, T. and Zaner, R. (1979) *The Structures of the Lifeworld*, Vol. I. Evanston, IL: Northwestern University Press.

Schwarz, M. and Thompson, M. (1990) *Divided We Stand: Redefining Politics, Technology and Social Choice*. New York: Harvester Wheatsheaf.

Scott, A. (1999) 'Risk or Angst Society', in B. Adam, U. Beck and J. van Loon (eds), *Positioning Risk*. London: Sage.

Senghaas-Knobloch, E. (1992) 'Industriezivilisatorische Risiken als Herausforderung für die Friedens- und Konfliktforschung', in H. Meyer and P. Wellman (eds), *Umweltzerstörung: Kriegsfolge und Kriegsursache*. Frankfurt am Main: Suhrkamp.

Short, J.F. and Clarke, L. (1992) ?? in *Organization, Uncertainty and Risk*. Boulder, CO: Westview.

Soros, G. (1998) *The Crisis of Global Capitalism*. Boston: Little Brown.

Spretnak, C. (1989) 'Towards an Ecofeminist Spirituality', in J. Plant (ed.), *Healing the Wounds: The Promise of Ecofeminism*. Philadelphia: Green Print.

Szerszynski, B., Lash, S. and Wynne, B. (1996) 'Ecologies, Realism and the Social Sciences', in S. Lash, B. Szerszynski and B. Wynne (eds), *Risk, Environment and Modernity: Towards a New Ecology*. London: Sage.

Tucker, A. (1996) 'The Fallout From the Fallout', *The Guardian Weekend*, 17 February: 12–16.

van den Daele, W. (1992) 'Concepts of Nature in Modern Societies', in M. Dierkes and B. Biervert (eds), *European Social Science in Transition*. Frankfurt am Main: Campus.

van den Daele, W. (1995) 'Politik in der ökologischen Krise', *Soziologische Revue*, 18(3): 501–8.

van Loon, J. (1999) 'Virtual Risks in an Age of Cybernetic Reproduction', in B. Adam, U. Beck and J. van Loon (eds), *Positioning Risk*. London: Sage.

van Steenbergen, B. (ed.) (1994) *The Conditions of Citizenship*. London: Sage.

Weber, M. (1968) *Economy and Society* (3 vols). New York: Bedminster Press.

Weber, M. (1991) 'Objektive Möglichkeit und adäquate Verursachung in der historischen Kausalbetrachtung', in *Schriften zur Wissenschaftslehre*. Stuttgart: Reclam.

Weizsäcker, E.U. von (1995) 'Hätte ein Dritter Weltkrieg ökologische Ursachen?', *Der Bürger im Staat*, 45(1): 57–8.

Wildavsky, A. (1994) *But Is It True? The Relationship between Knowledge and Action in the Great Environmental and Safety Issues of Our Time*. Chicago: University of Chicago Press.

Winner, L. (1992) *Autonomous Technology*. London: Sage.

Wolf, R. (1987) 'Die Antiquiertheit des Rechts in der Risikogesellschaft', *Leviathan*, 15: 357–91.

Wolf, R. (1988) ' "Herrschaft kraft Wissen" in der Risikogesellschaft', *Soziale Welt*, 2: 164–87.

World Commission on Environment and Development (1987) *Our Common Future*. Oxford: Oxford University Press.

Wuthnow, R. (1991) *Acts of Compassion*. Princeton, NJ: Princeton University Press.

Wynne, B. (1996a) 'May the Sheep Safely Graze?', in S. Lash, B. Szerszynski and B. Wynne (eds), *Risk, Environment and Modernity: Towards a New Ecology*. London: Sage.

Wynne, B. (1996b) 'The Identity Parades of SSK: Reflexivity, Engagement and Politics', *Social Studies of Science*, 26: 73–91.

Yearley, S. (1994) 'Social Movements and Environmental Change', in M. Redcliff and T. Benton (eds), *Social Theory and the Global Environment*. London: Routledge.

Zapf, W. (1992) 'Entwicklung und Zukunft moderner Gesellschaften seit den 70er Jahren', in H. Korte and B. Schäfers (eds), *Einführung in Hauptbegriffe der Soziologie*. Opladen: Campus.

Zimmermann, A.D. (1995) 'Towards a More Democratic Ethic of Technological Governance', *Science, Technology and Human Values*, 20(1): 86–107.

Zürn, M. (1995) 'Globale Gefährdungen und internationale Kooperation', *Der Bürger im Staat*, 45(1): 49–56.

Index

acceptability 42, 55, 58, 67, 138–9, 151: of error 123
access to information networks 117
accidents: 'normal' (Perrow) 56; scenarios 76, 140; *see also* WIA
accountability 50, 56, 70, 76, 77, 78: conflicts of 73–5; lack of 54, 149; rules of 52
achievement consciousness 95–6
action, and/or cognition 29–30
activism 14, 41
actor-network theory 27, 146
Adam, Barbara 1, 28, 31, 143, 148, 161
administration: collapse of 56; regulations 59; social acceptance of 100
Adorno, Theodor 108, 147: *Dialectic of Enlightenment* 85
aesthetic experiences, politicization of 136
aesthetic reflexivity 116, 131
after-care, provident 56, 76
air pollution policy 59
Albrow, Martin 1, 16

Altenstadt, lead crystal factory 54
alternatives 45, 70, 91–2, 98, 99, 100–1, 103, 104: professional of self-control 80
altruism 11
ambivalence 86–7, 88, 93, 108, 146
Amnesty International 38
anarchy 56
'and' thinking 4, 23, 26, 49, 134, 146
Anders, Günther 56, 81, 85: *Die Antiquiertheit des Menschen* 87
Arendt, Hannah 65
art, and politics 93
asbestos 145
'Asian crisis' 7
Asilomar conference, California (1975) 106
Atomic Energy Act, German 59
autonomy, social or technological 43, 58–9
awareness 66–7, 80–1, 87: *see also* unawareness

'bads' 8, 34–5, 63: distribution of the 73; opportunities of the 152

balloting, and purchase 44
Baudelaire, Charles 44
Bauman, Zygmunt 1: on the
    republic 12–13; on *Risk Society*
    (Beck) 86–7
Benjamin, Walter 27, 136
Benn, Gottfried 20–1, 108
Berger, P. L. 99
biography 5, 11–12, 75: reflexive
    119
biological hubris 107
biological warfare 106
'black-boxing' 146
Blair, Tony 106–7
blindness 4, 55, 81
Böhme, Gernot 1, 154
boundaries: confusion of 28;
    imposed by risk definitions 83;
    loss of 60–1, 143, 145–8
Bourdieu, Pierre 111
bourgeois social order 78, 101
bovine spongiform encephalopathy
    see BSE crisis
boycott movements 38, 40–7, 142
Brundtland Commission 35
BSE crisis 48–9, 106–8, 136–7,
    141, 144, 148
bureaucracies: autonomy of 95;
    criticism of 79; purposive-
    rational (Weber) 33, 38; safety
    56, 68; security 55–6
business: alternatives in 92; and
    ecological threats 52, 63–4;
    environmental morality and
    100–1; producer of and profiter
    from hazards 86, 102–5
business ethics 97, 100–1

calculability 4, 8, 50, 75–6, 88,
    95–6, 136–7
calculus of risk 50–2, 123, 137,
    140, 141
Calvinism 95–6
capital: as global 11; polarizations
    in 63–4

capitalism 2, 10, 69: Anglo-
    American 151; ecological
    questions in industrial 24;
    ecological reform of 89; global
    17; growth of industrial 51; and
    modernity 112; success of
    technologically advanced 11; and
    the work ethic 95–6; *see also*
    late capitalism
catastrophe threshold 84–5
categories 94, 133: either-or 146;
    mistakes 148–51
causality 52, 54, 84: *see also*
    'suspicion of cause'
centuries, confusion of 55–6
certainties, contradictory 125
certainty 2, 88, 140
chemical power 35–6, 53–4
Chernobyl disaster 8, 23, 60, 77,
    155, 158
Chirac, Jacques 40, 41
Christian morality 9–10, 95–6
citizens: recognition of patterns of
    misperception 124; reflexive
    116, 130; right of resistance 39,
    46, 79, 139
citizens' groups 68–9
citizenship: ecological 154; goals of
    43; and political freedom 10
citoyen 101
civic trust 18
civil rights, and techno-economic
    progress 65–6
civil society: global 13, 14, 18; and
    political freedom 10
civilization, artifical construction of
    145–8
class, new formations in reflexive
    society 117
class conflict 65
class issues 7, 24, 148
classification 93–5
climate change, and 'no-insurance'
    areas 156
climatic asylum-seekers 63

coalitions 81, 92, 102–3: *ad hoc*
of opposites 40, 41; *see also*
discourse coalitions
cognition, and/or action 29–30
cohesion 12, 13
collective identities 118–19
communicative rationality
(Habermas) 117
communicative society (Habermas)
101, 111
Communist Manifesto 14
communitarianism, new 116–19
community: global 13; Lash on
117–18; *see also* countermodern
communities; risk communities
compensation 34, 52, 56, 150:
meaninglessness of 8, 36, 54, 77,
142
Comte, Auguste 154
conflicts 92, 100: of accountability
73–5; and collapse of states 13;
ecological 61–5, 157; ethnic,
national and resource 37; of
industrial society 73–5; over
global goods and challenges 157;
transnational–national 7, 14
confrontation 104
congestion 130
consensus: building 33; of experts
125; Marxian 96–7
consent, modernity and 97–9
consequences: just distribution of
52; unforeseen *see* unintended
consequences
constellations 8, 75, 104: military
and economic 65; of subpolitics
20, 38
constructivism 24–5, 118–19,
133–4, 143–5: institutional 31–4;
reflexive realism and naïve 26
consumer society, and direct
democracy 42, 102, 142
consumerism 6, 86
contradictions, of hazard
administration 67–8, 80

control: collapse of the logic of
142; decisions about 82–3;
unintended consequences of the
logic of 139–40
controllability 2, 38, 76, 129:
limited 6–7
cooperation, supranational
institutions of 20, 33
corporate culture 97
corporate identity 97
corporate power, and ecological
issue 98, 100–8
cosmopolitan democracy 5, 13–14,
153–4: and ethical globalization
9; preconditions of 1
Cosmopolitan Manifesto, defined
14–18
cosmopolitan parties, features of
15–17
cosmopolitan society: goals, values
and structures of 14, 17; Kant
on 20, 43; the utopia of a
43–4; world risk society as
19–47
cosmopolitan world order, post-
national 13
cosmopolitanism, new 9, 14, 18
counter-experts 55, 79, 107: and
risk definition 4–5
countermodern communities (Lash)
131
creativity 13, 76, 88
crisis theory of social-natural
relations 29, 31
critical rationalism (Popper) 120
critical theory, standards 79–80
criticism, public 34, 66–9, 152
critique 79–81, 89
cultural differences 16, 22–3,
118–19
'cultural Red Cross consciousness'
44, 103
cultural studies 135
cultural theory 30, 118–19, 135,
154

culture: in the industrial society 74; loss of distinction between nature and 21, 145–8; science of 22
cybernetic reproduction 136

Daily Mirror 106
danger, risk distinguished from 84, 158
dangers 19, 26, 142: awareness of as political 22–3; denial of 53, 68; internal 46–7; knowledge-dependent 143; known and actual 128–9; levelling effect of 145–6; 'second-order' 12, 39, 153; as social constructs 22–3; uncontrollable 31–4; *see also* self-endangerment
de-individualization 51
debate: global 16; political 39–40
debt servicing 6
decidability 95
decision: dangers of wrong 76; freedom of 78; quality of 131
decision-making 30: democratization of 5, 131, 142, 152; hazards of political 53, 81–2; hierarchical autonomy of bureaucratic 98; and legitimation 92; in manufactured uncertainties 46–7, 105–8, 132; models of 125; and the nation-state 32; need to redefine rules for 78–9; 'palaver model' of 125; in post-national communities 1, 13, 16; responsibilities of 136–7; and risk 4; technocratic model 125; those affected by 84–5; in uncertainty 122–4
definition: and production 31; relations of 5, 135, 149–50, 152; *see also* risk definition
definitions: cultural 142; of hazards 66; need for new 74–5, 78
democracy 98, 152: culture of 5; objectives of industrial 70, 92;

possibility of in a global age 14–18, 71; science and the economy 107, 108; *see also* cosmopolitan democracy; direct democracy; representative democracy
democratic dilemma 14
democratization 7, 8, 61: of corporate action 98; of critique 79–81; of decision-making 5, 131, 142, 152; political, social and cultural 10; and political freedom 12–13; of transnational regimes 17
deregulation, national and transnational 15
destruction of nature: and destruction of markets 62, 64; and institutional constructivism 31–4
determinate judgement (Lash) 139–40
detoxification, symbolic 57
development, problem of 35
diagnoses 25, 36, 92, 139: monopoly of scientists and engineers 59–61
dialogue, between cultures 14, 22
difference, in first modernity 10
direct democracy, and consumer society 42, 102, 142
direct politics 39–40, 41, 44: and reliance on the symbolic politics of the media 44–6
discourse, and dramatization of risk 137–8
discourse coalitions 29–30, 31, 155: transnational 24–5
discourse-strategic action 30–3
discursive power (Foucault) 117
discursivity 95, 101
disembedding 111
dissent 125
distribution: conflicts 89; of consequences 52

diversity 9, 16, 17
division of powers 61, 70
Dobson, Andrew 1
domino effect 11–12
doubt 88, 107: liberation of 61;
  reflected 124
Douglas, Mary 93–4, 161: *Risk
  and Culture* 22–3
Dryzek, John S. 1
dualism: Enlightenment 150;
  society–nature 19, 27–31
Durkheim, Emile 2, 75, 94–5

'earth politics' 8
eco-refugees 63
'ecocracy' 22
ecofeminism 27–8, 31
ecological alliances 102
ecological consciousness 22
ecological crisis 5: as a discourse of
  self-confrontation 30–1; and the
  end of technocracy 92
ecological democracy, the utopia of
  69–71
ecological destruction: poverty-
  driven 35; threat of 53–4; wars
  and uncompleted modernization
  35–6; wealth driven 34–5
ecological enlightenment 48–71
ecological global movements 16
ecological labour movement 64–5
ecological question: and corporate
  power 98, 100–8; and
  developing industrial society
  24, 76; and manufactured
  uncertainties 19–47
ecology 19: and the disintegration
  of institutional power 91–108;
  and the economy 100–1;
  indeterminacy of concept of
  20–3
economic growth, destructive
  consequences of 102
economic interests, and
  autonomization of technological
  development 58–9

economy 2: and ecological conflict
  62–4, 100–1; science and
  democracy 107, 108; in world
  risk society 33–4, 114
education 97, 99, 159
Eichler, Margit 154
Ellul, Jacques 85
employment: and GDP growth 11;
  'precarious' 114–15; structure
  and ecological threats 64–5; *see
  also* underemployment
engineering sciences, in production
  of hazards 58–9
Enlightenment 111, 150
environment 8, 19: *see also* ecology
'environment tax' 42
environmental crimes 54–5, 65
environmental crisis 137–8: as
  inner crisis 77–9, 149
environmental destruction 14: side-
  effects of 61–5
environmental law 149, 160
Environmental Liability Law,
  Federal Germany 160
environmental policy,
  internationalization of 104–5
environmentalism 121–2
error 53, 122–4, 151: acceptability
  of 123
essentialism 29–30
ethical foreign policy 13–14
ethics: mathematical without
  morality 51; new of research
  58–9
Europe 79: BSE in 108, 141;
  Eastern 143; global domestic
  policy 65, 69–71; image of its
  future in 'Third World' 3; 'new
  unity' 68, 148; Western 151
European Union 14
evolutionary bias, in Western social
  science 2–3
Ewald, François 52, 76, 88, 140,
  151
exclusion 117
experiment, and theory 60

experimental identity 1
expert knowledge, as ecological
  neo-imperialism 25
expert rationality 99–100, 112,
  122, 124, 130, 141
experts 71, 82: consensus of 125;
  and counter-experts 55, 79, 107;
  powerlessness of 42, 58, 141–2;
  as producers, analysts and
  profiteers 140; and risk definition
  4–5, 122

fabricated uncertainty *see*
  manufactured uncertainties
Falk, Richard 38
family 148: and freedom 10; social
  changes in the 112–13
fatalism 47, 70, 87–8, 103, 140
feminism 16, 28, 99, 100
feminist eco-sociology 27–8
Fichte, Johann Gottlieb 111, 134
financial markets, global 111
financial risks, social explosiveness
  of global 7, 8
first modernity 1–2, 63, 133:
  institutional crisis of national
  environmental problem 33–4;
  and ontology of difference 10;
  see also industrial society
flexibility 12, 114–15
food safety 15, 145: *see also* BSE
  crisis; genetically modified food
Fordism 114
forests, dying *see* tropical
  rainforests; *Waldsterben*
Foucault, Michel 93, 117, 147
France, nuclear testing and 41, 148
Frankenfeld, Philip 43
Frankfurt School 147
free market: and ecological morality
  102–3; and environmental risks
  6; and genetically modified food
  107
freedom: creative uncertainty of
  13, 75, 78; *see also* political
  freedom

functional differentiation 2, 10
future: citizens' groups and themes
  of the 68–9; colonization of the
  139–40, 147; present and past
  137–8

Garfinkel, Harold 111
GDP growth, relationship with
  employment 11
Gehlen, Arnold 82, 85
gender issues 2, 148
gender research 27
generations, socialization of risk
  across 16–17
genetic engineering 34, 53–4, 124
genetically modified food 78,
  105–7, 142
genetics 105–8, 140
Genscher, Hans-Dietrich 65
geography, and threats 62–3, 64
geopolitical shifts 65
Germano-centrism 148
Germany 34, 40, 41, 42, 48, 68,
  69, 79: environmental crimes
  54–5; Greens in 4, 34, 42, 148;
  Institute for Standards 59;
  'motor car consensus' 157;
  Red-Green government: 'nuclear
  exit-politics' 53; socialism in
  former GDR 98
Giddens, Anthony 1, 49, 105, 119,
  124, 127, 134, 140: institutional
  reflection/reflexivity 109, 110–16,
  130–1
global age 1, 2, 5: possibility of
  democracy in a 14–18
'global citizenship' 17, 38
global governance 13
global market economy,
  politicization of 7–8
global movements 16
global risk society 2, 8, 90, 92–3,
  142, 151–2: *see also* world risk
  society
global subpolitics: case study 40–7;
  emergence of a 37–47

global threats, typology of 34–7
globality 17
globalization 2, 19, 115–16, 152:
cosmopolitan democracy and
ethical 9; discourses of 3;
dramatization of risks 137–8;
from above 37, 38; from below
37, 38; need for 'responsible' 8;
and state structures 13
'glocality' 15, 142, 147
Goffman, Erving 111
'goods' 8, 63: distribution of the
73
Gouldner, Alvin 111
government: and expert opinion
82; and manufactured
uncertainty 78; power and
legitimacy of 5
greenhouse effect 62–3: and
international insurance trade 159
Greenpeace 25, 38, 39, 44, 45–6,
159: and Shell 40–2
Greens, in Germany 4, 34, 42, 148
Grove-White, Robin 1
guilt: becomes acquittal 33, 36, 45,
105; collective 46; of world risk
society 129

Habermas, Jürgen 1, 101, 111,
117
Häfele, Wolf 60
Hajer, Maarten 1, 29–31, 125
Halfman, Jost 82
Haraway, Donna 1, 27, 28, 31
Harvey, D. 1, 142
Hayward, Tim 1
hazards: conflict game 102–5;
debates about 72–3; defined and
evaluated socially 64–5, 128–9;
incommensurability of 83–4; in
the industrial society 74; of
mega-technology, as a political
issue 50, 52–8; as quasi-subjects
150–1; and scientific logic
58–61; social birth of 57; social

explosiveness of 7, 8, 149,
150–1; transformed into risks
136–7; versus providentiality
77–9; and welfare 101
health management 51
Hegel, Georg Wilhelm Friedrich
134
Heidegger, Martin, *Being and Time*
118
Heine, Heinrich 94, 158–9
Held, David 1, 153–4
helper interests 104–5
history 108
Hobbes, Thomas 39, 139
Horkheimer, Max 147: *Dialectic of
Enlightenment* 85
humanity 8, 15, 17, 152
hybrids 27, 146–7
hypocrisy 14, 41

identities 118–19: and national
issues 148; *see also* collective
identities; experimental identity
IMF (International Monetary Fund)
7
impact, and knowledge 143–5,
147, 150–1
imperialism, disguised as humane
intervention 13–14, 25
inability to know 122, 124, 126,
127, 132, 141: denial of 131
incalculability 78, 79: of
consequences 54, 160; decision-
determined 88–9
inclusion 117
income: basic 12–13; diverse levels
16
indeterminacy 140–2
indifference 141: forced and learned
96–7, 98
individual: Adorno on the 108;
autonomy 5; and system 93–8
individualism: cooperative altruist
11; institutionalized 9, 10–11; of
Western societies 8–9

individualization 2, 19, 41, 68–9, 95, 132, 152: defined 9; and political culture 1; process of 74–5; and the social 118–19
indulgences, political sale of ecological 45, 105
industrial society: development into risk society 48–75; phases of development 24, 72–5; and a truncated democracy 70
industries: of the future 77; 'guardian angel' 104–5; regulation-intensive 15
inequality, new forms of social 117
information revolution 6
information society 113–15
inner world of society 19
insecurity 5, 38
institutional power, ecology and the disintegration of 91–108
institutional reflection/reflexivity (Giddens) 109, 110, 111–16, 130–1
institutions: change in 147–8; conflicts of 80–1; crisis of developing industrial society 76, 77–9, 130; failure in face of hazards 57; legitimacy of 123; nature of 93–8; politicization of 89; rationality of 33; risk management in 151–2; threat of public awareness to 66–7; *see also* international institutions; transnational institutions
instrumental rationality 76, 139
insurability 19: beyond 31–4, 36, 88–9
insurance 76: contracts 51; and genetically modified food industries 105; international and the greenhouse effect 159; limits of 8, 156; need for transnational 7; on a no-fault basis 51–2; refusal of 142; time

gap in 144–5; *see also* private insurance
insurers, and victims 145
interdependence: of threat definitions 66; transnational 3
interdisciplinarity 29
interest groups 92
international environmental agreements 38, 143
international institutions: cooperative 20; in world risk society 142–3
International Panel for Climate Change (IPCC) 25
international relations, anarchy of 5
invisibility, social 143
irony 152
issues, and consent 98–108

Jaspers, Karl 85, 88
Jonas, Hans 85

Kant, Immanuel 17, 20, 93, 116, 134: 'Perpetual Peace' 43
Keynesianism 114
King, Ynestra 28
Knight, Frank 112
knowledge: differences of 81, 120; expert vs. lay 24, 25, 29–31; gap between decision and 78; and impact 143–5, 147, 150–1; inequality of access to 117; key significance of 126; linear theories of 124–6; modes and types of 111; monopolies of 25; new and risk predictions 58; non-linear theories of 124–6; political theory of 81; potential 123–4, 140–1; in reflexive modernization 110, 115–16; selectivity of 117; sociology of 30; and unawareness 140–2; or unawareness 109–32, 147; uncertainty of 122; *see also*

inability to know; reflection; unawareness; unwillingness to know
Kohl, Helmut 40, 41, 42

labels 94
laboratory 60–1, 82, 107
labour: and ecological politicization 64–5; globalization of 137–8; transnational division of 16; *see also* social labour
labour contract 96–7
labour market 148
language, and separatism 37
Lash, Scott 1, 124, 127, 135: determinate judgement 139–40; reflexive community 109, 110, 116–19, 131–2
late capitalism 29, 101
late modernity 1
Latour, Bruno 27, 31, 146, 151, 155: quasi-objects 150
Lau, Christopher 83
law: and politics 70; and technology 43; and toleration thresholds 59; uncertainties in public 149
legal order, sanctions disadvantage 101
legitimacy 34, 40, 101
legitimation, and decision-making 92, 137
legitimation circle 33
Lenin, Vladimir Ilyich 114
liability 52, 121, 160
lifestyle: changes in 2, 121, 138–9; individualization and the collective 9
lifeworld 12, 117, 140: politicization of 89; structures of the 123–4
linear theories of knowledge 110, 124–6: defined 125
Lloyd's of London 144–5
Luckmann, Thomas 99: *The Structures of the Lifeworld* 123–4

Luhmann, Niklas 2, 10, 84, 96, 137, 158: self-referentiality of systems 111
Lyotard, François 1

Maffesoli, M. 1
Major, John 40, 141
management 97, 100–1: transnational 137–8
managerial class, global 17
manufactured uncertainties 5, 6, 78, 111–12, 140–2, 147: decision-making in 105–8, 132; and ecological questions 19–47; internalization by industries 145; and world risk society 31–4
marriage, and social changes 112–13
Marx, Karl 2, 3, 10, 95, 96, 135, 149, 154
Marxian theory 79
Mautz, R. 158–9
meaning, exhaustion of sources of 74–5
media: and global technological citizenship 44–6; manipulation by Greenpeace 45–6; and ministers of the environment re hazards 57; and perception 144; sensationalist 68; symbolic politics of the 44–6, 83, 122
mediation, symbolic 21, 44–6
Melucci 1
middle classes 12: *see also* bourgeois
military intervention, Western 13–14
ministers of the environment, media and hazards 57
modernity: as an age of values 13; and capitalism 112; defining 10; institutional aspects of political 120; need for redefinition of Western model of 33; pluralization of 2–3, 147; and political freedom 10–13;

radicalized (Giddens) 115–16;
rule-driven industrial 91–2;
self-endangering 131;
subpoliticization of 130;
uncertainty and 'security pact'
52; utopia of a responsible
147–8; *see also* first modernity;
late modernity; postmodernity;
second modernity
modernization: ambivalences of
86–7, 88; as autonomous
innovation 72; 'ecological' 92;
see also reflexive modernization;
simple modernization
Möglichkeitsurteile (probabilities)
136–7
money 112: for damages principle
52
monorationality 126
moral outrage 45
morality: ecological 101–8;
mathematicized 51, 138–9, 147;
and political freedom 9–10; and
politics 41–7; transnational 41;
and world risk society 8–11;
see also Christian morality
'motor-car consensus', Germany
157
multinational parties 17
Mumford, Lewis 43

NAFTA (North American Free
Trade Association) 6
nation-states 114, 148: collapse of
institutions 8; concept of the
political in 91–2; control by
139; and decision-making 32;
and first modernity 1–2; and
geopolitical shifts 65
national politics, sovereignty of
107
natural disasters 50
natural resources, and separatism
37
natural sciences 22: role in risk
society 58–61

naturalistic misunderstanding 21
nature 5, 19: defining 8; cultural
models of 21–2, 28; domination
over and abstraction of 154;
the end of 108; indeterminacy
of concept of 20–3; loss of
distinction between culture and
21, 145–8; politics of 1; science
of 22; social crisis in the
relationship to 29, 31; symbolic
mediations of 21; women's
special relationship with 27–8
nature conservation, perversion into
world-management 25
'nature state' 90
nature–society dualism, social
construction of 19, 27–31
NBC (nuclear, biological, chemical)
weapons of mass destruction
35–6
negotiation-constraints 34, 157
Nehru, Jawaharlal 3
neo-Spenglerism 146
'New International' 38
NGOs 16, 38
noise protection 59
non-linear theories of knowledge
119, 124–6, 127: defined 125
non-Western societies, in world risk
society 2–3, 7
nongovernmental organizations *see*
NGOs
normality, and exceptional
conditions 52–8
normalization: of hazards 57–8,
61; symbolic and destruction of
nature 32
norms: of calculability 4; failure of
industrial society 31–2;
renegotiation of 120
nuclear contamination, democracy
of 61–2
nuclear power 53–4, 67
nuclear reactor safety 59, 60
nuclear testing, in France 41,
148

Offe, Claus: self-endangerment 120
ontological security 115
openness 26, 40, 78, 125, 126, 147, 152
opportunities 26, 65–9, 128, 134, 151–2
options 113–14: for feminists 28
organization: forms of 10, 18, 70; societal measures of 78; *see also* self-organization
'organized irresponsibility' 6, 32, 54–8, 80–1, 152: and the power game of risk definitions 148–51
Other, the end of the 61–2
outsider perspective 126
overfishing of the oceans 157
ozone depletion 34, 144, 145, 157

paradigm shift 2, 113–14
Parsons, Talcott 2, 10, 139
participation 10, 42: ad hoc individual 39–40; technological 43–4
past, present and future 137–8
perception: of catastrophes 84–5; conflicts of 22–3, 25; cultural of dangers 71, 102–5, 143–4; global models of 23; of power 96; of risks 135–7, 138–9
Perrow, Charles 56
pessimism 32, 85–8
Pierson, C. 111–12, 115–16
pluralization 3, 95, 130–1, 132
political, concept of the 91
political community (Weber) 119
political culture, and individualization 1
political design 93
political economy of uncertainty 5, 11–12: and political freedom 12–13
political education 159
political expediency 45

political freedom: and cultural democratization 12–13; and morality 9–10, 119
political mobilization, risks and 4–5
politicians, resistance from citizens to 79
politicization 89: of aesthetic experiences 136; of assumptions and institutions 34; of the economy 100–2; of global market economy 7–8; via risk definitions 138
politics: and art 93; become unbound 130; category mistakes 148–51; disavowal of 15; formal in nation-state 91–2; and law 70; and morality 41–7; powerlessness of official 101–2; reinvention of 15–18, 47, 93, 155; and science 70–1
polluter-pays principle 54, 78, 142
pollution 61–2, 145
Popitz, Heinrich 120–1
Popper, Karl 120
post-national communities, decision-making in 1, 13, 16
'postmodern constellation' 8
postmodernism 126, 152
postmodernity 1, 133
poverty: and environmental destruction 35, 63; increase in world 5–6; and pollution 5–6; and unemployment 11
poverty trap 6
power, systems and 95–8
power game, of risk definitions 4–5, 64–5, 102–5, 122, 138, 141, 148–52
pragmatism 124, 134
praxis, self-assured life 118–19
pre-industrial society, threats of 75–6
predictability, of the unpredictable 56, 140

present, past and future 137–8
prion 136
Prittwitz, Volker von 104–5
private insurance 4, 129, 155–6: absence of 31–2, 77; refusal of 55–6
probability 84–5, 124, 136–7, 140–1: of improbable accidents 66; 'residual' 55
production: and definition 31; (*Herstellen*) and (*Produktion*) 29–30
profit 95–6, 102–5, 140
progress 148: antiquatedness of pessimism about 85–8; coalition of state, economy and science 34; consensus on 52, 73; techno-economic 65–6, 82
proof, burden of 34, 150, 160: redistribution of the 61, 70
protection, loosening of compulsion to work and social 97–8
protectionism 7, 8, 153
provident state and providing state 76
providentiality, hazards vs. 76, 77–9
public, authority of the 142
public opinion 14, 34
'public science' 70–1
public sphere 5, 20, 83: creation of a 70
publicity 101–2
purchase, and balloting 44

quasi-governmental power 66
quasi-objects (Latour) 150

racism, postmodern 132
radioactivity: itching of 71; tolerable levels of 59
Randeria, Shalini 3
rationality: collapse of techno-scientific and legal 56–8, 66, 147; conflicts of 80, 120, 122,

125, 131; economic of industrial society 77, 78, 84–5; of institutions 33; of probability 84–5; and reflexivity 86–7; risk society negates 88; *see also* communicative rationality; expert rationality; instrumental rationality; monorationality
rationalization (Weber) 10
re-embedding 111, 116
Reactor Safety Commission, 'Guidelines' 59
realism 23–4, 134: definitional power of 24; role of reflexive in strategies of power 26
realism–constructivism debate 23–37, 143–5
reality: 'crisis' 60; as project and product of acting 29–30, 155; *see also* virtual reality
reason (*Vernunft*) 152
recognition, conflicts of 144–5, 147
reflection 95: cognitive, moral and aesthetic (Lash) 116; concept of 111; and reflexivity 73–4, 81, 87, 89, 109–10, 121; *see also* knowledge
reflexive community (Lash) 109, 110, 116–19, 131–2
reflexive modernity, for Lash 117
reflexive modernization 1, 2, 33, 89, 92, 93, 147, 148: Bauman on 86–7; beginning of 125; concept of 73–5, 80–1; and 'second-order dangers' 39; as the self-criticism of society 79–81; and simple modernization 110, 159; and the social system 95–7; two perspectives on 109–32; and unintended consequences (Beck) 119–21
reflexive society 20
reflexive sociology (Gouldner) 111

reflexivity 78, 79, 109, 146:
Bourdieu on 111; narrow
concept of 127; political 65–9;
and rationality 86–7; and
reflection 73–4, 81, 87, 89,
109–10, 121; as a source of
productivity 113; *see also*
aesthetic reflexivity
refugees, flows of 37, 63
regional ecological treaties 16
reification, overcoming 47
Reiss, Albert 123
representation, by others 132
representative democracy,
despotism of 43
republicanism, Bauman on 12–13
research: logic of 59, 60–1; new
ethics of 58–9; reflexivity of
100
'residual risk society' 53–4, 72
'residual risks' 33, 49, 60, 72
resistance, right of 39, 79, 139
responsibility 6, 16–17, 50, 78,
121, 147–9: 'global' 8, 13–14,
42–3; of Western states 25; *see
also* 'organized irresponsibility'
revolutions 65, 66–7
rights, ecological crisis as
systematic violation of basic
39
Rio Earth Summit 24–5, 157
risk: defined 3–4; as an energizing
principle (Giddens) 49; 'and'
characteristic of immateriality
and materiality 4, 23, 26, 49,
134, 146; as a cognitive map
3–4; denial of 141, 150–1;
distinguished from danger 84,
137, 158; distribution of 83;
dramatization of 137–8; global
inequality of 5–6; limitation 56,
77; negative and positive facets
16–17; neglect of 144–5; and
responsibility 6; and security 6;
and threat 52–8; and trust 6;

and uncertainty 19, 112; 'vestigial'
129; *see also* calculus of risk
risk analysis, interdisciplinary
approach 4
risk assessment 82–4, 108, 140–2:
rules of 149–51
risk communities, global 5, 16–17,
41, 152
risk conflicts 34, 65–6, 107, 152
risk culture 149
risk definition 4, 66, 135:
architecture of 83–4; or
interpretation 58–9; mediated
and contested 4–5; metanorms
of 55; power game of 4–5,
64–5, 102–5, 122, 138, 148–52;
trust of insurers in socio-scientific
145
risk industries, and insurance
businesses 145
risk production: enforcing 55;
profit from 62, 102–5
risk science 4
risk society: concept of 72,
74–5; elements of a theory of
135–48; role of technology and
natural sciences in 58–61;
theory, politics, critiques and
research programmes 133–52;
and the welfare state 72–90;
see also global risk society; world
risk society
Risk Society (Beck) 8, 86–7, 134,
153
risk trap 141
risk-sharing 16–17
risks: are they timeless? 48–9;
constructed or real 22–3, 161;
decision-dependence 31–4, 50,
75–6; environmental 5–6; as
man-made hybrids 146–7; new
49; not the same as damages
135; public recognition of
144–5; *see also* 'residual risks'
Robertson, R. 142

rules: of accountability 52;
breakdown of allocation and
responsibility 32; changing or
inventing 92; emergence of a
system of industrial society 50–1;
legitimate of industrial society
91–2; need to redefine 78–9, 92;
standardized of behaviour 115

safety 102: acceptable levels of 59;
probability-based 57–8; security
becomes mere technical 56, 76;
and the welfare state 151
'safety circle' 60–1
Sandoz 160
Scandinavia 151
scepticism 9, 18, 124
Schelsky, Helmut 82
Schröder, Gerhard 4, 41, 42, 59
Schütz, Alfred: *The Structures of
the Lifeworld* 123–4
science: dependence on 98; and
doctrine of technological
infallibility 53, 59; economy and
democracy 107, 108; interaction
between different forms of
knowledge and 29; and new
types of risk 140; politics and
70–1; reflexivity in 99–100; and
risk assessment 58, 82–3; role in
manufactured uncertainties
105–8
scientific management (Taylor) 114
Scott, Alan 148, 161
second modernity 1–2, 117, 126,
131, 133, 152: challenges of
2–3, 160; and direct politics 41;
political freedom in 10–11
security 2, 33, 54: becomes mere
technical safety 55–6; creation of
151; and creativity 88; hazards
beyond 74; predictable in an
open future 50–2; risk and 6
'security pact' 52
selective inference 127

selectivity: of knowledge 117, 122;
of reception and transmission
122
self, religious concept of 95–6
self-criticism of societies 142–3,
152: reflexive modernization as
theory of 79–81
self-definition, reflexive 78
self-endangerment 80, 120, 128,
131: unawareness and
unintended consequences
126–30
self-limitation 80, 130
self-monitoring 71
self-organization 10, 39
self-representation, in US 131–2
Sellafield 155
Senghaas-Knobloch, Eva 37
senses, expropriation of the 55
separatism 37
services 113–14
shared significance (Lash) 118–19
Shell: and dumping at sea 42; and
Greenpeace 40–2
Shiva, Vandana 1
side-effects 9, 13, 19, 20, 80: of
environmental destruction 61–5;
knowledge of 120
Simmel, Georg 75, 111
simple modernization 110, 159
social, individualization and the
95, 118–19
social construction, of objective
indicators of hazard 64–5,
128–9
social ecology 29
social labour, in the industrial
society 74
social movements: dogmatization of
anti-expert knowledge 123, 131;
opportunities for influence 65–9,
128
social order, suspicion of the 139
social sciences: category mistakes
133, 148–51; challenges for 87;

evolutionary bias in Western
2–3; role of 152
social state 75, 78, 90
social structure 48–71: and
distribution of knowledge and
unawareness 125
social system, and modernity 95
social theory, category mistakes
148–51
socialism, in former GDR 98
sociality 1
socialization: different forms of 21;
forced global 23; of risk 16–17
Society of German Engineers 59
'socio-scapes' 16
sociological imagination 4, 134
sociology: of artefacts or hybrids
27; classical 94–5, 133; cognitive
127; and knowledge 110–11;
'nothing-but-society' 4, 23;
paradigm-shift for 2, 113–14
Soros, George 111
Spretnak, Charlene 27–8
standards: of acceptability of how
we want to live 138–9; defined
by experts 99–100; redefining
70, 74
state: power and globalization 13;
role of the 5, 11; *see also*
provident state; social state;
'technological state'; welfare state
'state of technology', and scientific
authority 59
statistics 51, 67, 76, 140
subpolitics 91–108, 130: the
concept of 37–40; *see also* global
subpolitics
subversion, democratic 68–9
suffrage, universal 97
survival 48–71, 139
'suspicion of cause' 160
sustainable development 24
symbolic mass boycott 40–7
symbolic politics, of the media
44–6

symbols 21, 32, 71, 117
symptoms: gap before they appear
144; not causes 71, 86–7
system: boundaries no longer apply
143; and individual 93–8;
reproduction of 93–4
systems, self-referentiality of
(Luhmann) 95–8, 100, 111
systems theory 2, 126

Taylor, Frederick 114
technocracy 15, 55: decision model
125; the end of 92; liberation of
politics from 61
technological alternatives 70
technological challenges 52–8
technological change 5, 148
'technological citizenship' 43–4
technological determinism 114
technological development,
autonomization of 58–9
technological infallibility, doctrine
of 53
technological moralization 51
'technological state' 82
technologies, obsolete 35
technology: critique 67–9; the end
of linear 81–5; internalization
of 82; and legislation 43; and
private insurance 4; and risk
assessment 82–3; role in risk
society 58–61; sociology of, and
feminist ecology 28; *see also*
'state of technology'
telecommunications industry 15
television 44
Terre des Hommes 38
territoriality 2, 153
terrorism, fundamentalist or private
36
Thatcher, Margaret 4
Thatcherism, 'reverse' 4
theory, and experiment 60
Third Way 52
'Third World' 3, 25

thought 94–5: autonomization of
modern 115–16; European
intellectual 134
threat: and opportunities for
influence of social movements
65–9; power of 61–2; and risk
52–8; social power of 66–7
threats: distinguished from risks
55–8; public visibility of 71;
see also global threats; hazards
time, natural and social 28
time-space distantiation (Harvey)
142
tolerability 17, 59, 138–9
Touraine, Alain 1
toxic threat 145–6
toxic waste 35
'toxin-absorbing regions' 62–3, 64
transmissability 45
transnational communities 16
transnational institutions 7, 8, 23,
24–5: cosmopolitanism of 17–18
Trittin, Jürgen 41, 59
tropical rainforests 35, 157
trust 12, 18, 44, 52, 101, 123,
135: active 116, 130; concept of
115–16; lack of 107, 155; post-
traditional 116; risk and 6
Tucker, Anthony 154–5

UK, BSE crisis 48–9, 106–7
unawareness: active 128–9; dealing
with 132; or knowledge 109–32,
147; and knowledge 140–2;
known 126; preventive effect of
(Popitz) 120–1; reflected 127;
selectivity of 117; types of
121–4; unintended consequences
as a conflict over (Beck) 119–21;
unintended consequences and
self-endangerment 126–30;
unknown or repressed 127,
130–1
uncertainty 5, 38, 93, 100:
constructed 126; decision-

making in 122–4; exposure of
scientific 61; political economy
of 11–13; repressed 129; and
risk 112; *see also* manufactured
uncertainties
underemployment 2
uninsurability 52–8, 77, 129
unintended consequences 2, 13, 73,
109–10, 119–21, 125:
intensification effect 128–9; of
the logic of control 139–40;
presuppose action 127–8; and
reflexive modernization 119–21;
unawareness and self-
endangerment 126–30; in
unintended consequences 148
United Nations 5–6, 38
unwillingness to know 122, 126
Urry, John 117
US: self-representation in 131–2;
'technological citizenship' 43
utopia: of a cosmopolitan society
43–4; of a responsible modernity
130, 147–8

'value ecology' 9
value orientations, new 10–11
values 17, 103: cosmopolitan 14,
17; debates about 5, 13, 100;
risks and 138–9
van den Daele, Wolfgang 155–6
van Loov, Joost 136, 150, 161
van Steenbergen, Bart 38
Veblen, Thorstein 82
victims: of decision-making 84–5;
and insurers 145
violence 118–19
virtual reality, and risk 136–7
virtuality 147, 150
visibility 71, 136–7, 144
voluntary organizations 18

wage labour 96–7
Waldsterben (dying forests) 128,
143, 148

war, and NBC weapons of mass destruction 35–6
waste management 104–5
water policy 59
'we' 10–11, 75, 117–18, 132
Weber, Max 2, 10, 33, 75, 82, 85, 111, 139: iron cage 115, 133, 147; *Möglichkeitsurteile* 136; political community 119; 'The Protestant Ethic and the Spirit of Capitalism' 95–6
Weizsäcker, Ernst Ulrich von 157
welfare state 69, 85, 89: hazards beyond safety systems of 76–7, 101, 151; individualization and the 9; and risk society 72–90; in world risk society 11–12
West: decline of model 2–3, 7–9; power to define and promote universal values 13
WIA (worst imaginable accident) 53–4, 57–8
Wildavsky, Aaron: *But Is It True?* 121–4; *Risk and Culture* 23
Winner, Langdon, *Autonomous Technology* 43
winners and losers 64–5, 102–5, 141
women, special relationship with nature 27–8
work: compulsion to 97–8; flexibilization of 12, 114–15; 'fragile' 11; as local 11; reflexive modernization of 113–16

work society, becomes risk society 12
world citizenship, self-conscious 17–18
world environment (*Umwelt*) 41
'world party' 17
world public, emergence of a 20, 37–47
world risk society 75, 114, 142–3: arenas and actors 37–40; concept of 6–8, 19, 25, 146–7; as cosmopolitan society 19–47; economic 6–8; elements of theory of 20–3; guilt of 129; and manufactured uncertainties 31–4; and morality 8–11; non-Western societies in 2–3; political economy of 11–12; politics and subpolitics of risk definition 4–5; self-critical 46–7
WTO (World Trade Organization) 6
Wynne, Brian 1, 24, 29

youth, issues of concern for 14

Zaner, Robert, *The Structures of the Lifeworld* 123–4
Zeit, Die 38
'zero risk' 82, 129
Zimmerman, Andrew 43
Zürn, Michael 35, 36